Alternative
Therapies
FOR MANAGING
Diabetes

Alternative
Therapies
FOR MANAGING
Diabetes

DAVID DRUM

AUTHOR OF *The Chronic Pain Management Sourcebook* AND
COAUTHOR OF *The Type 2 Diabetes Sourcebook*

Contemporary Books

Chicago New York San Francisco Lisbon London Madrid Mexico City
Milan New Delhi San Juan Seoul Singapore Sydney Toronto

Library of Congress Cataloging-in-Publication Data

Drum, David E.
    Alternative therapies for managing diabetes : everything you need to know
about / David Drum.
        p.   cm.
    Includes bibliographical references and index.
    ISBN 0-658-01380-7
    1. Diabetes—Alternative treatment.   I. Title.

    RC661.A47.D78   2002
    616.4′6206—dc21   2001035814

Contemporary Books

A Division of The McGraw·Hill Companies

1 2 3 4 5 6 7 8 9 0   AGM/AGM   0 9 8 7 6 5 4 3 2 1

ISBN 0-658-01380-7

This book was set in Sabon
Printed and bound by Quebecor Martinsburg

Cover design by Bill Stanton/Stanton Design
Cover illustration by Kathy Obringer

McGraw-Hill books are available at special quantity discounts to use as premiums and
sales promotions, or for use in corporate training programs. For more information, please
write to the Director of Special Sales, Professional Publishing, McGraw-Hill, Two Penn
Plaza, New York, NY 10121-2298. Or contact your local bookstore.

This book is printed acid-free paper.

For Koelle

"If we do not change our direction, we are liable to end up where we are headed." —Old Chinese proverb

Contents

PART III SPIRIT

Preface

Increasingly, people are taking charge of their own health. Individuals from all walks of life are educating themselves in order to make informed decisions about treating their ailments, including patients with Type 2, or maturity onset, diabetes. There is tremendous change under way in how we look at health and wellness, and it is reaching the status of a movement as more and more people look toward alternative therapies.

For the consumer of medical services, unfortunately, the task of looking into alternative therapies can be daunting. In the first place, there are a bewildering number of alternative therapies out there. More than six hundred alternative or complementary therapies have been identified by the Office of Alternative Medicine, but not all of these therapies are appropriate for every medical condition. In addition, many medical doctors are only slightly familiar with alternative therapies, and most are reluctant to recommend them. Since the research on many of these therapies is scanty or difficult to find, many people wishing to supplement conventional treatment may have a very difficult time distinguishing potentially interesting and useful therapies from those which have no value or might be harmful.

Alternative Therapies for Managing Diabetes provides a simplified and streamlined resource for making informed decisions. All of the alternative therapies presented in this book have potential benefits for people with Type 2 diabetes. All of them are best employed in a complementary way. When used judiciously and in tandem with good conventional medical treatment, the therapies presented in this book may offer a variety of benefits to Type 2 diabetics.

Acknowledgments

The author would like to thank the following individuals in the medical community for their generous help and assistance on this book: Paul Rosch, M.D., FACP, president, American Institute of Stress, Yonkers, New York; Mary L. Hardy, M.D., medical director, Cedars-Sinai Integrative Medicine Medical Group, Inc., Beverly Hills, California; Skip Shoden, CNN, New Health Resources, Marina Del Rey, California; Allen C. Neiswander, M.D., D.Ht., Alhambra, California; Susan Rush Michael, DNSc, R.N., CDE, Dept. of Nursing, University of Nevada at Las Vegas, Las Vegas, Nevada; Rosa Mantonti, RN, CDE, clinical nurse specialist, Presbyterian Health Care Services Hospital in Albuquerque, New Mexico; Nicole Salter, aromatherapist, Los Angeles, California; Terry Zierenberg, R.N., CDE, educational manager/marketing, Mini Med Inc., Beverly Hills, California; Susan Shaw, Certified Clinical Hypnotherapist, Hypnosis Motivation Institute, Tarzana, California; Frederick Travis, Ph.D., Chairman of the Psychology Department, and Ms. Sharon Starr, Mararishi University of Management, Fairfield, Iowa; Simon Chaitowitz and Doug Hall, Physician's Committee for Responsible Medicine, Washington, D.C.; Dana Ullman, Homeopathic Education Service, Berkeley, California; Norman Shealy, M.D., Ph.D., Holos Institutes of Health, Springfield, Missouri; Desire Stapley, USDA's Beltsville Research Facility, Beltsville, Maryland; and Florence Horn, spiritual healer and teacher of healing, North American Director for the Jewish Association of Spiritual Healers, New York, New York.

The author also owes a special debt of thanks to the individuals with diabetes who gave their time and experience during personal interviews.

Chapter 1

Alternative Therapies

More and more people are looking to add alternative therapies to conventional medical treatment. While even the most useful alternative therapies can't cure Type 2 or maturity onset diabetes, many therapies can complement good medical treatment and help control the worst effects of this common, debilitating disease.

Alternative treatments such as homeopathy, acupuncture, and naturopathy are based on a rationale that is different than conventional medicine. These and other treatments can greatly strengthen the natural energy of the body. Herbal medicines, hypnosis, certain vitamin and mineral supplements, biofeedback, and other therapies may help people cope with and manage diabetes more successfully. Some alternative therapies may help you control symptoms such as high blood sugar and high blood pressure, and ward off or manage particular complications.

Among the best existing alternative therapies, some may reduce stress, increase your energy, and buttress your overall health and well-being. Some may give you a greater perspective on yourself, the management of your disease, or an enhanced sense of well-being. Some supplements, herbs, and treatment systems covered in this book may help you control particular symptoms, or lose or maintain weight. A few alternative therapies may just help distract you from the drudgery of diabetes and help you feel a little better for a while.

Alternative therapies have strengths and weaknesses, which are highlighted in this book. They do not replace good, conventional medical treatment. If you use your common sense, educating yourself as you go along, you may find that alternative therapies open an entire new vista of good health for you.

Popularity

Alternative practitioners of all stripes are experiencing an unprecedented interest, often from well-educated, relatively affluent people. In 1993, a survey published in the *New England Journal of Medicine* found that about one in three adults had used an alternative therapy in the previous year. A recent Stanford University study found that while the number of visits to conventional medical doctors did not increase between 1990 and 1997, visits to alternative practitioners jumped a whopping 47 percent.

Health-care practitioners, including diabetes educators, are becoming more open to alternative therapies. A 1998 survey found that more than 60 percent of doctors had recommended alternative therapies to their patients at least once in the prior year. Certified diabetes educators include nurses and other medical specialists trained to educate people about diabetes self-management, and many recommend alternative therapies. According to a recent survey published in *The Diabetes Educator*, almost two-thirds of certified diabetes educators recommend alternative therapies to their patients with diabetes as an adjunct to good, basic medical care.

"People are interested in these therapies, and they want to know more about them," observes Dr. Susan Rush Michael, a professor of nursing at the University of Nevada-Las Vegas, and one of the authors of the survey. Dr. Michael says an even greater percentage of certified diabetes educators probably recommends alternative therapies today than when the survey was first published.

Support groups, meditation, lifestyle diets, laughter and humor, exercise, relaxation therapy, prayer, imagery and visualization, massage, music therapy, and homeopathy are among the therapies frequently recommended in the survey. Approximately 63 percent of diabetes educators recommend alternative therapies. Altogether, 87 percent of the educators surveyed thought the therapies they recommended were help-ful to people with diabetes.

Not surprisingly, the most frequently recommended alternative ther-apies have the greatest body of research data behind them. Rarely rec-ommended therapies such as hydrogen peroxide therapy, ozone therapy, Manchurian mushrooms, and crystal therapy have the least research data to support their use. According to the survey, older educators and female educators are more likely to recommend the use of humor ther-apy, relaxation therapy, and music therapy. Male educators, on the other hand, are more likely to recommend homeopathy and megavitamin therapy.

"Traditional medicine doesn't have all the answers," Dr. Michael observes. "Alternative therapies offer hope for a lot of people."

Dr. Michael refers clients with diabetes to alternative therapists based on each person's individual interests, whether they are experi-encing great stress, and other factors. Recently, she's referred several people to a local reflexologist, with excellent results. One older indi-vidual with balance problems was referred to tai chi classes. Several peo-ple have tried guided imagery, utilizing audio tapes made by a social worker to assist them. Others have benefited from therapeutic touch, aromatherapy, music therapy, and other alternative therapies, which complement their doctor's care, Dr. Michael says. However, she adds, referrals to alternative therapists do not always produce good results.

Rosa Mantonti, a certified diabetes educator and hospital adminis-trator in Albuquerque, New Mexico, where alternative therapies are quite popular, says, "People are going toward alternative therapies because they don't want to take insulin, they don't want to take pills, and they don't want to lose weight. Around here we have people who say that if it's easier to take an herb than to go for a walk, then I'm going to do the herb."

In New Mexico, Mantonti says, some alternative therapists have a problem with what might be called false advertising—promising patients a lot more than they can possibly deliver. Some therapists promise patients they may be able to get them off insulin or diabetes medica-tions, for instance, promises that can be impossible to fulfill.

Dr. Michael adds: "People in the health care professions had better become educated about these therapies so they can advise their clients, who are interested in them, and help keep them away from unsafe practices. Nurses are in a good position to help people understand these therapies."

Medical Progress

Conventional medicine has made extraordinary progress in the treatment of diabetes, a disease that has plagued humanity for thousands of years. Doctors now have a sophisticated understanding of the importance of diet, exercise, and powerful new medications. Extremely sensitive measuring devices have made Type 2 diabetes quite manageable. However, though conventional medicine has made great progress, diabetes remains difficult to live with and often difficult to manage. It is still one of the most frustrating and time-intensive of all chronic diseases. Western medicine is the best in the world, but is reductionist in its approach to health and disease. Type 2 diabetes, for instance, is typically diagnosed by symptoms such as high blood sugar and high insulin levels in the blood. These *symptoms* are then treated. Controlling these symptoms is of enormous benefit to people with the disease, but even the best conventional medical care doesn't make diabetes go away.

Look at the best-known symptom of diabetes, high blood glucose or high blood sugar. Normal levels of blood sugar are around 100 mg./dl.(milligrams per deciliter), increasing a little after eating, but normalizing quickly. In people with diabetes, blood sugar levels rise to dangerously high levels and remain there unless controlled. Lengthy periods of high blood sugar are linked to long-term complications affecting the heart, nerves, kidneys, eyes, and feet. Controlling this symptom with diet, exercise, and medications is the focus of good conventional medical care, and the wisdom of this strategy is well-documented. High blood pressure is another symptom that troubles medical doctors.

After we eat, insulin, a hormone secreted by the pancreas, is released by into the blood. Normally, insulin helps blood sugar enter the cells, but the bodies of people with diabetes resist this. This insulin resistance is the defining symptom of Type 2 diabetes, helping trigger high levels of blood sugar. Despite the presence of what should be adequate insulin, blood sugar levels remain high. Although there are exceptions, most people with Type 2 diabetes have two or three times the normal 30 units

Using Alternative Therapies

- Do some homework before you decide on an alternative therapy approach to try. Select an approach that interests you and that you think might be helpful.

- Ask your medical doctor, certified diabetes educator, or nurse for a referral to a practitioner. Many certified diabetes educators are familiar with useful alternative therapies. Nurses who are members of the American Holistic Nurses Association also receive special training in alternative therapies. Professional organizations, books, and support groups for people with diabetes may be other sources of referrals.

- Investigate the training and background of a practitioner you are thinking of consulting. Medical doctors, osteopathic physicians, naturopaths, and acupuncturists are licensed by individual districts or states and have credentials that may be checked. Hypnotists, biofeedback technicians, massage therapists, music therapists, and others can be certified by professional organizations.

- Meet with the practitioner. Ask about the risks and benefits of the therapy. Understand what you can reasonably expect to gain and what the therapy cannot do. Get an estimate of the costs and frequency of treatments, and inquire about possible side effects. Understand how you can tell if you are responding to the therapy, and how long it might take to see results. Trust your instincts.

- Inform your medical doctor that you are using the therapy. Many doctors will work with alternative practitioners in lowering levels of diabetes medications when appropriate.

- Report all adverse effects or reactions immediately to the practitioner, as you would with a medical doctor.

of insulin in their blood, but blood sugars remain too high unless steps are taken to control this symptom.

An important British research study, the United Kingdom Prospective Diabetes Study, followed 5,000 Britons with Type 2 diabetes for 20 years. When the study concluded in 1997, researchers found that people who kept their blood sugars close to the normal range reduced their risk of small vessel blood complications by 25 percent, lowered their heart attack risk by 16 percent, and lowered levels of damaged or glycosylated proteins in the blood by 11 percent. This study also concluded that people who kept their blood pressure near normal levels *significantly* reduced their incidence of complications involving the blood vessels, heart, and eyes.

This large, well-supervised study conclusively proves that controlling symptoms such as high blood sugar and high blood pressure is quite important for the long-term health of people with diabetes. However, results also indicate that there is more to managing diabetes than simply controlling these symptoms. If symptom control were all there was to it, people with good blood sugar control would not have experienced fewer complications, they would have experienced no complications at all.

Diabetes may be viewed as a metabolic disorder. A nutritional disease, diabetes interferes with the normal process of converting food to energy. It affects the endocrine system, which contains the pancreas, the adrenals, and other glands. Diabetes also affects the digestive system, the circulatory system, the immune system, and the nervous system. Diabetes may contribute to mental and physical stress and highly unpleasant emotions such as depression, anger, irritability, resentment, and fear. Therefore, a holistic approach is probably best.

Other Approaches

Other types of therapies look a bit beyond physical symptoms such as high blood sugar. Mind/body therapies, for instance, target their efforts mostly on the mind, aiming to lower stress levels, increase relaxation, and produce a number of positive, indirect effects on the body of the person with diabetes.

Naturopathy looks at some of the other symptoms that signal the onset of diabetes such as excessive thirst and excessive urination, regarding them as useful insights into the body's natural coping mechanisms at work, which may provide clues to treatment.

Other practitioners work with energies that aren't recognized by conventional medicine. Homeopathic practitioners might recommend remedies that strengthen a life energy they call the *vital force*. Practitioners of traditional Chinese medicine might suggest acupuncture or herbal treatments with an eye toward maximizing the strength of an invisible natural energy they call *chi*. Practitioners of an Indian folk medicine called Ayurvedic medicine might look at *prana*, an energy said to flow into the body through a series of seven invisible *chakras*, located in the trunk of the body and the head, which roughly correspond with the glands of the endocrine system. In Ayurvedic medicine, and in some other alternative therapies, practitioners might focus on the third chakra, where the pancreas, adrenal glands, and most of the digestive system is located. Even the emotions may factor into the onset of diabetes. Dr. Richard Gerber, author of the excellent book *Vibrational Medicine for the 21st Century*, notes that the pancreas is associated with obsessive worry in Chinese five-element theory. Worry itself could cause a kind of burnout of the pancreas, he suggests, expressed as symptoms such as high blood sugar and diseases such as diabetes.

Conventional medicine recognizes that hereditary factors, environmental factors, endocrine imbalances, dietary discretion, obesity, and stress all contribute to diabetes. But for the moment, the root cause of diabetes remains unknown.

Convergence

Conventional medicine has slowly begun to embrace the best alternative therapies, which many doctors call complementary or supportive therapies. In the past, one definition of alternative therapies was that they were therapies that weren't taught in medical schools. This definition no longer holds true. Alternative therapies are now popping up in medical school curriculums in the United States and Canada. More than half of North America's medical schools currently offer course work.

The American Medical Association's Resolution 514 did not endorse these therapies, but encouraged physician members to "become better informed regarding alternative (complementary) medicine and to par-

Most Recommended Therapies

A survey published in the *Diabetes Educator* in late 1999 found that almost two-thirds of certified diabetes educators now recommend alternative therapies to some of their clients with diabetes. Physical activity, lifestyle diets, and laughter and humor therapy were often recommended for use every day. The ten therapies most recommended by diabetes educators are:

1. Physical Activity

2. Self-help Groups

3. Lifestyle Diets

4. Laughter and Humor

5. Relaxation Therapy

6. Prayer

7. Imagery/Visualization

8. Meditation

9. Massage

10. Music Therapy

ticipate in appropriate studies of it." Some medical doctors are practicing alternative therapies alongside conventional medicine.

We are now witnessing the emergence of what might be called retromedicines. Older, gentler systems of folk medicine such as herbalism, Ayurvedic medicine, massage, light therapy, and homeopathy are being taken seriously again.

Traditional medicine is rapidly expanding its horizons, but the United States and Canada lag behind some European countries when it comes to the utilization of alternative therapies. In Germany and France, for instance, herbal medicine is well-established. It's said that people who visit a doctor in Germany are more likely to be prescribed herbs than conventional medications. In Great Britain, therapies such as homeopathy and spiritual healing are accepted. In many parts of Asia, medical doctors practice alongside practitioners of Ayurvedic medicine and Chinese traditional medicine. And in much of the third world, folk medicine remains all that is available to most people.

The public acceptance and growth of alternative therapies can be seen by looking at naturopathy, a treatment system combining diet therapy, exercise, counseling, homeopathy, herbal remedies, spinal manipulation, hydrotherapy, and massage. A few years ago naturopathy was virtually unheard of, and few states licensed naturopaths. But in July 2000 the North American Board of Naturopathic Examiners began certifying naturopaths by a clinical licensing process similar to that for doctors and chiropractors. More and more states now license naturopathic physicians, and naturopathic colleges are participating in research studies sponsored by the National Institutes of Health. In the field of health care, professional certification of many alternative practitioners is an established fact.

Some Precautions

It is necessary to discuss alternative therapies, *prior* to beginning them, with a good medical doctor. Some supplements can interact with existing medications and could require prompt medical treatment. Although many herbs may be useful in controlling diabetes, a few are quite dangerous and should be avoided. If supplements or alternative therapy treatments lower blood sugar levels, your doses of medications will have to be adjusted or you will be at risk of low blood sugar reactions. If you do achieve better control of blood sugars, reducing or discontinuing medication under your doctor's supervision is the safest and most conservative way to proceed, with the least possible risk to you.

Note also that a few of the alternative therapies mentioned in this book are considered dangerous by some conventional medical doctors and should be carefully investigated beforehand. Chelation therapy, for instance, has potential benefits as a treatment for vascular problems, and some strong advocates. But before you try this therapy, you should fully understand what it might do for you, and the potential dangers of treatment. And, of course, it should be administered only by a medical doctor trained in its use.

Alternative therapies work quite slowly compared to conventional medical treatment. Since so many therapies take a long time to achieve results, you should allow a reasonable amount of time to evaluate them. It can take several weeks, and even months, before you know whether some alternative therapies are having a positive effect.

Of course, if you have an adverse reaction in the first week, stop the therapy right away. And if you try something for a while and it doesn't work, try something else. Work with both your alternative practitioner and your doctor to gradually reduce doses of diabetes pills or insulin when that is possible.

Unfortunately, there are quack alternative practitioners at work in the world. If someone promises you something that sounds too good to be true, it probably is. The chance that you might abandon good, conventional medical treatment for an alternative therapy is the biggest single danger in seeking help from an alternative practitioner, and the easiest way to harm yourself.

Mild side effects from alternative treatment are not uncommon. In 1994, a survey published in the magazine *Nature* found that nearly 16 percent of British users of alternative therapies reported a mild to moderate adverse reaction to the therapies they utilized. More than 12 percent using acupuncture reported an aggravation of their symptoms, fatigue, pain, and mental or needle trauma. Almost 10 percent of patients who had tried homeopathy indicated symptom aggravation or adverse mental and digestive effects. Almost 8 percent of users of herbal therapies reported mild to moderate digestive problems or effects.

Of more concern are the horror stories that have appeared in medical journals concerning people with diabetes. For instance, two people with Type 2 diabetes and undiagnosed peripheral neuropathy consulted two different practitioners of Chinese medicine, complaining of cold feet. Both were treated with moxibustion, a treatment that involves burning a bit of material near an acupuncture site. Both people developed ulcers on their feet and legs at the site of the treatment.

In India, a man treated for hepatitis, who was also taking an ethnic herbal remedy for diabetes, came down with lead poisoning due to a high concentration of lead in the herbal remedy, a common problem in the Indian subcontinent. In the United States and Canada, unfortunately, many supplements are also of questionable purity.

In Eastern Europe, a 21-year-old female Type 1 diabetic went to a popular faith healer in her country, and when the faith healer withdrew her from insulin, she went into a diabetic coma.

As previously stated, the biggest danger with alternative therapies is abandoning good medical treatment. Begin any alternative treatment while remaining under the care of a good medical doctor. Make sure the practitioner consults with your physician, and vice versa. As an alternative, consult an alternative practitioner who is also a medical doctor.

Holistic Treatment

The best conventional medical care already involves recommendations for diet, exercise, and medications as needed. A few holistic practitioners are already going a bit further.

At the Holos Institutes of Health in Springfield, Missouri, holistic physician Dr. C. Norman Shealy, treats diabetes not only with a natural, high fiber diet and aerobic exercise, but also with electroacupuncture on "Ring of Fire" acupuncture points to restore DHEA. His patients utilize a deep relaxation therapy called Biogenics, which consists of autogenic exercises and biofeedback at a rate of twenty minutes twice a day, or more. Zinc picolinate, chromium, and magnesium supplements are utilized if needed. Some clients are advised to try hypnosis with past life therapy. Recently, Dr. Shealy has added three capsules per day of the Ayurvedic herb gymnema to this regimen. All together, he estimates that 80 percent of his clients with Type 2 diabetes have come off all diabetes medications.

Increasingly, Western medical treatments are being combined with alternative approaches, in attempts to utilize the best from each. In the United States, relaxation therapies, support groups, hypnosis, biofeedback, visual imagery, counseling, Reiki, tai chi, yoga, art therapy, aromatherapy, humor therapy, therapeutic touch, and more are offered as support therapies at many major treatment centers for chronic diseases. In addition, a great deal of research on alternative therapies is under way.

There are potential benefits in combining appropriate therapies. A study of people with diabetes at Hengyang Municipal Hospital in

Hunan, China, utilized Western medications to control blood sugar levels, and then added Chinese traditional medicine with the aim of supplementing chi energy, nourishing yin, and promoting the circulation of the blood to remove blood stasis. Results published in 1997 showed that the group whose treatment combined Western and Eastern approaches was more than twice as effective, 77 percent to 33 percent, as the control group that received a single therapy alone.

Research Support

It is an unfortunate cliché among some doctors that alternative medicine is all unscientific bunk, because the therapies are not backed by rigorous, double-blind studies in peer review journals that are the highest standard of proof to the skeptical but inquisitive scientific mind. Genuine improvements reported by patients are sometimes dismissed as "anecdotal," "placebo effects," or worse. This attitude is unfortunate, and increasingly old-fashioned, since there is a growing body of research support for some alternative therapies.

Research presented in this book includes many good, double-blind, randomized research studies as well as many smaller studies from around the world. Only a few therapies have been widely studied. Mind/body medicine, for instance, has an extremely large body of research support, estimated at perhaps ten times that of any other area of alternative therapy.

In addition, some forms of alternative medicine do not easily adapt to the randomized, double-blind format that is ideal for studying pharmacological drugs. Double-blind trials can't easily be designed for treatment modalities such as homeopathy or Ayurvedic medicine, which attempt to *individualize* their treatment recommendations to particular individuals or particular personality types. It is also difficult to design a good placebo for some modalities, such as acupuncture. Although a lot of these modalities are difficult to assess even with double-blind trials, evidence is accumulating that some alternative therapies can help you.

And research continues.

Least Recommended Therapies

The following alternative therapies were recommended *least* frequently by diabetes educators surveyed in 1999. Hydrogen peroxide therapy, the least popular, was recommended less than 1 percent of the time.

1. Hydrogen Peroxide Therapy
2. Manchurian Mushrooms
3. Ozone Therapy
4. Crystal Therapy
5. Magnetic Therapy
6. Wheat Grass
7. Ayurveda
8. Chakra Balancing
9. Reiki
10. Macrobiotic Diets

About This Book

This book is written for people who are curious, and perhaps a little skeptical, about alternative treatments for Type 2 diabetes. It examines some of the more potentially useful alternative therapies, and presents some of the evidence that supports their use.

This first chapter provides a general overview of alternative therapies. The remainder of *Alternative Therapies for Managing Diabetes* is divided into three parts focusing on different types of alternative treatments.

Part I, "Body Therapies," focuses on alternative therapies that help the body.

Lower Blood Sugar

Here are a few of the herbs and foods discussed in this book that lower blood sugar or relieve other symptoms of diabetes:

Aloe Vera

American Ginseng

Artichokes

Bitter Melon

Cinnamon

Fenugreek

Garlic

Guar

Guava

Gymnema

Legumes

Nopal

Onions

In Chapter 2, we take a fresh look at dietary strategies that help control blood sugar and other symptoms. Chapter 3 recommends particular foods to eat or to avoid.

Chapter 4 evaluates vitamin and mineral supplements that may be helpful to people with diabetes, and Chapter 5 continues this examination with other potentially useful supplements.

Chapter 6 looks at the herbs that may be useful in the treatment of diabetes and in controlling symptoms such as high blood sugar.

Chapter 7 takes a new look at exercise—an effective way to combat insulin resistance and lower blood sugar. Chapter 8 examines bodywork or massage that may increase blood and lymph circulation, relax tense muscles, and relieve stress.

Chapter 9 covers chelation therapy and DMSO, two potentially useful but controversial treatments.

Part II, Mind/Body Therapies, begins with Chapter 10, which examines the impact of stress on diabetes.

Chapter 11 discusses the benefits of meditation, and the relaxation response that is the opposite of stress. Chapter 12 covers hypnosis, autogenic therapy, and affirmations. Chapter 13 explains the potential benefits of biofeedback.

Chapter 14 taps into the important but often unrecognized health benefits of social support.

Chapter 15 presents yoga, tai chi, and other exotic mind/body therapies that may benefit people with diabetes. Chapter 16 attends to the sounds of music therapy. Chapter 17 sniffs out aromatherapy, which delivers health benefits through its direct yet subtle effect on the mind.

Part III, Spirit, covering energy therapies, begins with Chapter 18 which looks at the potential benefits of acupuncture.

Chapter 19 examines homeopathy and how it can strengthen the body. Chapter 20 takes a peek at gentle Bach flower remedies and crystals that may provide emotional solace.

Chapter 21 looks at light and color therapies, which may be helpful with depression and other symptoms. Chapter 22 covers magnet therapy.

Chapter 23 covers therapeutic touch and other therapies that are modern variations of the "laying on of hands." Chapter 24, the final chapter, covers faith healing and spiritual healing.

A wonderfully useful Resources section in Appendix A, provides information on medical and support organizations for various alternative therapies. Appendix B contains World Wide Web sites of possible interest.

Toward Wellness

The great 19th-century French physiologist Claude Bernard made important discoveries that sharpened our understanding of diabetes.

Widely considered the father of experimental medicine, Dr. Bernard did crucial and important research on the role of the pancreas and the glyco-genic function of the liver. In perhaps his greatest single achievement, the esteemed French physician artfully described what he called the body's *interieux milieu*: the natural healing environment within the interior of the human body, which constantly battles the organisms of disease. Treatments that strengthen the internal environment of the body, Dr. Bernard believed, are ultimately of greater benefit to patients than powerful drugs that kill pathogens that cause disease. Dr. Bernard was quoted as saying that if there is any treatment that may be of benefit to the patient, and if the treatment itself is not harmful, then the physician was obligated to try it.

With Dr. Bernard's words in mind, it is the author's wish that this book will help you begin a new journey into healing. The author hopes that you will find the information presented here of use in improving your mental, physical, and spiritual health. Ultimately, in partnership with your doctor, the best available knowledge may propel you forward to a state of enhanced physical and emotional wellness, the greatest and most tangible reward of all.

Part I

BODY THERAPIES

"The significant problems we have cannot be solved at the same level of thinking with which we created them." —Albert Einstein

PART I FOCUSES ON ALTERNATIVE therapies which directly strengthen the body, and whose inputs and effects are easily measurable.

Chapter 2 looks at the vital importance of a good diet. Chapter 3 includes a summary of particular foods that have been proven to benefit people with diabetes, and includes suggestions on what to eat and what not to eat.

Chapters 4 and 5 examine vitamin and mineral supplements which may be of benefit to people with diabetes, and other useful supplements which strengthen the body.

Herbs which can lower blood sugar and relieve other symptoms of diabetes are included in Chapter 6.

Chapter 7 covers exercise, and Chapter 8 discusses bodywork or massage that can relieve stress, increase blood circulation, and provide other tangible physical benefits.

Chelation therapy and DMSO, two controversial but possibly useful alternative therapies, round out this section on the body.

Chapter 2

Nutrition

Foods have a role in the management of diabetes in many alternative therapy systems and in Western medicine. This chapter looks at some strategies for healthy eating. Eating properly helps you maintain your weight, reduce physical stress, and keep blood sugar and other symptoms of diabetes under control.

It's no secret that obesity rates in the United States are galloping into the sky. The soaring statistical increase in Type 2 diabetes roughly parallels this trend. More than 90 percent of people with Type 2 diabetes are overweight. In fact, poor eating habits and sedentary lifestyles probably help bring on Type 2 diabetes. On the other hand, losing a little weight will help most people control it.

Much North American corpulence has to do with our stressful lifestyles, the quantity and the quality of the food we eat, and the exercise we don't do to burn off the excess calories.

In order to maintain your particular weight, you must burn off the same amount of calories you take in every day. To lose weight, you must burn more calories than you consume. The foods you put into your own mouth constitute the calories you must burn off. Mostly, we burn calories by moving our bodies. Most of us don't work as hard as our primitive ancestors, so we need to eat less. In addition, as we grow older our metabolism slows by approximately 5 percent per decade. Meanwhile, our ability to absorb nutrients from food diminishes. To maintain a normal weight, older people need to eat more nutrients and less calories, which is most easily done with natural, unprocessed foods.

Healthy Eating

Diets recommended for people with Type 2 diabetes aren't much different than those recommended for all people who wish to remain healthy and minimize the incidence of disease.

While it's important to control *how much* food you eat if you want to lose weight, the *quality* of foods is also crucial to good health, and in controlling blood sugar. Our national eating habits are poor. The third National Health and Nutrition Examination Survey in 1994 revealed that Americans continue eating immense quantities of energy-dense, nutrient-poor foods, popularly described as junk foods. The American appetite for junk foods is huge—27 percent of our total calories, or 31 percent if alcohol, a calorie-laden drug, is included. Junk food gives us quick carbohydrate energy, but it doesn't have many real nutrients. Although artificial flavors and smells provide the illusion that we are eating nutritious food, much junk food actually *depletes* vitamin and mineral levels.

In one small research study, a group of people ate four snacks that were about equal in fat and carbohydrate content. Blood sugar and insulin responses were measured after eating. According to results published in the *American Journal of Clinical Nutrition*, when people ate the manufactured snacks (a chocolate-coated candy bar or cola drink with crisps) their blood sugar levels rose highest and fell lowest afterward. When consuming whole-food snacks (raisins and peanuts or bananas and peanuts) their blood sugars didn't rise as high and didn't have so far to fall back. These types of blood sugar fluctuations are important. One person had what researchers characterized as *pathological* insulin responses to the manufactured snacks, and completely normal responses to the whole foods. In a related animal experiment, insulin sensitivity plummeted when six-week-old rats were fed high-sugar diets, but improved either with the addition of fiber to the diet or with exercise on an exercise wheel. The quality of the food we eat is quite important in controlling symptoms such as high blood sugar, and is important for overall health.

Many studies have found that groups with simple, traditional diets, such as the Seventh Day Adventists and Mormons, have unusually high longevity and much lower rates of diabetes, cancer, and other diseases. For instance, a study of Seventh Day Adventist men published in the *American Journal of Public Health* found they had only *half* the risk of dying with diabetes than the national average for men of similar age. Within this group, vegetarians had a substantially lower risk than non-vegetarians. Other studies of the Amish, Hutterites, and other religious groups who stress healthy dietary habits have found that these groups have greater longevity, lower rates of heart disease, and a higher level of overall health. Eating simple, unprocessed foods that are dense in real nutrients and low in calories is one of the keys to good health.

Any program to modify the diet is a change in behavior, of course, and is more likely to succeed if it is supported by family members and friends. Preparing and serving wholesome foods that are appealing in color, taste, and smell always helps make them good to eat and also assures a good mix of nutrients in the food. Taking adequate time to prepare good meals, and plenty of time to eat them, can prevent overeating and improve health. A number of suggestions for good eating strategies for people with diabetes may be found in the book *The Type 2 Diabetes Sourcebook*, cowritten with Terry Zierenberg, R.N., C.D.E.

Balance

Most dietitians would agree that you need a balanced diet, one containing enough carbohydrates, proteins, and fats to nourish you and give you energy, as well as an adequate intake of vitamins and minerals. However, some nutritional experts estimate that as many as 97 percent of Americans don't eat a balanced diet.

In terms of your body chemistry, you are what you eat. Scientists tell us that the 10 trillion or so specialized cells in your body will *all* be replaced over a period of about seven years. Your new cells will be constructed from the foods you consume during that time. Vitamin and mineral supplements can help bolster deficiencies, but supplements cannot replace the perfectly balanced combination of nutrients you get from good, nutritious food and from an adequate consumption of ordinary water.

Carbohydrates, protein, and fats provide the energy you need to live, which is expressed as calories. All these macronutrients convert to glucose, a simple sugar that provides energy. Since carbohydrates, proteins, and fats are absorbed by the body at different rates of speed, a balanced diet that contains all three is crucial in spreading out the absorption of glucose and the accompanying insulin response over time.

The human body can store only 1,500 calories as carbohydrates. This is about a two-day supply. Beyond this, glucose converts to fat. The human body can store a whopping 100,000 calories in the form of fat, the most concentrated form of energy storage.

Packing extra calories as fat was probably quite useful to our primitive ancestors, who sometimes went for a long time between meals. But the calorie-storing body that kept the cavemen alive is dysfunctional today. Fats are scarce in nature, but in our incredibly rich culture, they are everywhere you look. Fat is fattening. Furthermore, the fats you eat, chemically similar to body fat, convert into body fat with only a small expenditure of energy, estimated at about 3 percent. By contrast, carbohydrates and proteins burn 25 percent or more of their own calories converting into fats. Dr. Art Ulene has estimated that the average American diet is 40 to 45 percent fat, much of it from meat and diary products, which gives us too much fat and also twice the protein we actually need.

Vegetarian Diets

Switching to a well-planned vegetarian diet could possibly help control diabetes, even without stepping up your present level of exercise. This was suggested by a small pilot study conducted at Georgetown University Medical Center in 1999, which was published in the magazine *Preventive Medicine*. The Georgetown study found a 28 percent mean reduction in fasting blood glucose on subjects with Type 2 diabetes who were given low-fat, high-fiber vegetarian diets for three months, versus a 12 percent reduction in fasting blood glucose for subjects given a good, balanced American Dietetic Association (ADA) diet emphasizing fish and chicken rather than meat. Subjects on vegetarian diets also lost more weight than the control group, an average weight loss of approximately 16 pounds over the three months, compared with an 8-pound loss by the control group. Several of the subjects on vegetarian diets were able to reduce their oral hypoglycemic medications, and one was able to discontinue them. The group who ate vegetarian meals also lowered their serum cholesterol and reduced the rate of protein loss in their urine, which was not true of the control group.

In a 1997 position paper, the American Dietetic Association took note of scientific evidence regarding the benefits of appropriately planned vegetarian diets to people with many chronic diseases. Appropriate planning is necessary to reduce the possibilities of deficiencies in nutrients like Vitamin B_{12} and Vitamin D, which can occur in some types of vegetarian diets. The ADA position paper states in part:

> Scientific data suggest positive relationships between a vegetarian diet and reduced risk for several chronic degenerative diseases and conditions, including obesity, coronary artery disease, hypertension, diabetes mellitus, and some types of cancer. Vegetarian diets, like all diets, need to be planned appropriately to be nutritionally adequate. It is the position of the American Dietetic Association (ADA) that appropriately planned vegetarian diets are healthful, are nutritionally adequate, and provide health benefits in the prevention and treatment of certain diseases . . .
>
> Vegetarian diets low in fat or saturated fat have been used successfully as part of comprehensive health programs to reverse severe coronary artery disease. Vegetarian diets offer disease protection benefits because of their lower saturated fat, cholesterol, and animal protein content and often higher concentration of folate (which reduces serum homocysteine levels), antioxidants such as vitamins C and E, carotenoids, and phytochemicals. Not only is mortality from coronary artery disease lower in vegetarians than in nonvegetarians, but vegetarian diets have also been successful in arresting coronary artery disease. Total serum cholesterol and low-density lipoprotein cholesterol levels are usually lower in vegetarians, but high-density lipoprotein cholesterol and triglyceride levels vary depending on the type of vegetarian diet followed.
>
> Vegetarians tend to have a lower incidence of hypertension than nonvegetarians. This effect appears to be independent of both body weight and sodium intake. Type 2 diabetes mellitus is much less likely to be a cause of death in vegetarians than nonvegetarians, perhaps

because of their higher intake of complex carbohydrates and lower body mass index . . .

A well-planned vegetarian diet may be useful in the prevention and treatment of renal disease. Studies using human being and animal models suggest that some plant proteins may increase survival rates and decrease proteinuria, glomerular filtration rate, renal blood flow, and histologic renal damage compared with nonvegetarian diet.

Major health organizations recommend the consumption of at least five servings of vegetables and fruits per day for optimal health. This is a conservative recommendation, but more than most Americans currently consume. According to Dr. Bruce Ames, head of the University of California's Environmental Health Center, only about 9 percent of the U.S. population actually eats the recommended five servings per day. According to the American Dietetic Association, a full 11 percent of the U.S. population eats *no* fresh fruits or vegetables daily.

Many research studies affirm the value of eating more vegetables and fruits. For instance, a five-year study of middle-age female health professionals, published in the October 2000 *American Journal of Clinical Nutrition*, found that women who ate ten or more servings of fruits and vegetables had only 68 percent of the risk of cardiovascular disease as women who ate only one serving per day. Women who ate five to ten servings per day had 30 percent less risk than women who ate two and a half servings per day.

William J. McCarthy, an associate professor of nutrition at the University of California in Los Angeles, says our ancestors ate twelve servings of fruits and vegetables per day in Paleolithic times. Today, McCarthy says, seven servings per day for women and nine for men is ideal. While it is difficult for most people to be completely vegetarian, he says it's not difficult to become a *casual vegetarian*, eating mostly vegetables, grains, legumes, and fruit, and every once in a while eating fish, chicken, or meat.

People concerned about their vitamins and minerals should first eat more vegetables and fruits, the best natural source of such nutrients. Three servings of vegetables and two of fruit, for instance, will give you about 250 milligrams (mg.) of Vitamin C, more than the average daily requirement, and adequate supplies of most other vitamins and minerals in their most natural form. To demonstrate the point that real food is superior to vitamin supplements, Dr. Kenneth Pelletier, director of the Complementary and Alternative Medicine Program at Stanford University, cites research that three-quarters of a cup of kale can neutralize more free radicals than supplements containing 500 mg. of Vitamin C or 800 IU of Vitamin E, even though the kale actually only contains 40 mg. of Vitamin C and less than 10 IU of Vitamin E. Nutrients in natural foods may be much more potent, since they are naturally balanced with phytochemicals and other beneficial substances.

Diets, Diets Everywhere

If you are overweight, experts agree that reducing your intake of calories and exercising regularly are the two best ways to assure healthy weight loss. Despite a gaggle of diet gurus promising instant weight loss on particular fad diets, slow and steady almost always wins the race. Advocates of particular diets do recommend avoiding or minimizing refined sugar and processed products, and eating more unprocessed foods. Beyond that, the experts give conflicting advice.

Anyone who has attempted to lose weight knows it is much easier to find dietary advice than to actually lose weight. It is extremely difficult to lose weight and keep it off. Losing weight is a slow, frustrating, habit-breaking process at best. Every person's body chemistry is different, so no particular diet is appropriate for every person. Some trial and error is necessary to find what works for you.

Many different diets are out there. All are a little different in what they recommend and how they recommend accomplishing it. Some of the more popular diet plans include:

ADA Diet. The American Diabetes Association and the American Dietetic Association together recommend a diet consisting of 30 percent or less fat (mostly monounsaturated), 50 to 60 percent carbohydrates, and the balance protein. Exchange lists, constant carbohydrates, food points, and fat and carbohydrate counting are among the approaches commonly used by registered dietitians to follow these basic and somewhat general ADA guidelines. This is a healthful, basic approach. The American Diabetes Association suggests that vegetables

from its "Food Exchange Group A," such as spinach, asparagus, broccoli, cabbage, string beans, and celery, should be abundantly included
in the diet.

Atkins Diet. Dr. Robert Atkins, of the Atkins Center for Complementary Medicine in New York City, contends that a high-fat, low-
carbohydrate diet will help people lose weight. Dr. Atkins's diet throws
the body into a state of ketosis, which burns fat cells for energy. When
fat is burned, insulin levels will fall, he says. Dr. Atkins says his diet may
correct diabetes, high blood pressure, and other conditions. His diet
calls for the consumption of 45 grams or less of carbohydrates per day
for weight loss, and 90 grams or less for maintenance. Dr. Atkins
restricts all white sugar and white flour—he says these make up as much
as half of many people's calories, and that both increase the production
of insulin. Dr. Atkins claims that people who follow his diet lose weight,
experience improved blood pressure and lower cholesterol, and may
reduce their doses of prescription drugs. People with diabetes are
advised to take supplements such as those sold by his Center for Complementary Medicine, containing nutrients such as chromium, vanadium, Vitamins B complex, C, Coenzyme Q_{10}, alpha lipoic acid, and
essential fatty acids GLA and EPA.

Bernstein Diet. Developed by Dr. Richard K. Bernstein, a brilliant
New York physician who has Type 1 diabetes, the Bernstein diet involves
severely limiting carbohydrate consumption, to perhaps 6 grams of
slow-acting carbohydrate at breakfast, 12 grams at lunch, and 12 grams
at dinner. Dr. Bernstein's books recommend eliminating simple sugars
such as those contained in some powdered artificial sweeteners, fruits,
fruit juices, desserts, milk and cottage cheese, snack foods, candy, cold
and hot cereal, commercial prepared soups, and cooked beets, carrots,
potatoes, and corn. He recommends eating more vegetables, meat, fish,
fowl, cheeses, soy milk, nuts, yogurt, soybean products, bran crackers,
and low carbohydrate desserts, and allows only limited amounts of
alcohol.

The HCF Diet. Dr. James Anderson of Lexington, Kentucky, an
early enthusiast of oat bran, is an advocate of high fiber diets for people with Type 2 diabetes who are overweight. His high carbohydrate
fiber nutrition plan, or HCF diet, recommends the consumption of up
to 70 grams of fiber per day, particularly soluble fibers such as those
found in oat bran, legumes, some vegetables, blackberries, and barley.

The Ezrin Diet. Los Angeles research endocrinologist Dr. Calvin Ezrin recommends a low carbohydrate diet with appropriate supplements for people with Type 2 diabetes. During the weight loss portion of his diet, dieters are limited to a maximum of 1,000 calories per day, including a maximum of 40 grams of carbohydrate, creating a state of ketosis in which the body burns fats for energy. Every day, 55 to 75 grams of protein, 1,000 mg. of calcium, a multivitamin and mineral supplement containing 100 percent of the RDA, and a teaspoon of salt are advised. According to *The Type 2 Diabetes Diet Book*, which Dr. Ezrin cowrote with Robert Kowalski, this diet is safe and effective but must be supervised by a physician.

The Mediterranean Diet. The so-called Mediterranean diet, high in monounsaturated fats like olive oil, as well as vegetables and fruits, is touted as preventive to heart problems. This diet has a beneficial effect on insulin sensitivity and improves blood circulation in people with Type 2 diabetes, according to research done at Trinity College in Dublin, Ireland, and published in the year 2000. A review of diets high in monounsaturated fat, published in the *American Journal of Clinical Nutrition* in 1998, found that such diets generally improved lipoprotein profiles and blood sugar control. There is no evidence that such diets induce weight gain if calories are controlled, the authors stated.

The Ornish Diet. Dr. Dean Ornish of the Preventive Medicine Research Institute in San Francisco, California, developed a multidisciplinary program to reduce heart disease without surgery or drugs. Dr. Ornish's recommended diet is basically vegetarian, a low fat, high carbohydrate strategy. He says the typical American diet consists of 40 to 50 percent fats, 25 to 35 percent carbohydrates, and 25 percent protein. His reversal diet is basically vegetarian, with fats composing a maximum of 10 percent of the diet, protein 25 percent, and perhaps 70 to 75 percent carbohydrates. His prevention diet allows 20 percent of calories from fat. Dr. Ornish recommends consuming grains, legumes, and possibly small amounts of nonfat yogurt or skim milk to assure adequate protein, and avoiding refined sugars and highly processed food products. Exercise, yoga, and support groups are other aspects of his program. This diet is similar to the Pritikin Diet, which was popular during the 1970s.

The Zone Diet. Barry Sears, Ph.D., author of *The Zone: A Dietary Road Map*, calls his diet "a protein adequate, low fat, moderate carbohydrate program." Sears cites a small study that compared his "zone diet" to an ADA diet on a group of fifteen people with Type 2 diabetes. The two diets have different ratios of protein to carbohydrate—the zone diet group ate a ratio of 3 grams of protein to 4 grams of carbohydrate, while the ADA diet group ate 1 gram of protein for every 3 grams of carbohydrate. At the end of eight weeks certain parameters such as weight, fat, fasting insulin, and triglycerides were lower on the zone diet group. Both groups had a 12 percent drop in fasting glucose. In the ADA diet group, Dr. Sears says, triglyceride and fasting insulin levels actually increased.

High Fiber

High fiber diets have many benefits for people with diabetes seeking to lose or maintain weight. The act of chewing fiber stimulates the production of saliva, which improves digestion. The fiber abundant in plant foods helps in both digestion and excretion, and it produces a *full* feeling after eating. The bulk that fiber provides in the stomach and intestines also slows down the movement of food through the intestines and provides more time for the absorption of nutrients. This slows the normal blood sugar rise after eating, among other benefits.

The Third National Health and Nutrition Examination Survey states that the average American with diabetes consumes 16 grams of fiber per day. However, an intake of 20 to 60 grams of fiber per day taken in the form of food may be ideal for most people with Type 2 diabetes, according to several research studies.

There is considerable evidence that consuming a high-fiber diet can help in weight loss, lower blood sugar, and reduce the production of cholesterol in the body. The downside is that many people experience an increase in flatulence when they increase their intake of fiber, but the additional farting is a harmless if sometimes embarrassing side effect.

An interesting crossover study conducted at the University of Texas Southwestern Medical Center in Dallas was published in the *New England Journal of Medicine* in 2000. Researchers put a dozen people with Type 2 diabetes on high fiber diets containing about 50 grams of fiber, or the equivalent to seven to eight servings of fruits and vegeta-

Alkaline Diets

In treating people with diabetes, some practitioners, including naturopath Skip Shoden, recommend an alkaline diet. The body's pH is neutral at a measurement of 7. Alkaline diets are designed to increase it to just over 7, a slightly alkaline state that is the natural pH of the cell. One expert has noted that as many as 90 percent of Americans become overly acidic at some point in their lifetimes, mainly due to poor diets.

When the body's pH is acidic, Shoden says, it is a sign of inflammation, which will benefit from being controlled. On the other hand, when the body is slightly alkaline, maximum oxygenation of the blood occurs, levels of pathogens decrease, and better health occurs. Reducing saturated fats and eating an abundance of green vegetables, he adds, helps make the body more alkaline, protecting the lining of blood vessels and providing many general health benefits.

Shoden often recommends an old naturopathic remedy for people with diabetes. It is a broth made from four green vegetables—asparagus, zucchini, celery, and green beans. Consumed every day in reasonable quantities, he says, this alkaline broth can help reduce blood sugar levels and improve overall health.

Dr. Susan Lark, a nutritionist who teaches at Stanford University Medical School and the author of several books, has observed that stress, certain medications, long airplane flights, strenuous athletic activity, and even the many items in the standard American diet such as red meat, dairy products, caffeine, refined sugar, and flour can tip a person's body chemistry toward acidity.

To maintain a proper acid-alkaline balance, Dr. Lark recommends eating more alkaline foods, such as vegetables, grains, beans, a few seeds and nuts, and cold water fish, and supplementing this with high chlorophyll green foods such as alfalfa, barley grass, spirulina, and cholorella, which promote alkalinity. For people over the age of forty, she recommends restoring alkaline mineral reserves in the body with supplements such as calcium, magnesium, potassium, zinc, manganese, chromium, selenium, copper, iodine, boron, and buffered Vitamin C as needed.

bles per day. Subjects stayed on the high fiber diets for six weeks, then spent another six weeks on a standard ADA-recommended diet. When subjects ate the high fiber diets, they reduced their blood sugar levels about 10 percent, and also improved their cholesterol levels when compared to people who followed the ADA diet.

Dr. James Anderson was one of the first medical doctors to advocate complex carbohydrate, high fiber diets, which are high in cereal grains, legumes, and root vegetables. Dr. Anderson recommends fiber be taken in the natural form, that is, as food rather than in supplements.

Consuming fiber restricts simple sugar and fat intake, he notes, since you can't eat one thing if you're eating another. Both sugar and fat consumption are strongly linked with diabetes in scientific studies, and high fiber foods don't have much of either. Anderson's HCF diet calls for 65 to 75 percent of total calories from mostly complex carbohydrates, only 10 to 15 percent of calories from fats, and 10 to 15 percent from protein. He personally recommends consuming at least 50 grams of fiber per day, much more than is consumed by the average American.

Anderson writes that among people with Type 2 diabetes who have followed an HCF diet, 60 percent were able to discontinue insulin therapy, while insulin doses were significantly reduced for the other 40 percent. His high fiber diet reduces the blood sugar rise after a meal, lowers insulin resistance, reduces LDL (bad cholesterol), increases HDL (good cholesterol), reduces triglycerides, and helps dieters progressively lose weight. Of course, much more water than usual should be consumed by people on high fiber diets, to help digest it and speed it through the system. Drinking adequate water also prevents dehydration, a problem for people with diabetes.

There are two basic types of fiber found in plants: one type is soluble in water, the other isn't. Water-soluble fiber is believed to be the most beneficial. It binds in the gut with cholesterol-containing bile acids, preventing their reabsorption. Soluble fiber slows the absorption of glucose, and is less likely to cause diarrhea. According to Michael Murray, a naturopath who is the author of several books on nutrition, soluble fiber increases sensitivity of tissues to insulin, prevents excessive insulin secretion, and improves the uptake of glucose by the liver. Insoluble fiber provides bulk, absorbs water in the gut, and dilutes concentrations of toxic bile acids. According to statistical research conducted at the

Department of Nutrition at the Harvard School of Public Health, even insoluble fiber may have a role in reducing the incidence of diabetes. Insoluble fiber intake also has a statistical correlation with reduced heart disease.

Better Quality Foods

Eating better quality foods increases the intake of fiber and nutrients. Food processing often removes fiber, along with vitamins, minerals, and beneficial phytochemicals. Good natural sources of fiber, energy, and nutrients are unprocessed foods, particularly legumes, vegetables, fruits, whole grains and cereals, and nuts and seeds. These are excellent foods to include in the diet for many reasons, and may help control blood sugar. But probably the prime nutrient of all, which is especially essential to people with diabetes, is plain old water.

Water

Life as we know it first appeared in the magic elixir of water, and our bodies are almost two-thirds water. After oxygen, water is the most crucial element in maintaining health. Water plays an important if unacknowledged role in diabetes control.

We should all drink six to eight 8-ounce glasses of water per day. Water is necessary for every chemical reaction in the body, and it carries nutrients in and waste out of our cells. A major component of blood, lymph, and saliva, water is crucial for digestion, the absorption of food, blood circulation, the utilization of water-soluble vitamins, the excretion of waste matter, and many other unsung benefits. As we age, we have a reduced sense of thirst, decreased kidney function, and retain lower amounts of water in the body. A lack of water in the body is called dehydration, and it is very dangerous.

Dehydration is one of the most common causes of hospitalization in people over 65, according to the American Dietetic Association, and about half those hospitalized for dehydration die within a year. Dehydration may accompany diarrhea, vomiting, fever, or sweating. It can occur at any time—especially during the summer or during exercise sessions. The worst dehydration scenario is a *diabetic coma*, which requires hospitalization and aggressive replacement of fluids.

High blood sugar both *causes* dehydration and makes it worse. According to Dr. Bernstein, high blood sugar creates a fleeting insulin resistance that causes further rises in blood sugar. High blood sugar also triggers glycosuria—the kidneys excrete water and glucose, which further intensifies dehydration. People with diabetes who are dehydrated are more susceptible to infection, which can raise blood sugars and trigger the onset of complications, or aggravate complications that already exist. Dr. Bernstein advises patients to drink fluids without carbohydrate, adding back salt, potassium, and chloride electrolytes if fluids are lost from vomiting or diarrhea.

Research in the United Arab Emirates showed that mice with diabetes developed neuropathy faster when they were dehydrated.

Dr. Fereydoon Batmanghelidj, the Iranian-born author of *Your Body's Many Cries for Water*, believes that diabetes, depression, high blood pressure, and obesity are all partially diseases of dehydration. Dehydration narrows the arteries and shuts off the blood supply to some of the capillary beds, he says, responses that conserve water for the most vital organs, but which can worsen many health problems.

For one thing, dehydration forces the body to conserve salt. This thickens the urine and stresses the kidneys. The pancreas is stressed without adequate water for its primary role in digestion, which is the secretion of an alkaline solution into the intestines. The pancreas also needs adequate water for the production of insulin and other hormones. Stress and dehydration also form a vicious circle, Dr. Batmanghelidj notes. Dehydration triggers the release of stress hormones, while lack of water contributes to and intensifies the effects of stress.

The body's signals for thirst and hunger are the same, Dr. Batmanghelidj says, and people sometimes eat when their body actually only needs a drink of water. Dr. Batmanghelidj advises that the six 8-ounce glasses of water a day should include a glass of water a half hour before eating for people seeking to lose weight.

A few nutritionists focus some of their efforts on the quality of water. Skip Shoden, a naturopath specializing in nutrition who practices in Marina del Rey, California, recommends that his patients with diabetes drink specially hydrated waters, which he says help them fully

A Balanced Diet

Figure 2.1 **USDA Food Pyramid**

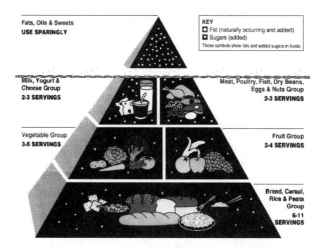

Source: The U.S. Department of Agriculture and the U.S. Department of Health and Human Services

The Food Guide Pyramid, pictured above, is a good place to begin thinking about what proportions of foods to eat to balance your diet. Prepared by the U.S. Department of Agriculture, this diagram recommends a specific number of servings of from various food groups every day. Healthiest foods at the base of the pyramid are recommended in largest amounts. Note that one portion of food in both diagrams is approximately the amount of that food you can hold in the palm of your hand.

Bread, cereal, rice, pasta, vegetables, and fruits should be eaten most frequently. For a balanced diet, aim for six to eleven servings from the whole grain group and two to five servings of vegetables and fruit.

digest their food. Problems with digestion are common in people with diabetes, he adds, adding that truly hydrating waters tend to carry nutrients more effectively into the cells, rather than allowing them to pass through the system. One older brand of hydrating water is Willard Water, developed a few years ago by a retired South Dakota chemist. Chickens who were given Willard Water almost completely digested all the nutrients they were fed, according to research, and this doesn't often occur when chickens are given regular tap water. Anecdotal reports claim some healing effects for people drinking Willard Water. Other hydrating waters on the market are molecularly altered by lasers and electromagnetic fields. However, Dr. Batmanghelidj does not recommend any waters of this type; he says regular tap water is just fine if you let it sit out for half an hour, which allows the chlorine to dissipate. Some holistically oriented doctors advocate the use of inexpensive charcoal filters that remove chlorine and certain heavy metals from tap water.

Although health experts recommend drinking six to eight 8-ounce glasses of water per day, not all of us drink this much water. A survey by Rockefeller University in New York found that 10 percent of respondents drank no water at all each day, and that only a third of us drink the recommended amount. Sodas and coffee are consumed in large quantities, but these are actually diuretics that rob the body of water, contributing to many incidences of mild, chronic dehydration.

Legumes

Legumes are one of the oldest human foods, and one of the first cultivated. A legume is a plant with a pod that splits, such as beans or peanuts. Often called "the poor people's meat," legumes have about the same number of calories as grains, but they provide two to four times as much protein. Legumes may help blood sugar control. A study in 1987 concluded that simply adding more legumes to the diet lowered blood sugar levels after eating and reduced the excretion of glucose in the urine. Legumes improve liver function and lower cholesterol. Green beans and lentils are good sources of amino acids, and legumes in general are good sources of iron, copper, and zinc, as well as the B complex and Vitamin B_6 necessary for good liver function. Beans and peas are good sources of calcium, magnesium, and potassium. Soybeans and products made from soybeans, such as tofu and soy yogurt, are good sources of bioflavonoids. Soybeans also contain isoflavones such as genistein, a substance that may protect against heart disease as well as breast and prostate cancer. A study of 175 elderly men showed that the ones who ate the most legumes had the least glucose intolerance and the least diabetes. The closer to nature the better—research in Canada has shown that cooked dried beans elicit a more favorable glycemic response than beans from a can.

Vegetables

Vegetables, which means "to enliven" in Latin, are the richest source of antioxidants, especially when eaten raw. Vegetables such as garlic, kale, onions, leafy greens, and spinach have an extremely high ratio of antioxidants to carbohydrates, higher than most fruits, with the exception of berries, according to research conducted at Tufts University. Vegetables are complex carbohydrates that provide fiber, delay the emptying of the stomach, and level out the absorption of sugars into the blood. Many vegetables contain high levels of Vitamin C, or heady combinations of other vitamins and minerals. For example, one sweet potato or one cup of carrot juice contains more than 20,000 IU of beta carotene, the preferred form of Vitamin A. Vegetables contain only tiny amounts of fat, in the form of essential fatty acids, and large amounts of other vitamins and minerals such as calcium and magnesium. Carrots, potatoes, sweet potatoes, winter squash, and parsnips are high in potassium, an important mineral.

Eating certain vegetables may help lower blood sugar. Bitter melon, cabbage, green leafy vegetables, okra, and tubers have documented blood sugar lowering effects in humans and test animals. Cucumbers lower blood sugar. Spinach leaves can lower blood sugar. Artichokes, which contain inulin, have a mild blood sugar lowering effect on people who have eaten a meal high in the fruit sugar, fructose; artichokes may also prevent the oxidation of cholesterol and protect the liver. A study published in 1994 showed reductions in blood sugar in research animals fed Maitake mushrooms. *Agaricus bisporus* mushrooms and Reishi mushrooms also lower blood sugar in some animal studies. Celery may help lower blood pressure, perhaps because of the compound 3-n-butyl phthalide. In animal studies, celery also slightly lowered cholesterol.

If you're trying to lose weight, note that a few vegetables contain no calories at all.

Fruits

Fruits are good sources of fiber, and contain many minerals and vitamins, such as potassium and Vitamin C. Figs, raisins, blackberries, bananas, and oranges are good sources of calcium, magnesium, and potassium. Apples, a folk remedy for diabetes, contain pectin, a potent soluble fiber that absorbs water in the intestinal tract and helps to control either constipation or diarrhea. Fruit contains fructose, a form of sugar digested more slowly than refined sugar.

A glass of grapefruit juice every day suppresses the appetite and helps break down fats, according to *The Illustrated Encyclopedia of Natural Remedies*. Eating a grapefruit would probably have a similar effect, while adding fiber to the diet. Despite claims made by salesmen of juicing machines, turning fruits into fruit juice is not recommended at all times; juicing degrades some nutrients, and removes the fiber but not the sugar. According to UCLA nutritionist McCarthy, new federal guidelines advise that only one-third of fruits and vegetables be consumed in the form of juice.

Whole Grains

Whole grains are good sources of fiber, the B vitamins, and Vitamin E, as well as magnesium, calcium, and potassium. Oat bran's ability to lower cholesterol is well-documented. For the highest concentration of nutrients and fiber, foods may be prepared with whole wheat flour, as well as buckwheat and rice flour, millet, or oats. Bread made with whole meal barley flour is one of the slowest to convert to glucose. According to research in Sweden, people who ate whole meal barley bread had lower sugar and insulin levels than subjects who ingested pumpernickel or white bread. Research animals with diabetes who had barley added to their diets had lower blood sugar and lower water consumption than animals fed regular starch or sucrose-based diets, perhaps because of

A Balanced Vegetarian Diet

The Food Guide Pyramid for Vegetarian Meal Planning, pictured below, was prepared by the American Dietetic Association, a large professional association whose registered dietitian members specialize in nutrition and meal planning. The American Dietetic Association does not advocate vegetarian diets per se, but it does have an official position citing some of the health benefits of eating in this fashion. While this pyramid eliminates meats, it does include meat substitutes such as legumes, eggs, and nuts, and permits some consumption of dairy products from the milk, yogurt, and cheese group. The Physicians Committee for Responsible Medicine recommends even more drastic alterations to the USDA Food Guide Pyramid. The PCRM would eliminate dairy products from this pyramid, but retain the meat substitutes that contain protein.

Figure 2.2 **Food Guide Pyramid for Vegetarian Meal Planning**

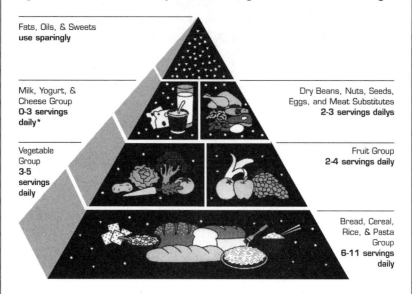

Fats, Oils, & Sweets
use sparingly

Milk, Yogurt, &
Cheese Group
**0-3 servings
daily***

Dry Beans, Nuts, Seeds,
Eggs, and Meat Substitutes
2-3 servings dailys

Vegetable
Group
**3-5
servings
daily**

Fruit Group
2-4 servings daily

Bread, Cereal,
Rice, & Pasta
Group
**6-11 servings
daily**

* Vegetarians who choose not to use milk, yogurt, or cheese need to select other food sources rich in calcium.

Source: National Center for Nutrition and Diatetics, The American Diatetic Association.

the chromium content of barley. Barley sprouts lower blood sugar. Some of the richest sources of amino acids may be found in the germinating sprouts of grains and other plants.

Seeds and Nuts

Seeds and nuts are good sources of fiber, B complex vitamins and Vitamin E, protein, fiber, essential fatty acids, and minerals such as magnesium, calcium, and potassium. Although these foods are high in oil, they may help with weight loss programs, since a few nuts may help produce a feeling of being full. A large study of more than 25,000 Americans showed that those who ate the most nuts were the least obese and suffered the fewest heart attacks. A study of walnut consumption published in the *New England Journal of Medicine* showed reduced cholesterol, LDL cholesterol, and triglyceride levels in men with normal blood lipid levels who were given additional walnuts. One study showed that horse chestnuts can lower blood sugar.

Eating a well-balanced diet, including lots of vegetables, fruits, legumes, and whole grains will bolster your health, reduce the physical stress of diabetes, and help you control your weight. The next chapter recommends particular foods to eat or avoid, and examines some of the research that supports the recommendations.

Chapter 3

Foods to Eat and Foods to Avoid

A few foods are particularly good to include in the diet if you have Type 2 diabetes, according to research, while other foods and food ingredients have a highly negative effect on diabetic control. Foods containing refined sugar, white flour, and other substances have proven negative effects on the person with diabetes, but some substitutes for these substances are suggested here.

Good Foods to Eat

Excellent foods to include in the diet are brewer's yeast, cold water fish, garlic and onions, karella, nopal, and tropical guava.

Brewer's Yeast

Real brewer's yeast is nontoxic, and it often reduces the craving for sweets. Although it has a bitter taste, brewer's yeast is the best natural source of the important trace mineral chromium. The chromium in brewer's yeast is in the highly usable form of glucose tolerance factor, or GTF. This easily absorbed form of chromium makes insulin more potent and helps the body metabolize glucose. Real brewer's yeast contains 50 to 60 micrograms of chromium per tablespoonful, a good amount.

Brewer's yeast is also an excellent source of B vitamins. It supplies all the essential amino acids, and some minerals such as selenium. One tablespoon also contains more than 100 percent of a day's supply of Vitamin B_1, and between 20 to 40 percent of the RDA of Vitamins B_2, B_3, B_6, and folic acid, along with biotin and inositol. Brewer's yeast also contains many useful amino acids and naturally occurring nucleic acids (DNA and RNA), which are believed to enhance immune system function and increase energy.

One study of people with diabetes who were given 1.6 grams of brewer's yeast per day saw glycosylated hemoglobin, or HbA1C, levels decrease 17 percent, and LDL, or "bad" cholesterol, decrease 36 percent.

Brewer's yeast is sold as a fine powder, or in tablets or capsules. The powder has an odd, airy, bitter taste, but can be added to shakes or other foods, or sprinkled over other dishes. Some doctors recommend two to three tablespoons per day for people with diabetes.

Precautions: Other commercial yeasts such as baker's yeast, tortula yeast, and nutritional yeast are low in chromium and don't have the nutritional benefits of real brewer's yeast. "Debittered" yeast sold in some health food stores is not real brewer's yeast. Approximately 30 percent of women with candida yeast infections may be allergic to brewer's yeast, and experience symptoms if it is consumed, according to Dr. Robert Atkins.

Cold-Water Fish

Many studies have shown reasons to eat more foods containing essential omega-3 fatty acids, which are found in large amounts in cold-water fish like salmon, mackerel, and herring. Eating more fish is believed to have cardiovascular benefits, to reduce cholesterol and high blood pressure, to help reduce obesity, and to lessen incidences of cancer, autoimmune diseases, and other health problems. In Sweden, where longevity is the highest of all the countries in the world, fish is plentiful while sugar and meat are scarce.

Fish oil contains about 30 percent of beneficial omega-3 oils such as eicosapentaenoic acid (EPA) and docosahexaenoic acid (DHA). These essential fatty acids can lower triglycerides and are generally anti-inflammatory. Many people with diabetes have problems metabolizing some of the essential fatty acids, which are the only forms of fat that can be increased in the diet for health benefits. Essential fatty acids help modulate parts of the immune system, dampen the generation of free radicals, and reduce the fat oxidation that contributes to vascular and heart problems.

Human life evolved on a diet that contained approximately equal amounts of the omega-6 and omega-3 essential fatty acids, experts say, but the balance went out of whack in the past century or so, coinciding with the increased incidence of Type 2 diabetes. Today, the Western diet contains perhaps twenty or thirty times more omega-6 than omega-3. Too much omega-6 fatty acid, found in vegetable oils such as corn and sunflower oil, can have the effect of clogging up blood vessels, which omega-3 fatty acids help keep in good working order.

Essential fatty acids are so called because they must be consumed to maintain health. They are needed by the body in relatively large amounts—by every cell in the body, as components in cell membranes—and they cannot be manufactured in the body. The World Health Organization recommends that 5 percent of calories come from essential fatty acids for pregnant women and children. Various authorities recommend from 1 to 5 percent of calories come from essential fatty acids for all people.

Eating real fish is better than taking fish oil capsules. One study of men with high cholesterol found that both fish and fish oil supplements lowered LDL cholesterol and triglyceride levels. However, eating real fish was superior to fish oil: real fish reduced the "stickiness" of platelets, which can create blood clots in small arteries and lead to a heart attack or stroke.

While studies of normal people have shown a blood sugar lowering effect, two studies of fish oil supplements given to people with Type 2 diabetes yielded unimpressive results. One study gave subjects 10 grams of fish oil per day for three weeks, which actually *raised* blood sugars a bit. A second study produced no change in either blood sugar levels or insulin resistance. Because of the chance that they can raise blood sugars, nutritionally oriented doctors often do not recommend fish oil supplements. Dr. James Anderson recommends eating fish twice a week and using fish oil supplements only if fish can't be consumed that frequently.

Precautions: Some fish oil capsules contain large amounts of para-aminobenzoic acid (PABA), a chemical that can elevate blood sugar. Some fish oil capsules have been found to contain chemical contaminates, unsafe levels of Vitamins A or D, or high levels of lipid peroxides produced by fats going rancid. Vitamin E added to supplements by manufacturers can help keep capsules from turning rancid, and may also aid in holding down the rise in blood sugar seen in some studies. Vitamin E protects the EPA and DHA from oxidation within the body.

Garlic and Onions

Garlic and onions have been used as a folk medicines for many years. Eating one or both daily is recommended for people at risk for heart disease or circulatory disorders. Consuming these foods may help lower blood sugar in people with diabetes and provide other nutritional benefits.

There have been more than 1,000 scientific studies of the medicinal effects of garlic. Among its documented beneficial properties, garlic is a natural antibiotic, antioxidant, fungicide, expectorant, antiseptic, and antihistamine. Garlic cleanses the blood, discourages internal parasites, and helps to create a healthy population of bacteria in the gut. The active compound is allylpropyl-disulfide, which apparently lowers blood sugar because it competes with sites that inactivate insulin in the liver.

Garlic has been shown to reduce blood sugar in both human and animal studies, according to the *Lawrence Review of Natural Products*. In one study, researchers noted an increase in insulin in the blood and an improvement in the storage of glycogen in the liver after the administration of garlic. Another study compared two groups of diabetic rats fed high sugar diets. Rats who received garlic oil showed decreases or stable cholesterol and triglyceride levels, while rats fed no garlic saw those levels rise 50 percent.

Antioxidant garlic is high in sulfur and contains small amounts of many useful vitamins, minerals, and trace elements, including germanium and selenium. In crushed, cooked, or juice form, some studies have

No-Calorie Vegetables

The following list of vegetables may be eaten as often as desired, and can be valuable in weight-loss plans as snack items. They are virtually calorie-free, since the calories they contain are entirely used up by the body in their digestion. They are a bit more nutritious when eaten raw.

Alfalfa Sprouts

Bell Peppers

Bok Choy

Cabbage

Celery

Chicory

Chinese Cabbage

Cucumbers

Endive

Escarole

Lettuce

Parsley

Radishes

Spinach

Turnips

Watercress

shown that garlic can help lower blood sugar, blood pressure, and cholesterol. Eating garlic may help prevent heart disease and arteriosclerosis. Garlic may help clear up a candida yeast infection or ward off cancer. Fresh garlic is pungent and bracing. Powdered garlic tablets are

Culinary Herbs

Several herbs often used in food preparation have been found to lower blood sugar or have other beneficial effects, mostly in animal studies. These culinary herbs are safe, and may be good alternatives to sugar or salt.

Cinnamon is used in traditional Chinese medicine to invigorate circulation, warm the body, and harmonize the top part of the body with the lower part of the body. Cinnamon may help lower insulin requirements, according to one study of people with Type 2 diabetes conducted at the USDA's Beltsville Human Nutrition Research Center in Beltsville, Maryland. Cinnamon makes insulin three times more potent, according to researchers. Seasoning with 1/4–1 teaspoonful of cinnamon per day may help keep blood sugar under control. Note that too much cinnamon can irritate the liver in very large quantities, and it should be avoided by people with inflammatory liver disease. Other spices that have some documented blood sugar lowering effect include **apple pie spice**, **cloves**, and **bay leaves**, as well as **tumeric**, the key ingredient in many Indian curries. Tumeric is a powerful antioxidant, which reduces inflammation, protects the liver, and improves blood circulation by reducing the clumping together of platelets.

Cilantro is a folk treatment for diabetes. It is used in Chinese and Mexican cooking and in Chinese medicine for medicinal purposes. Cilantro stimulates digestion and blood circulation. It is a nerve stimulant it is therefore beneficial for apathy and fatigue, as well as being a mild aphrodisiac. When incorporated into the diets and drinking water of diabetic mice, cilantro reduced blood sugar levels and increased the conversion of glucose into glycogen, according to a 1999 study published in *British Journal of Nutrition*. As an essential aromatic oil, when added to massage oil, coriander's sweet, musky scent is said to relieve tired or sore muscles.

A study in India of people with diabetes who were given an extract of **holy basil** saw fasting blood sugars reduced by an average of 21 mg./dl., postprandial blood sugar reduced by 15 mg./dl., and slight reductions in cholesterol. Holy basil has also been studied as a stress-relieving adaptogenic.

The ingredient that gives gin its characteristic flavor, **juniper berries** are high in fiber, and also have a hypoglycemic action. A study at the University of Granada in Spain showed that juniper created a significant reduction in blood sugar, prevented weight loss, and resulted in greater longevity in diabetic rats. Juniper is also a diuretic—it apparently acts by irritating the tissue of the kidneys, and should not be used with people with impaired kidney function.

Kelp, a sea vegetable that may be substituted for salt, is sometimes recommended to increase metabolism in people seeking to lose weight, according to Time-Life's *Medical Advisor*. Kelp contains amounts of natural iodine, and comes in powdered form, or in tablets. From three to four tablets per day are often recommended for people seeking to lose weight.

Sage may make insulin more potent, according to one study. A dash of **vinegar** on a starchy meal may help reduce blood sugar and insulin responses after the meal, according to research conducted in Sweden on ten people without diabetes.

Rosemary, on the other hand, may actually raise blood sugar. Rosemary oil increased fasting blood sugar levels 17 percent and inhibited the release of insulin in diabetic rabbits, according to research published in 1994. Francis Brinker, author of *Herb Contraindications and Drug Interactions*, says **coffee**, **tea**, **cocoa**, and **cola seeds** all raise blood sugar.

available for those who don't like the taste of garlic cloves or who don't include real garlic in their diet.

In clinical trials involving human beings, the strongest body of research focuses on garlic's ability to lower blood cholesterol, particularly "bad," or LDL, cholesterol. Several analyses of research on garlic have confirmed this. A meta-analysis conducted at the University of Oxford in England of sixteen trials involving garlic showed a 12 percent average reduction in cholesterol beyond placebo after one month of therapy. Another study of garlic powder showed more mixed results, but the authors at Flingers University of South Australia, Adelaide, concluded that garlic powder might be of clinical use in cases of mild hypertension. In general, benefits of this type seem to be best confirmed for fresh garlic, according to an analysis in the *British Journal of Clinical Pharmacology* in 1989.

Onions, also from the allium plant family, have similar beneficial properties. Some studies have shown that onions help lower blood sugar and cholesterol and may provide some protection against certain types of cancer and other disorders. Onions increase the blood circulation and help relax muscles. Regular consumption also reduces nervous debility. The "weeping" stimulated by raw onions helps the body release toxins.

Eating either raw or boiled onions reduces blood sugar during glucose tolerance tests, possibly by increasing the supply of insulin in circulation. Other experts believe onions help metabolize sugar in the blood, thereby lowering blood sugar. Research has demonstrated that blood sugar reductions with onion consumption are dose-dependent; that is, eating more onions results in greater reductions of blood sugar. Onions contain *quercetin*, a useful bioflavonoid that blocks the "sorbitol pathway" associated with some complications of diabetes.

Precautions: Garlic does thin the blood and could cause adverse reactions in those taking anticoagulant drugs. Although fresh garlic has been used for centuries as an ingredient in cooking, the safety of concentrated garlic extracts is not completely proven; occasional cases of stomach upset, nausea, and lightheadedness have resulted from a 25 milliliter dose of fresh extract. Garlic dust, inhaled, is also known to induce asthmatic reactions.

Karella

Karella, a bitter-tasting melon from India, may help lower blood sugar. Also known as bitter melon, bitter gourd, or *Momordica charantia*, it is a traditional Ayurvedic recommendation for mild Type 2 diabetes and is said to have a calming, tonic effect. Found in South America, Africa, and Asia, karella is shaped like a cucumber but covered with bumps like a gourd. It is green when unripened, but the fruit turns yellow-orange when ripe.

Although a couple of studies have shown karella has no effect on blood sugar, a majority of the studies conducted in India so far have found that a single dose of karella lowers blood sugar, perhaps by modulating the secretion of insulin. In studies in India in which normal and Type 2 diabetic people were fed various vegetable fibers, karella was more effective at lowering blood sugar than the leafy vegetables.

As the name "bitter melon" suggests, this vegetable is quite bitter. If you can tolerate the taste, some practitioners advise boiling one or two karella, cut into small pieces, and eat it in the morning, and perhaps in the evening. As a medicinal herb, it may also be utilized in the extract form.

Prickly Pear Cactus

Prickly pear cactus, or *Opuntia streptacantha*, is a Mexican folk remedy for diabetes. Also known as nopal, it has one of the lowest ratings on the glycemic index, meaning that it converts to glucose very slowly in the body. Nopal is quite nutritious, containing high amounts of calcium, potassium, Vitamin C, and iron. Celebrity doctor Andrew Weil suggests it.

A small Mexican study of people with Type 2 diabetes, published in 1989, assessed the effects of eating broiled nopal on blood sugar. Consumption of 100, 300, and 500 grams of nopal resulted in decreases in blood sugar, with maximum decreases three hours after eating. The biggest portions of nopal produced the best results. Blood sugar reductions of 30 mg./dl. and 40 to 60 mg./dl. were achieved from eating 300 grams and 500 grams (about a pound) of nopal. However, another study published the same year found no effect using dried extract of nopal.

In a 1991 study, 500 grams of nopal stems were given to people with and without Type 2 diabetes. Subjects were tested several times over three hours. Significant reductions in blood sugar and serum insulin levels were noted in people with diabetes, but not in normal subjects.

A 1996 study in Michoacan, Mexico, with nopal extract on diabetic rats found that blood sugar and glycosolated hemoglobin levels were reduced to normal when insulin and extract were combined for seven weeks. When insulin was withdrawn and nopal extract continued, the blood sugar of the rats remained normal, according to results published in *The Journal of Ethnopharmacology*.

Tropical Guava

Chinese folk medicine holds that eating guava helps people with diabetes. Researchers in Taiwan gave 3 ounces of guava juice to normal subjects and to people with diabetes. The guava juice reduced blood sugar. In diabetic subjects, blood glucose fell from 214 mg./dl. to 165 mg./dl., and the effects lasted for about three hours. Another study, published in the *American Journal of Cardiology*, in which subjects ate one guava per day before a meal, showed an 8 to 10 percent reduction in triglycerides, serum cholesterol, and HDL cholesterol, as well as a reduction in blood pressure.

Bad News Foods

Refined sugar, white flour, salt, and a few other commonly eaten food ingredients may be minimized to great benefit in the diet, since they contribute to obesity, mental blowsiness, vitamin deficiencies, high blood sugar, high blood pressure, and excess alkalinity. Foods containing caffeine, alcohol, and smoked meats may also be avoided or minimized to great benefit.

Refined Sugar

Refined sugar is a cheap, hugely overused food additive, the obvious culprit in rising levels of obesity. Eating lots of sugar raises blood sugar, to say nothing of tooth decay and periodontal disease. Sugar addiction is common in the United States, where many people use sweet foods as a way to handle stress and frustration. Americans consume an average of 120 pounds of sugar per person per year, roughly twenty teaspoons or about a third of a pound of sugar every day. Most of it doesn't come from the sugar bowl. If you read food labels, you realize that processed foods are *loaded* with refined sugar. Most doctors and dietitians say people with diabetes should avoid or minimize their intake of white, refined sugar, which can lower glucose tolerance and make circulation problems worse. Sugar burns up B vitamins and minerals as it is digested, resulting in a nutritional gain of less than zero.

Many Americans eat their body weight in refined or white sugar every year, most of it hidden in processed foods such as soda pop, TV dinners, and breakfast cereal. Processed foods contain massive amounts of sugar. One doughnut contains the equivalent of two teaspoons of added refined sugar, an average-sized piece of cake contains six teaspoons, and 12 ounces of cola contains nine teaspoons, according to the U.S. Department of Agriculture. According to Dr. C. Norman Shealy, a holistic physician, sugar triggers the release of excess insulin, which "excessively interferes" with important hormones such as DHEA.

Health organizations recommend that a maximum of 10 percent of total calories come from refined sugars, which even have an effect on behavior. One study of juvenile delinquents who were incarcerated showed that incidents of antisocial behavior decreased by 40 percent when the kids were put on sugar-restricted diets.

Because it is chemically similar to glucose, white sugar rockets immediately into the bloodstream, triggering the release of insulin. Fructose, a more natural form of sugar found in fruit, does not cause as rapid a rise in blood sugar because it must be converted to glucose in the liver before utilization. A 1993 study found that when fructose was given to people with Type 2 diabetes over four weeks, it enhanced insulin sensitivity by 34 percent. Some double-blind studies have found that people who eat food sweetened with fructose eat fewer calories than do people who eat food sweetened with aspartame, sucrose, or glucose, when allowed to eat at all-you-can-eat buffet tables from half an hour to two and one-half hours later. Since fruits contain fructose, eating a piece of fruit at least half an hour before a meal may help reduce the total calories you eat. Fruit can also be substituted for sugar in pastries, cookies, and muffins.

Stevia, an herbal sweetener that is very popular in Japan and South America, is a South American folk remedy for diabetes. Some research suggests that substituting stevia for refined sugar might reduce blood sugar, although not all research has affirmed this. One study found that stevia dilated blood vessels, and therefore reduced blood pressure, in research animals. Stevia powder or tablets, available at health food stores, may be added directly to food or to tea. Cinnamon is another excellent herbal substitute for sugar, since it has made insulin more potent in animal studies. Nutmeg, another substitute for sugar, may have some beneficial blood sugar lowering effects.

Raw honey raises blood sugar, but it contains trace amounts of many nutrients. Honey contains some levulose, a form of sugar that breaks down slowly and therefore doesn't tend to overload the pancreas. Raw, unprocessed honey, which is preferred, is dark and thick rather than pale and watery.

Highly concentrated artificial sweeteners are not a particularly good alternative to sugar. Many powdered sweetener packets actually contain a great deal of glucose, according to Dr. Bernstein. Artificial sweeteners are much sweeter than sugar, but they may leave you hungrier than after consuming glucose, actually contributing to overeating, according to some research.

White Flour

White flour is ubiquitous in our society, another cheap, mass-produced, un-nutritious ingredient in many processed foods. Wheat itself is fairly nutritious, but processing it into white flour removes all the nutrients contained in the wheat germ and all the fiber in the husk. Only a few nutrients are added back into "enriched" flour, leaving white flour deficient in fiber, selenium, Vitamin E, and Vitamin B_6. Both diabetes and cancer of the colon are more common among people who eat white flour and don't eat whole grains, according to Dr. Shealy.

Guar flour or konjac flour, available at some health food stores, may be substituted or added to other flours for a possible glucose-lowering effect due to fiber content. Whole grain or whole wheat flour is also a nutritious substitute for white flour in breads and recipes. Whole grain rice flour or barley flours are a bit higher in the B vitamins and minerals than other flours, and they also contain more fiber. Rice flour can be used for cookies and pastries, barley flour for pie crusts. In cooking, one cup of any flour is equal to one cup of white flour.

Salt

Salt is a necessary mineral, but it may be reduced in many diets to great benefit. Most Americans eat about four times the amount of salt they actually need every day. Not surprisingly, processed food provides 70 percent of the sodium we eat, and only a little comes from the salt shaker.

Lowering consumption of salt is often recommended to help control high blood pressure. This works for about one person out of three—following a low-salt diet for three or four weeks is long enough to see if cutting your salt intake favorably affects your blood pressure. In most people, the body efficiently throws off excess salt.

Probably the most important thing to watch is the amount of sodium you take in relative to potassium. Ratios of sodium to potassium can be out of whack in people with diabetes, who often take in much more sodium than potassium. Including some potassium-based salt, such as Morton's Salt Substitute, may be a good idea if this is the case. Powdered seaweeds such as kelp or *nori*, which are high in iodine, can be used as salt substitutes and to season vegetables and salads. Certain culinary herbs such as basil, cilantro, or sage can sometimes be substituted for salt and may lower blood sugar or provide other benefits. In cooking, a half a teaspoon of salt equals one-half teaspoon herbs, or half a teaspoon of potassium chloride salt substitute.

Caffeine

Caffeine, a stimulant drug more widely used than tobacco or alcohol, depletes stores of B-complex vitamins and many minerals. Used in excess, it increases anxiety and irritability. Cells in the brain, liver, pancreas, and endocrine glands are stimulated by caffeine. Caffeine acts on the kidneys to increase urine production, dehydrating the body and draining away nutrients. High levels of caffeine in coffee, black tea, chocolate, and soft drinks act to inhibit the absorption of iron. Water is the best substitute for caffeinated drinks. Grain-based beverages like Pero and Postum may be substituted. Ginger is a natural stimulant that's healthy and can be used to make a tea. Decaffeinated teas and herb teas are good, caffeine-free alternatives. Decaffeinated green tea is an interesting possibility. With a long history as an aid to meditation in 12th-century Buddhist monasteries, green tea has lately been found to contain high levels of beneficial antioxidants such as epicatechin. A study published in the prestigious British medical journal *The Lancet* found that epicatechin regenerates beta cell function in rats with induced diabetes. Naturopath Michael Murray recommends that people with diabetes drink two cups of green tea per day. Black teas, to their credit, also contain antioxidants. Carob, a legume that contains no caffeine, can be substituted for chocolate, but it is high in calories.

Alcohol

Alcohol intake is correlated with diabetes, as people who drink are more likely to have diabetes. Alcohol improves glucose tolerance in healthy people, but it has the *opposite* effect in people with diabetes and older people. Alcohol lowers blood sugar, but it increases the secretion of insulin and can produce a craving for food, especially very sweet food. It also contains empty calories in the form of sugar.

A 1991 study conducted at an Italian hospital found that people with Type 2 diabetes who drank had higher fasting and postprandial blood sugar than people who didn't drink, but these differences disappeared after about three days of abstinence by the drinkers. A study of older men conducted at Temple University School of Medicine in Philadelphia found that a drink of ethanol *decreased* glucose tolerance by 23 percent when compared with a drink of saline solution. Other research has concluded that people with diabetes who drink have a statistically higher instance of eye and nerve complications.

Low alcohol or nonalcoholic wine or beer can be used for cooking, retaining the flavor but reducing the alcohol. If you want to stop drinking but cannot, groups such as Alcoholics Anonymous can be quite helpful.

Smoked Meats

Smoked or cured meat should be minimized or avoided, most health organizations now advise. Meats cured in this manner are heavy with chemical compounds that can lead to the formation of dangerous nitrosamines. These chemicals can actually damage the beta cells of the pancreas, which produce insulin. A compound that is chemically similar to nitrosamine, called streptozotocin, is used to induce diabetes in experimental animals; it works by destroying beta cells.

Blood Pressure

Here are some foods that might help lower blood pressure because of the beneficial nutrients they contain:

Celery

Garlic

Nuts and Seeds

Green Leafy Vegetables

Whole Grains

Legumes

Broccoli

Citrus Fruits

People with diabetes may lower blood sugar levels and maintain a healthy weight by careful eating. Eating good foods like brewer's yeast, fish, garlic, onions, and nopal containing fiber and natural nutrients strengthens the body, while highly processed foods containing too much sugar or salt have an opposite effect. Many people with diabetes are deficient in particular vitamins and minerals. They may benefit from vitamin or mineral supplementation, the topic of the next chapter.

Chapter 4

Vitamins and Minerals

The idea that people who live in our rich, afflu-
ent society can be deficient in vitamins and minerals is still heresy to a
few doctors, but nutritional deficiencies occur, and supplements can
help fix them. This chapter looks at some of the vitamins and minerals
that may be depleted in people with diabetes, some relevant research,
and precautions if any are advised.

Vitamin and mineral deficiencies can spring from chronic illnesses
like diabetes, stress, poor nutrition, smoking, depression, medications,
overconsumption of diuretics such as soft drinks and coffee, and poor
absorption of nutrients. Dieters are at great risk, particularly those consuming less than 1,200 calories per day. Older people often have trouble absorbing nutrients. Smokers and vegetarians can have vitamin
deficiencies. Some diabetes medications deplete the body of nutrients
such as folic acid and magnesium, and medications for other conditions
can also impact nutritional status. Deficiencies, marginal deficiencies,
or imbalances in ratios between certain vitamins and minerals can
weaken the body and cause additional health problems.

People with diabetes who have high blood sugar urinate more often
than usual. When blood sugar levels top approximately 160 mg./dl., the
kidneys lose their ability to reabsorb glucose and water soluble nutrients, and the excretion of sugar, vitamins, and minerals begins. Water

soluble vitamins such as B_1, B_6, B_{12}, and C, as well as chromium, magnesium, and zinc, can all be lost.

Vitamin and mineral supplements are still controversial. Some doctors scorn them, while other doctors recommend a few key supplements routinely, or after relevant tests. The American Diabetes Association does not endorse the use of supplements, citing only "theoretical reasons" for their use.

All people with diabetes certainly need the recommended daily levels of major vitamins and minerals, and some need more. Good tests of nutritional status are available. If you are low, supplements may be recommended. If your nutritional status is extraordinarily poor, intravenous vitamins and minerals may be advised.

Vitamins are not a substitute for real food, which gives us calories and energy. Vitamins provide no energy. However, vitamins and minerals are crucial for proper metabolism, growth, and development as well as to prevent deficiency diseases and sustain life. The judicious use of supplements can help you manage diabetes.

Gail's Story

Just two years ago, in rural Georgia, a woman we'll call Gail was diagnosed with Type 2 diabetes. Before Gail saw a doctor, she suddenly lost 22 pounds. She had a yeast infection that wouldn't go away. When a medical doctor diagnosed diabetes, Gail had blood sugar readings of almost 300 mg./dl., and HbA1c test readings of 10.5, which are dangerously high. Her cholesterol and her blood pressure were also elevated.

Gail's physician urged her to get more exercise. She attended educational classes at his suggestion. The doctor also gave her a prescription for glyburide, a diabetes medication, and asked her to take 5 milligrams twice a day. He prescribed another medication to bring down her blood pressure.

Gail and her husband ran a health food store. She decided to educate herself and see what she could do to help control her diabetes with supplements and herbs, while keeping her medical doctor apprised.

"On the day that I was told I was Type 2, I started taking a supplement from Enzyme Therapy called Doctor's Choice for Diabetics, which has vitamins and herbs that a diabetic needs," she recalls. This supplement contains antioxidant vitamins; minerals such as chromium, copper, and vanadium; and blood sugar lowering herbs such as fenugreek, gymnema, and bilberry. In addition to the commercial supplement package, Gail takes a Vitamin B complex, acidopholis supplements to prevent yeast infections, and juniper berries, which she says are good for the adrenals and pancreas.

"I have things available in my store, and I also read up on them while I am at work," she states. "I have found out by trial and error what works for me."

Gail was overweight when she was diagnosed with Type 2 diabetes. She says she is still a bit heavy, although she has lost ten pounds. In the summer she swims. She tries to walk two or three times a week, although this is sometimes difficult since she is running a business. As she experimented with supplements and herbs, she talked about what she was doing with her medical doctor.

"I go to a doctor of internal medicine, and he doesn't know anything about herbs and only a little about vitamins for diabetes," she says. "I told him I would try to help educate him about them, but he just looks at me funny. I don't think he is too interested."

A few months ago Gail also began to take flaxseed oil, one tablespoon per day, which she says has given her energy and helped her lower her cholesterol from a reading of 225 to 190 in about eight months. She also takes alpha lipoic acid, an antioxidant that also seems to help.

"I have done really great on this," she says of her supplement program. "It seems to keep my blood sugar count low, and I feel good, with lots of energy."

Her test results have shown great improvement. Her recent HbA1c tests have run 5.4 percent, 6.2 percent, and 6.4 percent, which are significantly improved. As a result, her doctor cut her dose of diabetes medications in half. She continues to take blood pressure medication, and other supplements for arthritis, and she continues working with her medical doctor.

"I have had diabetes for two years now," she says, pleased at her progress in controlling it so far. "I feel very good. I have not had any complications from my diabetes."

Antioxidants

Glycosylation occurs with high blood sugar, as glucose molecules attach to amino acids or protein molecules in the blood. Among its harmful effects, glycosylation has the effect of slowly choking off the blood circulation. The attachment of glucose molecules to protein molecules is believed to be caused by the *oxidation* of free radicals. By one estimate, oxidation occurs 10,000 times per day in every cell in the human body. Automatic repair enzymes in the body rapidly cut out parts of DNA that are damaged, but over time this process eventually takes its toll, particularly if oxidation is accelerated by conditions such as high blood sugar. Oxidation can be countered by *antioxidants*, chemical substances that reverse this process.

Antioxidants include Vitamin A, Vitamins B_3 and B_6, Vitamin C, Vitamin E, selenium, Coenzyme Q_{10}, amino acids such as L-carnitine, and herbs such as bilberry and ginkgo biloba. Supplements of these antioxidants are sometimes advised. Some nutritionally oriented practitioners recommend even more potent antioxidants, such as grapeseed oil or pine bark extract. Grapeseed extract, for one, is said to be an antioxidant twenty times more powerful than Vitamin C. Minerals such as magnesium, zinc, and copper are not antioxidants in themselves, but they help form other antioxidants.

Diabetes research physician Dr. James W. Anderson of Lexington, Kentucky, is among those who have written on the importance of antioxidants to general health. In his book, *Live Longer Better*, Dr. Anderson says antioxidant Vitamins A, C, and E are of prime importance in preventing free radical damage to the beta calls of the pancreas, which produce insulin. Type 2 diabetes springs from a premature aging of the beta cells, Dr. Anderson observes. Antioxidants also help prevent complications such as heart disease and stroke, which are much more common to people who have diabetes. Among their other beneficial effects, Vitamins C and E, as well as beta carotene, delay the oxidation of "bad," or LDL, cholesterol, which sets the stage for hardening of the arteries.

High blood sugar promotes excessive oxidation of proteins in the kidneys and eyes, but Vitamin C or Vitamin E supplements apparently help prevent diabetes-related kidney problems, or eye problems such as age-related macular degeneration and cataracts, Dr. Anderson says. Vitamin E prevents the development of diabetes in research animals. For optimum health, Dr. Anderson believes every person with diabetes should eat at least three servings of vegetables and two of fruits every day, and regularly exercise, in addition to taking antioxidant supplements.

Eating foods high in antioxidant vitamins and minerals is probably the best, safest way to get them into the body. Nutrients in foods are balanced in the ways our bodies have evolved to utilize them. But in some cases, as when it is difficult to take in adequate amounts in food, supplements are advisable. Use supplements only with the full knowledge and consent of your medical doctor, since some affect the efficacy of medications, and vice versa.

Simply taking a good multivitamin and mineral supplement (without added iron) every day may be helpful for every person with diabetes, since needs for certain nutrients may be higher, levels in most supplements are safe, and small marginal deficiencies are difficult to detect with current tests. However, not all practitioners agree with this "shotgun" approach.

Some of the most commonly recommended vitamin and mineral supplements for people with diabetes are listed here. Some of the research that supports their use, natural food sources of each nutrient, and safety considerations are included.

Vitamins

Vitamins are necessary to sustain life. Fat soluble vitamins such as Vitamins A, D, E, and K are stored in fat cells and remain in the body for long periods of time. Water soluble vitamins such as the B vitamins and Vitamin C dissolve in water and can more easily be excreted and depleted in people with diabetes.

Vitamin A

Vitamin A is an antioxidant vitamin, vital to the immune system. It has an important role in regulating the secretion of insulin by islet cells in the pancreas and is an essential nutrient for the liver and for the eyes. At low concentrations Vitamin A stimulates insulin secretion, but at very high concentrations it inhibits it. Vitamin A, in the safe beta carotene form that comes from plants, probably protects against heart attacks.

Research at the University of Illinois in Chicago examined the diets of 3,000 senior citizens and found the ones who consumed the most beta carotene had a 40 percent lower risk of macular degeneration than those whose diets included the least beta carotene. In another study, published in the *American Journal of Clinical Nutrition* in 1979, people who ate two medium-size, vitamin A rich carrots at breakfast every day for three weeks reduced their LDL cholesterol by 11 percent.

The U.S. RDA for Vitamin A is 3,300 IU for men and 2,640 IU for women. As part of an antioxidant program, Dr. Anderson recommends 10,000 IU (6 mg.) of Vitamin A in beta carotene form each day. This amount is relatively easy to get from food, by eating fruits or vegetables rich in beta carotene. For instance, a half cup of carrot juice, half a raw carrot, ten halves of dried apricot, three-quarters of a cup of cooked spinach, half a medium sweet potato, or a half cup of gazpacho all contain more than 10,000 IUs of Vitamin A in the beta carotene form.

Note that supplements contain a synthetic form of beta carotene, which may have slightly different effects on the body than beta carotene in its natural state.

Many plant foods such as carrots and sweet potatoes contain beta carotene. Sources of Vitamin A include liver, fish liver oils, milk, eggs, butter, cheese, cream, egg yolk, and whole milk.

Precautions: Vitamin A itself should be used carefully, since it can be toxic when consumed at levels over 25,000 IU per day. The U.S. Food and Drug Administration (FDA) says that overuse of Vitamin A has resulted in severe liver injury, as well as bone and cartilage pathologies. Elevated intracranial pressure and birth defects as a result of Vitamin A overuse have also been reported to the FDA. Especially vulnerable to risk are people with liver disease, children, pregnant women, and people with severe protein-energy malnutrition.

In beta carotene form, the potential for adverse effects (beyond a yellowing of the skin on hands and feet) is not there. However, beta carotene must be converted to Vitamin A in the liver before use—a problem if liver function is poor.

Vitamin B Complex

A number of doctors routinely recommend a B complex vitamin for people with diabetes. Vitamin B complex contains eleven factors that perform important functions in the body, such as stabilizing brain chemistry and blood sugar. Many B vitamins, including B_1, B_2, B_3, B_6, and B_{12}, play important roles in the metabolism of glucose. Since B vitamins are water soluble, they can all be excreted in the urine during periods of high blood sugar or high stress. Increased intakes of folic acid, Vitamin B_6, and Vitamin B_{12} help bring dangerously high levels of the amino acid *homocysteine* into the normal range, thereby helping prevent heart attacks and strokes.

Vitamin B complex pills are sold everywhere; the best include folic acid and adequate levels of Vitamin B_{12}. A folic acid deficiency, for example, is not common in people with diabetes, but 3 percent of individuals with diabetes have it, according to one study. Elderly people with diabetes, particularly poor people, are at higher risk for a deficiency in folic acid. Folic acid is found in green plant tissue, liver, and yeast.

The B vitamins are found in many foods. Normal cooking or heat doesn't destroy them, but they are destroyed when foods are cooked for a long period of time or at very high temperature. B vitamins have a synergistic action, working well together. Occasionally, doctors will recommend additional supplements of one of the B vitamins listed here.

Vitamin B₁ (Thiamin)

Vitamin B_1 or thiamin supplementation for diabetes is safe but somewhat controversial. Water soluble B_1 is not stored in the body. Studies have shown that patients with Type 1 diabetes often have low blood levels of B_1, but older patients with Type 2 diabetes usually have normal levels.

Thiamin deficiency can result from alcoholism, and deficiencies may be treated by supplementation or injection. There is some evidence that B_1 improves nerve function and reduces pain of neuropathy. According to John Senneff, author of *Numb Toes and Aching Soles: Coping with Peripheral Neuropathy*, one study reported a 50 percent benefit for patients with neuropathy when thiamin was injected. A study in Germany where B complex, including B_1, were given in high doses of 320 mg. per day resulted in some improvement in neuropathy.

The RDA of B_1 for men is 1.2 to 1.5 mg.; for females it's 1 to 5 mg.

Natural sources of Vitamin B_1 include brewer's yeast, where it occurs in high concentrations. Other good sources include cereal grains, peas, beans, peanuts, oranges, organ meats, pork, and many vegetables, fruits, and nuts.

Precautions: Although it may be unnecessary, Vitamin B_1 is safe. It has been taken in doses of 500 mg. daily for more than a month with no toxicity. It is easily cleared by the kidneys.

Vitamin B₂ (Riboflavin)

A powerful antioxidant, Vitamin B_2, or riboflavin, works with other B vitamins. It requires the presence of Vitamin E and selenium to be effective. A deficiency of riboflavin can result in nerve disorders and cause degeneration of the myelin sheaths, which are the outer layer of nerves. People who use certain medications are advised to increase their intake of Vitamin B_2.

The RDA is 1.7 mg. per day, although people who exercise may require 2.0 to 2.5 mg.

Natural sources include eggs, green vegetables, liver, kidney, lean meat, milk, wheat germ, and brewer's yeast.

Vitamin B₃ (Niacin)

Niacin, niacinamide, or Vitamin B_3 is a controversial vitamin in diabetes treatment, with proven benefits and risks. Enzymes that contain niacin play a role in many body processes, including metabolism, energy production, and the manufacture of sex and adrenal hormones. Niacin facilitates the uptake of glucose, and some studies suggest it can restore the integrity of beta cells in the pancreas, or slow their deterioration. Vitamin B_3 prevents the development of Type 1 diabetes in experimental animals. However, too much niacin can adversely affect blood sugar, so it should be taken under the supervision of the doctor who manages your diabetes. Levels of this vitamin are sometimes too high in people with Type 2 diabetes, so test results should be examined before beginning supplements.

Medical doctors sometimes recommend Vitamin B$_3$ to reduce cholesterol, for weight reduction, high blood pressure, acne, and alcoholism. Niacin gives the characteristic *flush*, a feeling of overheated skin in the facial area, usually at a dose above 35 mg. In the niacinamide form there is no flush. In the United States the recommended daily allowance is 20 mg.

Administered at the rate of one gram three times a day, niacin lowers cholesterol. In the Coronary Drug Project, niacin was the only substance that decreased mortality—11 percent lower than placebo in this study. But since niacin can raise blood sugar, a safer form is inositol hexaniacinate, composed of six molecules of niacin and one molecule of inositol, which is tolerated better by the body, according to the *Encyclopedia of Natural Medicine*.

In some cases, niacin supplements may be useful. Research published in the *Journal of the American Medical Association* found that people with diabetes who were given up to 3 grams, or their maximum tolerated dosage, for up to 60 weeks experienced small increases in blood sugar of between 8 to 9 mg./dl. However, they also experienced significant decreases of about 8 percent in triglycerides; a 23 percent reduction in low density lipoprotein, or "bad" cholesterol levels; and increases of almost 30 percent in high density lipoprotein, or "good" cholesterol. The authors concluded niacin could be used safely in patients with diabetes, as an alternative to statin drugs such as fluvastatin and lovastatin or fibrates when these drugs don't work to accomplish the desired effects.

According to the American Diabetes Association's *101 Medication Tips for People with Diabetes*, niacin can *increase* blood sugar in large amounts. Some practitioners don't use this vitamin for people with Type 2 diabetes. However, if liver function is strong, some nutritionally oriented doctors may recommend it for its beneficial effects.

Precautions: The amount of niacin in a multivitamin is not harmful, but people with diabetes who are considering taking more than 35 mg. per day should consult their doctors because of possible adverse effect on blood sugar levels. According to the FDA, some people taking daily doses of 500 mg. in slow-release form and 750 mg. in immediate-release form have reported gastrointestinal distress and mild to severe liver damage. Rare side effects are liver injuries, muscle disease, maculopathy of the eyes, heart injuries from low blood pressure, and metabolic acidosis—increased acidity in the blood and urine. The FDA reports that most observed adverse reactions occurred when patients switched from prescription forms of niacin in immediate-release form to over-the-counter formulations without the knowledge of their doctors.

Vitamin B$_6$ (Pyridoxine)

Vitamin B$_6$, or pyridoxine, one of the water soluble B vitamin complex, is necessary for the functioning of more than 60 enzymes, for protein synthesis, and for the production of white blood cells and antibodies. Vitamin B$_6$ can help control Type 2 diabetes, perhaps by decreasing insulin demands. It can be helpful in controlling the pain of diabetic neuropathy. As an antioxidant, B$_6$ inhibits the glycosylation of proteins. Vitamin B$_6$ is believed to be the most important vitamin of all for the maintenance of a healthy immune system, and it's important in maintaining healthy teeth and gums, and healthy skin. It also helps the body absorb Vitamin B$_{12}$.

Some studies have shown a deficiency of Vitamin B$_6$ in people with diabetes. One study found lower levels of B$_6$ among people treated with insulin than those taking diabetes pills. A deficiency in Vitamin B$_6$ is associated with an impaired secretion of insulin, as well as glucose intolerance. However, research with B$_6$ is inconclusive. One study of people with Type 2 diabetes who received supplements for six weeks resulted in lower glycosylated hemoglobin levels, but not all studies show this.

The neuropathy that develops as a result of B$_6$ deficiency is identical to diabetic neuropathy. According to naturopath Michael Murray, B$_6$ supplements may offer protection against development of neuropathy because some people with neuropathy have been shown to be short of Vitamin B$_6$. Doses of 150 mg. per day have been used as preventative doses against the development of neuropathy.

A study in Tanzania, published in the *East African Medical Journal* in 1997, showed reduced signs of peripheral neuropathy in almost 50 percent of patients treated daily with 25 mg. of B$_1$ and 50 mg. of B$_6$, compared with about 11 percent improvement in the control group.

Supplementation with 100 mg. of B$_6$ for two weeks eliminated gestational diabetes in 12 of 14 women with gestational diabetes in one study.

The U.S. RDA is 2 milligrams. Vitamin B_6 should be taken as part of a B complex supplement that contains equal amounts of Vitamins B_1 and B_2.

Natural sources of Vitamin B_6 include chicken, fish, brown rice, soybean products, and eggs. Other sources include meat, fish, milk, eggs, whole grain cereals, and vegetables.

Precautions: Vitamin B_6 is toxic in very high doses, and can cause nerve damage when taken in quantities of more than 2,000 mg. per day, which is 1,000 times the RDA. Some people have reported side effects at levels as low as 100 mg. per day, and the FDA says that Vitamin B_6 has been associated with balance problems and sensory neuropathy in some people taking these supplements at that level. Some doctors advise this be taken only as part of a B complex.

B_{12}

Vitamin B_{12}, or cobalamin, which is found in all the body's cells, is said to help prevent heart disease and to help relieve depression and low blood pressure. Vitamin B_{12} levels are often low in older people.

A deficiency of B_{12} has a link to peripheral neuropathy, and a test of B_{12} levels is a standard test for neuropathy. A Vitamin B_{12} deficiency also results in pernicious anemia, which can occur simultaneously with Type 2 diabetes. The biguanide medications such as metformin and phenformin are believed to partially block the absorption of B_{12}, but taking an appropriate supplement containing B_{12} or B_{12} shots may remedy this problem.

The RDA for Vitamin B_{12} is 2 micrograms for men and 20 micrograms for women. However, some authorities say 100 to 200 micrograms per day are needed for optimum health. People with deficiencies are given much larger amounts than the RDA. Muscle injections of B_{12} allow for speedy absorption.

Natural sources of Vitamin B_{12} include meats and other animal products.

Inositol

Inositol is a B vitamin present in the leaves and seeds of most plants, and also found in the human brain, liver, kidneys, and skeletal and heart muscles. People with diabetes excrete more inositol than most people. A sweet-tasting vitamin, inositol has been shown by research to protect people with diabetes from complications such as peripheral neuropathy, and to relieve symptoms such as tingling and numbness.

Levels of inositol are often low in the nerve cells in people with diabetes. High blood sugar causes a form of sugar called sorbitol, which is normally excreted, to build up in nerve cells, and this results in inositol's excretion. Dr. Atkins has treated peripheral neuropathy using 2 to 6 grams of inositol per day, but most authorities don't recommend supplements over 1 gram per day, taken in 500 mg. doses twice a day.

Author John Seneff says research at the University of Alabama found a statistically significant improvement in nerve function among people with diabetes placed on a diet high in inositol, containing foods such as cantaloupe, peanuts, grapefruit, and whole grains.

Natural sources of inositol include liver, wheat germ, brown rice, citrus fruits, nuts, and vegetables. Lethicin, a widely used food additive and supplement, contains inositol, as do foods containing lethicin, such as egg yolks, soybeans, liver, fish, cauliflower, and cabbage.

Precaution: No toxicity has been reported with inositol, but it should be taken under doctor's supervision. According to Time-Life's *Medical Advisor: The Complete Guide to Alternative and Conventional Treatments,* inositol may change blood sugar levels, so a practitioner should be consulted before taking supplements.

Biotin

Biotin is a B vitamin that may help lower blood sugar and protect against neuropathy in people who are deficient. Also called Vitamin H, biotin is a coenzyme in the metabolism of food, and it helps maintain skin, nerves, hair, sweat glands, and bone marrow. Biotin is manufactured in the intestines by certain bacteria, and most people consume adequate amounts in food. However, biotin may improve the metabolism of glucose in people who lack an adequate amount in their bodies.

A study in Japan using 3 mg. biotin per day lowered fasting glucose levels in research subjects with Type 2 diabetes, without side effects, according to M. F. McCarty, of Nutriguard Research in Encinitas, California. Biotin stimulates glucokinase expression in liver and pancreatic beta cells. Glucokinase, an enzyme used by the pancreas and liver, is often low in people with diabetes, according to McCarty, and biotin helps regulate the metabolism of glucose.

In one study of people with Type 2 diabetes, supplements of 9 mg. of biotin per day lowered fasting blood sugar levels and improved blood sugar control.

In a study at the University of Athens, patients with neuropathy were given 10 mg. of biotin per day intramuscularly three times a week for six weeks, then oral supplements of 5 mg. daily. Symptoms of neuropathy were reported to have decreased within four to eight weeks without side effects.

Another small study published in 1996, also conducted in Athens, examined the effect of large doses of biotin (50 mg. given intravenously after dialysis) on patients undergoing hemodialysis. Oral glucose tolerance tests established that subjects who had taken biotin had better glucose metabolism.

No RDA for biotin has been established. Natural sources of biotin include brewer's yeast, oatmeal, liver, egg yolks, mushrooms, bananas, soy, and peanuts.

Biotin is not toxic. Excesses are excreted in the urine.

Vitamin C

As the best-known antioxidant, Vitamin C is the most commonly taken dietary supplement in the United States. A powerful antioxidant that fights free radical activity associated with diabetes, Vitamin C is not produced in the body. It complements many other nutrients, including chromium, and may help the body fight off infection by beefing up the immune system, and help prevent cataracts. Vitamin C is also needed for healthy blood vessels, bones, teeth, and gums, and it may have a protective effect against cancer.

The turnover of Vitamin C is faster than normal in people with Type 2 diabetes, since it is spilled out in urine during periods of high blood sugar. Data published in the *American Journal of Clinical Nutrition* in July 1999 found that serum concentrations of Vitamin C were lower in people with diabetes. Earlier research found a deficiency of Vitamin C levels in the white blood cells and platelets in people with diabetes. Low levels of Vitamin C have been found in people with diabetes even when diets contain adequate amounts. Several studies have shown benefits in Vitamin C supplementation, but not all have.

As an antioxidant, Vitamin C inhibits harmful glycosylation. In England, researchers at the University of Cambridge's Department of Community Medicine found that Vitamin C levels were "considerably higher" in people with HbA1c of less than 7, and lower in those with HbA1c higher than 7. In *Diabetes Care* in June 2000, researchers concluded that increasing Vitamin C levels in plasma might help prevent diabetes.

In a study published in 1995, researchers studying supplementation with magnesium and ascorbic acid noted that supplements of 2 grams of Vitamin C per day improved fasting glucose levels by about 10 percent and also reduced HbA1c levels to 8.5 from 9.3.

Supplementation with 1 to 2 grams per day of Vitamin C can reduce the concentration of sorbitol, a harmful form of sugar that can build up in red blood cells. Vitamin C reduces levels of enzyme aldose reductase, which contributes to the accumulation of sorbitol in the eyes, nerves, and kidneys.

A study published in *Diabetes Residential Clinical Practice* in 1995 measured the effects of 1 gram of Vitamin C per day for two weeks on red blood cells. Although fasting blood sugar wasn't affected, the study showed a 12 percent reduction of sorbitol and a 20 percent drop in the ratio between sorbitol and plasma glucose. In a second study, sorbitol reductions were found to be greater when Vitamin C was taken in a citrus fruit medium such as orange juice. In another study, published in *Diabetes* in 1992, twelve normal people showed 18 percent reductions in glycosylated hemoglobin levels, and a 33 percent decrease in glycosylated albumin after consumption of 1 gram of Vitamin C for three months.

A National Health and Nutrition Examination Survey that examined the role of Vitamin C intake found that those who ingested more than 50 mg. per day had almost a 50 percent lower chance of death from all causes than those who took less than 50 mg. per day.

Vitamin C supplementation could help you lose weight. In 1985 a double-blind controlled study of severely obese women who had failed previous weight loss efforts found that six weeks of supplementation with 3 grams of ascorbic acid per day produced greater weight loss than achieved with placebo—approximately a six-pound loss for women taking Vitamin C, compared to a two-pound loss for the control group.

The RDA for Vitamin C is 60 mg. per day. Supplementation of 100 mg. per day is recommended for people who smoke. Some practitioners recommend from 1 to 10 grams per day.

Citrus fruits and other fruits, strawberries, tomatoes, broccoli, brussels sprouts, green peppers, and onions contain Vitamin C, which is easily destroyed by heat and cooking.

Precautions: Supplementation with Vitamin C is not very risky, but supplements can precipitate oxalate stones. Supplementation with over 500 mg. of Vitamin C per day may throw off glucose strip test results. Very high intakes of Vitamin C can cause upset stomach and diarrhea, but intake can be lowered to a level that doesn't cause this side effect.

Vitamin E

Vitamin E is an important antioxidant that lowers insulin resistance, improving the action of insulin in people with Type 2 diabetes. It may lower insulin requirements in large doses. Vitamin E helps prevent damage to cell membranes and nerve cells, assists enzyme function, helps preserve skin and tissues, and also protects against the effects of air pollution. Note that it is very difficult to get even the recommended daily allowance of Vitamin E from food. For instance, you would have to eat more than 200 slices of whole wheat bread to get even the 15 International Units (IUs) that are the recommended daily allowance.

Several large studies have shown that Vitamin E provides significant protection against heart disease. In the Cambridge Heart Antioxidant Study, 2,000 men and women with narrowed arteries who were given 400 or 800 IU per day of Vitamin E cut their risk of heart attack in half. A Harvard University study of health professionals who took Vitamin E supplements daily found they had 25 to 35 percent less coronary risk than those who didn't take Vitamin E.

Research at the University of Utah published in the year 2000 demonstrated that people with Type 2 diabetes have increased inflammation, as shown by activity of a pivotal cell called a circulating monocyte in plaque formation on artery walls. Supplements of 1,200 IU of natural Vitamin E for three months reduced this inflammation. Researchers concluded that supplemental Vitamin E could be useful in preventing vascular complications associated with diabetes.

In a trial conducted at the University of Naples, Italy, 25 elderly people with Type 2 diabetes took 900 mg. of Vitamin E per day over three months found that the vitamin resulted in a "minimal but significant improvement" in metabolic control, including lower blood sugar, triglycerides, free fatty acids, cholesterol, and more. HbA1c levels fell from 7.8 to 7.1. However, one trial involving obese Type 2 patients in the Czech Republic who took 600 IU of Vitamin E per day for three months found that Vitamin E supplements actually made insulin resistance worse.

Supplements of Vitamin E at levels far above the RDA are often recommended. Dr. Kenneth Cooper, founder of the Cooper Institute, recommends 400 IU per day, and more for people who are overweight, heavy exercisers, or in other high-risk categories. Dr. Anderson recommends 400 IU per day. Dr. Bernstein, who does not favor supplements of most vitamins, recommends from 400 to 1,200 IU of Vitamin E per day to many of his patients.

The RDA for Vitamin E is 30 IU. The natural alpha tocopherol form is often recommended, but other forms of Vitamin E may also have benefits. Gamma tocopherol, for instance, which is found in soybeans and nuts, can protect against nitrogen oxides that can cause DNA damage as free radicals; alpha tocopherol doesn't affect these free radicals and can even cause elimination of gamma tocopherol.

Foods that contain Vitamin E include vegetable and seed oils such as wheat germ oil, walnut oil, and soybean oil.

Precautions: Vitamin E is generally safe. However, according to Kenneth Pelletier, Director of the Complementary and Alternative Medicine Program at Stanford University, some researchers worry that Vitamin E supplements over 400 IU per day may increase the risk of hemorrhagic stroke. People taking medications that inhibit their blood clotting should check with their doctors before using Vitamin E supplements.

Flavonoids

The more than 4,000 identified bioflavonoids or flavonoids, responsible for the color of flowers and fruits, are also the active ingredients in many herbal medicines. Antioxidant flavonoids protect the small blood vessels called capillaries against small breaks and leaks, and also buffer the body against the effects of environmental stress. Some flavonoids, such as quercetin, promote insulin secretion and also inhibit sorbitol accumulation. Flavonoids help prevent the body from bruising, and generally support the immune system.

Flavonoids can increase the Vitamin C levels within cells. They are considered excellent in combination with Vitamin C, where they have maximum effect. Many Vitamin C supplements contain bioflavonoids.

A five-year study of elderly Dutch men, reported in the British medical journal *The Lancet*, concluded that men who consumed the most flavonoids had a 68 percent lower rate of heart attacks during the study than men whose intake was low, independent of other risk factors for heart attacks. The most common source of flavonoids for these men, who were from 65 to 84 years of age, was tea.

Some naturopathic physicians recommend 1 to 2 grams of a mixture of flavonoids per day for people with diabetes.

The small white core of citrus fruits is the richest known source of flavonoids. Flavonoids are found in many vegetables such as broccoli, green peppers, and onions; fruits such as apricots, cranberries, grapefruit, and apples; and beverages such as green tea and red wine.

Minerals

Minerals are necessary inorganic substances that form most of the bones, teeth, and other hard parts of the body. Found in every cell, and important as enzymes to many processes, minerals regulate the permeability of cell membranes and capillaries, and help maintain the crucial acid/alkali balance in the body.

Calcium

Calcium is the most plentiful mineral in the body, which contains two or three pounds of it. Calcium helps maintain bones and teeth, where 99 percent of the body's supply is located. Calcium also has a role in the clotting of blood, muscle growth, heart and nerve functioning, and in cell membranes. Adequate calcium in the body helps normalize blood pressure, although doctors don't understand exactly why.

The typical American diet supplies only 450 to 550 mg. of calcium, less than the recommended minimum amount. Studies have shown benefits for people with high blood pressure from supplements of 800 mg. of calcium per day, according to Time-Life's *Medical Advisor*.

One study on people without diabetes, but with high blood pressure, showed an increase in insulin sensitivity and a decrease in fasting insulin levels with calcium supplementation of 1,500 mg. per day for eight weeks.

Some people with Type 2 diabetes, particularly women, may have reduced levels of calcium content in their bones. The National Institutes of Health Consensus Development Conference on Osteoporosis recommends supplementation of 1,000 mg. of elemental calcium per day for elderly individuals, a bit higher than the RDA. The National Academy of Sciences recommends an intake of 1,200 mg. per day for adults over the age of 51.

Good food sources of calcium in the diet include leafy green vegetables, beans, peas, seeds and nuts, seafood, tofu, and blackstrap molasses.

Precautions: Calcium competes with other minerals for absorption, so if you are taking calcium for a period of time, it might be prudent to take a multimineral supplement. Calcium needs Vitamin D to be absorbed into the body, so some nutritionally oriented doctors also recommend Vitamin D supplements along with calcium.

Chromium

Chromium is a very important trace mineral for people with diabetes but is needed only in small quantities. It has been estimated that about half the U.S. population has a chromium deficiency, particularly older people, athletes, pregnant women, and people who live in areas where water or soils are chromium deficient. Chromium is an important regulator of blood sugar, necessary in the production of insulin. It is believed to make circulating insulin more potent, and to increase the binding of insulin to cells by increasing insulin receptors.

The stress of diabetes, poor diets or diets containing sweet and sugary foods, and exercise all increase the body's chromium needs.

Vitamin Tests

Certain vitamins and mineral levels can be low in people with diabetes, but good tests have been developed to measure vitamin and mineral levels in the body. Practitioners who use tests can more accurately recommend vitamin and mineral supplements to correct deficiencies in nutritional status. A full battery of nutritional status tests might cost around $500, depending on the lab and the practitioner.

The best tests examine vitamin and mineral levels in red and white blood cells, rather than levels in the serum. Tests of red blood cells can provide an accurate reading of magnesium levels, for instance, and determine if supplementation might be of benefit. For Vitamin B1, a good reading is the level of red blood cell transkelotase. Vitamin B12 is tested with a methylmalonic acid assay of the urine, which provides a good read on B12 levels. New cellular tests can uncover deficiencies of essential fatty acids such as EPA and GLA.

Tests of vitamin levels in blood serum have been available for some time, but these do not provide readings on deficiencies of vitamins and minerals within the cells, which are likely to be more accurate. Serum tests also have very wide variations in what is considered to be normal results. Hair analysis, once touted as the best test, has proved to be unreliable, but some practitioners still use it to determine heavy metal toxicity in the body.

Chromium is excreted through the kidneys during periods of high blood sugar, and with the stress hormone cortisol. There is speculation that a deficiency in chromium helps trigger the onset of Type 2 diabetes. Chromium also has a minor effect on suppressing hunger pains. Chromium picolinate, the preferred form, is utilized efficiently by the body.

In a study published in the medical journal *Diabetes*, in November 1997, subjects with Type 2 diabetes were given 200 and 1,000 micrograms of chromium for four months. Chromium had beneficial effects on the subjects' HbA1c, glucose, insulin, and cholesterol levels. HbA1c values after two months were 7.4 in people taking the larger dose versus 8.6 for placebo group. After another two months, HbA1c levels fell almost another point for both groups taking chromium picolate, while remaining about the same for placebo.

Another study, conducted at Wake Forest University, used 1,000 micrograms of chromium picolinate added to nutritional regimens. Over the eight months of the study, which was published in 1999, insulin sensitivity was significantly increased in subjects deemed to be at high risk for Type 2 diabetes.

There is no RDA for chromium, but 25 micrograms per day is probably adequate. Supplements of up to 200 micrograms per day have been recommended. Amounts in excess of this should be cleared through your doctor or a registered practitioner. Since chromium increases insulin sensitivity, some nutritionists recommend starting chromium supplements at 100 micrograms per day, then gradually increasing the dose.

Brewer's yeast is the best natural source of chromium. Other sources include whole grain cereals, liver, American cheese, wheat germ, molasses, egg yolks, potatoes, apples with skins, spinach, oysters, carrots, and chicken breast. Some varieties of barley grown in Mesopotamia are among the world's richest sources of chromium, according to recent research.

Precautions: Chromium is basically safe, since excess chromium is excreted by the body. However, chromium competes with iron in the body, and chromium supplements of more than 200 micrograms per day have been linked to iron deficiencies, according to Dr. Pelletier. Some doctors speculate that chromium could accumulate in the tissues and possibly contribute to chromosome damage or cancer, but this is unproven.

Manganese

Manganese is an antioxidant mineral needed in small quantities for brain and nervous system functioning. Diabetes may have a link to a deficiency of manganese, which helps the body metabolize glucose. According to Time-Life's *Medical Advisor*, people with diabetes *often* have a serious manganese deficiency, frequently half the normal levels. Deficiencies in manganese are related to high intakes of processed or refined food, since food processing removes manganese. In guinea pigs,

Safe Supplements

The biggest problem with buying vitamin and mineral supplements is that you might not get what you pay for. The U.S. 1994 Dietary Supplement Act looks good on paper, but it is not really enforced. A few companies have high quality standards—GNC, for instance, owned by a drug company, has pharmaceutical grade products. Problems of adulteration and mislabeling pop up *frequently* in perhaps one-third of over-the-counter products. Here are some things to look for:

- Supplements that carry a U.S. Pharmacopoeia or USP notation indicate the manufacturer has followed established quality and safety standards. The approved Quality Product Seal from ConsumerLab.com, or the TruLabel from the National Nutritional Foods Association, are also indicators of good quality content.

- Supplements by a nationally known food and drug manufacturer with manufacturing controls already in place are probably safest. Conversely, deeply discounted supplements might raise suspicion, since they may contain a substitute ingredient that is inferior or cheaper.

- If you are curious about the quality of particular supplements, write or call the manufacturer and ask about the conditions under which its product is made. The response you receive may tell you quite a lot about the products you want to buy.

a deficiency of manganese results in diabetes, the birth of offspring that have no pancreas, or pancreatic abnormalities. Supplementation with manganese may help control diabetic retinopathy and reduce the possibility of cardiovascular damage.

Some naturopaths recommend supplements of 30 mg. per day for people with diabetes, but most recommend 2 to 4 mg. per day, below the U.S. RDA of manganese of 2.5 to 7 mg.

Good natural sources of manganese are cereals, tea, green leafy vegetables, whole wheat bread, wheat germ, pulses, nuts, and seeds.

Precautions: Manganese toxicity is quite rare, but symptoms can include lethargy, involuntary movements, posture problems, and coma.

Magnesium

Magnesium is involved in the metabolism of glucose, in maintaining energy, and it assists the action of calcium, Vitamins B_1 and B_6, and Vitamin C. One of the most abundant ions present in living cells, magnesium plays a role in the release of insulin from the pancreas and in regulating blood pressure. Insulin, too, is a factor in regulating magnesium concentrations in the blood serum and within individual cells. In a perfect world, adequate magnesium would be consumed in foods, but it is refined away by food processing.

Although not all people with diabetes have a measurable magnesium deficiency, statistical studies show a correlation between low levels of magnesium in the diet and diabetes. According to a 1998 study published in *Diabetes Care*, between 25 to 38 percent of people with Type 2 diabetes have low magnesium levels. Some doctors claim much greater percentages of people are deficient in magnesium. Adequate magnesium may prevent some complications such as heart disease and especially retinopathy.

Studies have shown that supplementation at the rate of 300 mg. magnesium per day can lower high blood pressure, although some people benefit more from calcium for this purpose. Magnesium optimizes usable calcium because it increases its absorption. On the other hand, calcium can interfere with magnesium absorption. A ratio of about two to one between calcium and magnesium is believed ideal.

People with diabetes often take in less magnesium than necessary. Magnesium depletion is believed to be caused by a combination of factors in people with diabetes: secretion in the urine, altered Vitamin D metabolism, decreases in Vitamin B_6 and taurine levels, and treatment with high levels of insulin and biguanide diabetes medications. Potassium depletion, also common in diabetes, comes from many of the same mechanisms as magnesium depletion; adverse effects on heart and liver can increase if both are depleted, according to a 1984 Swiss study.

Administration of magnesium salts to people with Type 2 diabetes tends to reduce insulin resistance, according to a 1994 French study. A

German study published in the European medical journal *Diabetologia* in 1990 showed that chronic magnesium supplementation can contribute to an improvement in beta-cell response in the pancreas and improved insulin action in people with Type 2 diabetes.

A landmark research study in 1978 showed that people with diabetes who had the lowest magnesium levels also had the most severe cases of diabetic retinopathy. Researchers found that the link between low magnesium and retinopathy was stronger than any other factor. The study concluded that magnesium supplementation would help protect the eyes of people with diabetes.

Magnesium deficiency may contribute to heart disease, according to research published in the medical journal *Hypertension* in 1993.

In England, magnesium sulfate injected into muscle and then infused into patients with peripheral vascular disease—suffering gangrene, ulcers, claudication, as well as angina, acute myocardial infarction, and congestive cardiac failure—produced "excellent results," according to the authors of a 1994 study published in the *Journal of Nutritional Medicine.*

The RDA for magnesium is 350 mg. per day for men and 300 mg. for women. In the United States, average intakes of magnesium are low, estimated at between 143 to 266 mg. per day for healthy adults.

Many practitioners recommend magnesium supplements for people with diabetes, between 300 to 800 mg. per day. Some practitioners recommend magnesium in the more absorbable forms of magnesium aspartame or magnesium citrate. These are often combined with at least 50 mg. of Vitamin B_6, which is needed for magnesium to penetrate the cell and become useful.

Naturopath Skip Shoden often recommends 500 mg. per day for people with diabetes, a level he says is safe unless the person has a kidney problem. He says magnesium is crucially important to the heart and nervous system, and sometimes recommends 1,000 to 1,500 mg. per day for people with diabetes with cardiovascular symptoms.

Legumes, beans, tofu, seeds, nuts, whole grains, and green leafy vegetables, as well as fish and meat, are good dietary sources of magnesium.

Precautions: People with impaired kidney function who also take big doses of drugs containing magnesium should not supplement with magnesium. Magnesium supplements may increase the absorption of sulfonylurea drugs, and require a dose reduction. Too much magnesium causes diarrhea in some individuals.

Potassium

Highly alkaline potassium helps regulate levels of acidity in the blood, water balance in the body, and blood pressure. Potassium is needed for nervous system function, and it helps the body convert blood sugar into glycogen. Potassium is stored in the liver and muscles; a potassium shortage results in less stored glycogen, which is used during exercise for energy. Potassium helps regulate blood pressure, heart and blood function, and the actions of muscles and kidneys. According to naturopath Michael Murray, potassium affects the secretion of insulin, insulin sensitivity, and its responsiveness. The administration of insulin causes the body to lose potassium, as do potassium-depleting prescription drugs. Symptoms of a potassium deficiency include fatigue and muscle weakness.

Potassium is an important electrolyte that assists in the transmission of nerve impulses and muscle contraction. Within the cell, the constant electrical exchange of potassium and sodium ions, called the "sodium potassium pump," is an elemental process that moves food in and waste out of the cell. Sodium and potassium work together to maintain such things as blood pressure and water balance. Many people have ratios of sodium and potassium that are out of balance because of high salt consumption.

Although the average American diet consists of a ratio of one part potassium to two parts salt, some nutritionists recommend a five-to-one ratio of potassium to sodium, which is ten times more potassium than the average person consumes. Many studies have found that a diet high in potassium and low in sodium or salt protects against heart disease and high blood pressure.

A European study put two groups of people who were obese on a protein-modified fast. Subjects who were given potassium supplements had higher levels of insulin in the bloodstream in peripheral areas, and showed an improved utilization of glucose. In subjects who did not take potassium, insulin levels decreased and insulin resistance increased. The RDA is 1.9 to 5.6 grams per day.

Try to get your potassium from food. Fruits and vegetables are good sources of potassium, as are some dairy products, according to the U.S. Department of Agriculture. Many fruits and vegetables contain a ratio of potassium to sodium of 50 to 1 or higher. Bananas have a ratio of 440 to 1, oranges 260 to 1, potatoes 110 to 1, apples 90 to 1, and carrots 75 to 1, for instance. Since the average person takes in approximately 70 percent of their sodium from processed foods, rather than adding it from the salt shaker, substituting a potassium-based table salt such as Morton Lite Salt for regular table salt might help right the balance between potassium and sodium in the body if that balance is askew. Other products such as Antisalt, from Finland, contain magnesium and potassium in beneficial ratios.

Good natural sources of potassium include dulse, kelp, sunflower seeds, wheat germ, almonds, raisins, parsley, Brazil nuts, prunes, peanuts, dates, figs, mangoes, dried apricots, Swiss chard, avocados, pecans, yams, potatoes, dried beans, peas, lentils, milk, and yogurt. Orange juice and grapefruit juice are fairly good sources.

Precautions: Most people with diabetes can handle a high potassium diet, but before undertaking one, check with your doctor. Your physician should definitely be consulted if you are considering taking a potassium supplement, which entails more risk than eating more potassium-rich foods. People with kidney disease can't handle an excess of potassium, which can cause heart disturbances and potassium toxicity. People with kidney problems are often asked to curtail their potassium intake. People who are taking potassium-sparing diuretics should avoid products containing potassium chloride, and they should not increase their potassium intake.

By law, the amount of potassium in supplements is unusually small, a maximum of 99 mg. Multiple potassium pills can irritate the stomach—a problem that doesn't occur when potassium is taken with food.

Precautions: The side effects of too much potassium salts can include nausea, vomiting, diarrhea, and ulcers.

Vanadium

Vanadium is a naturally occurring trace element needed in very tiny amounts by the human body. The oxidized forms of vanadium have chemical properties similar to insulin. Vanadium supplements may help lower blood sugar and reduce body fat levels.

Vanadium compounds dramatically improve or normalize blood glucose in animal models of Type 1 and Type 2 diabetes, according to Dr. Allison B. Goldfine, a leading researcher in this area. In the form of vanadyl sulfate or sodium metavanadate, vanadium may benefit people with diabetes, according to preliminary research.

In one study, moderately obese people with and without Type 2 diabetes were given 50 micrograms of vanadyl sulfate twice a day for four weeks, and a placebo for four weeks afterward. A significant improvement in insulin sensitivity was found in the subjects with diabetes who took vanadium, but no change occurred in nondiabetic subjects. In a study of vanadium conducted at the Joslin Diabetes Center in Boston, patients with Type 2 diabetes showed improved insulin sensitivity and lower insulin requirements; some patients with Type 1 diabetes also improved with supplements. Serum cholesterol dropped in both groups.

A trial of people with Type 2 diabetes conducted at the Temple University Schools of Medicine and Pharmacy in Philadelphia, using 50 micrograms of vanadyl sulfate, found decreases in fasting blood sugar, and a decrease in insulin resistance in the liver after four weeks of supplementation. Another study of people with Type 2 diabetes using 100 micrograms of vanadyl sulfate per day for three weeks suggested that both liver and peripheral insulin sensitivity were increased with vanadium supplements, and that those effects remained for up to two weeks after the supplements were discontinued.

Good natural food sources of vanadium are parsley, black pepper, dill, mushrooms, shellfish, soy, corn, and gelatin.

Precautions: The safe and adequate dietary intake of vanadium is about 100 micrograms per day. Much larger doses of up to 25 mg. per day for adult males have been taken in clinical trials, with only minor side effects such as green tongue and upset stomach. The effects of long-term supplementation with this trace mineral are unknown.

Zinc

People with diabetes are often deficient in zinc because zinc is excreted in the urine during periods of high blood sugar. Zinc is involved in insulin metabolism, and it protects against the destruction of beta cells in the pancreas. It may help increase glucose tolerance and help the body utilize insulin, since about 0.5 percent of crystalized insulin is composed of zinc. Zinc's effect on insulin secretion is *biphasic*—that is, either too little or too much can adversely effect it.

Zinc is also involved in wound healing, immune system function, digestion, and sexual organ function. It is a cofactor for many necessary enzymes, including those involved in the synthesis of proteins, the preservation of vision, and the action of antioxidants.

The average American diet does not provide adequate zinc, and many elderly people are zinc deficient. Statistical studies show that populations whose diets are low in zinc have more dysfunctions involving insulin resistance. Problems resulting from zinc deficiency include slow wound healing, greater susceptibility to infection, decreased sensations of taste or smell, and skin problems.

A deficiency of zinc has been linked to abnormalities in insulin-like growth factor. In a study of people with Type 2 diabetes who took a 30 mg. zinc supplement every day for three weeks, published in the *American Journal of Clinical Nutrition* in 1997, people who had low levels of IGF saw these levels rise significantly. Some studies have shown that zinc deficiencies are associated with increased tissue resistance to insulin as well as a decreased secretion of insulin.

One study involving elderly people showed that zinc supplementation helped heal leg ulcers.

Most multivitamin and mineral tablets contain zinc. The RDA for men is 15 mg. per day, and for women it's 12 mg. Some practitioners recommend 30 mg. per day for people with diabetes.

Foods containing high levels of zinc include seafood, meat, eggs, tofu, wheat germ, whole grain foods, legumes, nuts and seeds, and black-eyed peas.

Precautions: Although zinc supplements may help people who are deficient, zinc is toxic in large doses and can cause nausea as well as diarrhea. More than 50 mg. per day of zinc is unnecessary and may cause side effects, including the suppression of the immune system. Too much zinc may interfere with the absorption of iron, calcium, chromium, and magnesium. Upset stomach and vomiting has been reported with large intakes of zinc in zinc sulfate form. Also, consuming too much zinc can deplete levels of copper, a small amount of which is needed to balance zinc. Copper is a trace element believed to improve glucose tolerance; 2 mg. per day are sometimes recommended to balance zinc supplement intake.

In addition to the vitamin and mineral supplements discussed here, other supplements with helpful effects are sometimes recommended for people with diabetes, as the following chapter reveals.

Chapter 5

Other Supplements

A few other nutritional supplements are sometimes recommended for people with Type 2 diabetes. These include alpha lipoic acid; the essential fatty acid gamma linolenic acid; the amino acids L-arginine, L-carnitine, and taurine; and DHEA and Coenzyme Q_{10}. Tests can be employed to check levels of some of these nutrients in the body. A fatty acid profile, for instance, can show a doctor a deficiency or ratios of fatty acids that are out of balance and might benefit from supplementation.

Alpha Lipoic Acid

Alpha lipoic acid, or ALA, also called thioctic acid, is a natural antioxidant that increases the utilization of glucose in peripheral areas such as the arms and legs, improves insulin action, and also raises levels of the enzyme glutathione. Unlike most antioxidants, ALA is both water and fat soluble. The antioxidant effects of ALA occur despite blood sugar fluctuations and protein in the urine. ALA is produced in the body in small amounts, but the amount obtained from a normal diet may be insufficient. It's been used as a treatment for diabetic neuropathy in Europe for some time. One study showed some benefit for people with glaucoma.

A Mayo Clinic study published in the September 1997 *Diabetes* found that patients with neuropathy experienced significant improvements in nerve conducting ability after three months of supplementation with 20, 50, and 150 milligrams of ALA per kilogram of body weight.

A study at Heinrich-Heine University in Dusseldorf, Germany, of 328 people with Type 2 diabetes who had either peripheral neuropathy or cardiac autonomic neuropathy concluded that supplementation with 600 mg. ALA per day over three weeks safely reduced the symptoms of peripheral neuropathy. It was also observed that 800 mg. of ALA per day for four months could improve cardiac autonomic dysfunction. Researchers suggested that ALA induced the regeneration or "sprouting" of nerve fibers, and a diminishing of pain in patients treated with ALA for three weeks, without side effects.

In 1995 a Russian study of 45 people with glaucoma found that supplementation with 150 mg. of ALA per day for a month improved the biochemical parameters and visual function.

ALA has been used intravenously in cases involving acute liver failure, producing dramatic results, including at least one incidence of preventing liver transplantation, according to Kirk Hamilton, a naturopath.

Dr. Ray Sahelian, author of *Lipoic Acid: The Unique Antioxidant*, recommends 10 to 30 mg. in the morning for people with diabetes. Some practitioners recommend supplementation from 100 to 600 mg. per day or higher for people with Type 2 diabetes who need it. Naturopath Skip Shoden says Vitamin B_{12} must be taken along with ALA. A commercial standardized form of ALA called AlphaBetic is being imported from Germany, where it is more widely used.

Meat is believed to be a rich natural source of this nutrient.

Gamma Linolenic Acid

Gamma linolenic acid, or GLA, an omega-6 essential fatty acid, is normally produced by enzyme action on linoleic acid found in vegetable oil. People with diabetes may not be able to properly break down linoleic acid into GLA, some research suggests, because they lack certain enzymes that break it down. Further along in this process, GLA normally converts to prostaglandin E1, a substance that reduces inflammation in the body, dilates blood vessels, and thins the blood. GLA has

---

Two Supplements to Avoid

Human Growth Hormone. Celebrity doctor Andrew Weil says too much of human growth hormone can actually bring on diabetes.

Glucosamin. Dr. Paul Rosch of the American Institute of Stress reports some evidence indicates that this popular arthritis "cure" may bring on Type 2 diabetes.

---

170 times the cholesterol-lowering power of linoleic acid, which itself reduces serum cholesterol. GLA regulates some hormones. GLA may reduce blood pressure and aid in weight loss, according to unpublished data cited in *The Lawrence Review of Natural Products*. Several recent studies have concluded that supplements of GLA can improve diabetic neuropathy.

A randomized, double-blind study conducted at seven centers in London was reported in a 1993 issue of *Diabetes Care*. In this study, people with diabetes who had peripheral neuropathy took 480 mg. of GLA per day for one year and reported improvement in symptoms of neuropathy, while a placebo group described their symptoms as worse. Researchers said that subjects with better blood sugar control benefited more from supplementation than those with poor control.

A 1990 study at Glasgow University in Scotland used 360 mg. of GLA daily on 12 of 22 patients with distal diabetic polyneuropathy. Patients who received supplements for six months showed improvement in symptoms compared with the placebo group.

A prime source of GLA is evening primrose oil, which contains one of the richest concentrations of GLA in plants. The maximum recommended daily dose of evening primrose oil, according to nutritional supplement labels, is 4 grams per day, which contains from 300 to 360 mg. of GLA. Expeller-pressed, organic oils in light-resistant bottles are said to be superior. According to *The Lawrence Review of Natural Products*, evening primrose oil appears devoid of adverse effects.

Flaxseed oil, another supplement, has a ratio of four to one omega-3 to omega-6 oils, and is said to be useful in rebalancing the body's essential fatty acid ratios. As a dietary supplement for people with diabetes, Skip Shoden recommends black current oil or borage oil rather than fish oil, which he says can have an adverse effect on blood sugar levels in some people. Borage oil contains about 24 percent GLA, while black current oil contains about 18 percent GLA by volume.

Precaution: Evening primrose oil is quite safe. However, some borage seed oils sometimes contain dangerous alkaloids—avoid borage oils with 0.5 mg. or more pyrrolizidine alkaloids per gram since these are toxic to the liver and often to livestock, and are not considered safe for human consumption.

Amino Acids

Digestion breaks protein down into amino acids, which are reformed as needed inside the body. Twenty amino acids combine in different sequences to form proteins, enzymes, and other necessary substances. Eight of these are classified as essential, because they aren't manufactured in the body and must be consumed in food. Three more are manufactured in limited quantities. Most people consume adequate amino acids, except for dieters and certain athletes. However, supplements of L-carnitine, L-arginine, and taurine are sometimes recommended.

Note that some doctors believe the amino acids should not be taken individually, but rather, in food sources that contain them all.

L-Carnitine

Acetyl-L-Carnitine, or ALC, is an amino acid normally found in high concentrations in the muscles. A powerful antioxidant, L-carnitine is naturally produced in the body, where it is essential for the transportation of long-chain fatty acids into the mitochondria, which are small power plants inside individual cells. L-carnitine is believed to help regulate the oxidation of fats in the body, although some studies dispute this. People apparently become deficient in carnitine when it is excreted from the body, sometimes a result of infection, surgery, or other stress.

A study in Italy found that levels of L-carnitine in the blood were lower in people with diabetes, and that less L-carnitine was excreted in people with diabetes than in subjects without diabetes.

Three small, short-term studies of L-carnitine *infusion* (not supplementation) also conducted in Italy on people with Type 2 diabetes show that L-carnitine beneficially affects the utilization of glucose. One study found that glucose disposal increased with an infusion of L-carnitine. Another found that glucose uptake was significantly higher in Type 2 subjects given a two-hour infusion of L-carnitine when compared with subjects given a saline solution. The same study concluded that the infusion of L-carnitine improved insulin sensitivity in insulin-resistant subjects. A third Italian study found that glucose utilization was higher during intravenous infusion of L-carnitine.

In a study conducted in Rome, two dozen elderly patients who were depressed showed significant improvement when given a gram of L-carnitine per day for a month.

According to the book *Numb Toes and Aching Soles: Coping with Peripheral Neuropathy*, studies have found that L-carnitine protects the nerves from free radical damage. One small study found double the nerve fiber regeneration when small mammals were treated with ALC for sixteen weeks.

Several studies have shown that L-carnitine has a protective effect on heart patients, helping to reduce angina and improve the duration of exercise. L-carnitine supplements unarguably help people with heart muscle disease who are deficient in L-carnitine and people on dialysis who are deficient.

Dr. Robert Atkins of the Atkins Center for Complementary Medicine suggests that reasonably healthy people should take 500 to 1,000 mg. of ALC daily, and from 1,500 to 3,000 mg. for therapeutic purposes under care of doctor. Other practitioners suggest 500 mg. twice a day, up to 1,000 mg. twice a day, depending on the person and their individual needs.

L-carnitine is found naturally in red meat, especially lamb and beef. It is also found in dairy products.

Precautions: Only the L-carnitine form should be taken as a supplement. The DL form called DL-carnitine can cause muscle weakness syndrome in some people. Like many other supplements, standardization is a problem. A study of twelve over-the-counter brands conducted at Duke University in 1992 found that two brands contained little or no carnitine, and most of the rest were poorly manufactured.

L-Arginine

L-arginine is an amino acid that is usually classified as "nonessential," meaning the body usually produces adequate amounts. L-arginine is considered an essential amino acid for infants because it cannot be produced in adequate quantities for the first few years of life. An antioxidant, it assists in the metabolism of essential fatty acids and may help protect the insulin-producing cells of the pancreas against damage.

A small Australian study published in 1997 studied three groups—a group of healthy subjects, a second group who were obese, and a third group with Type 2 diabetes. Low doses of L-arginine, when infused, improved insulin sensitivity in all three groups. Blood vessel expansion, normally impaired by insulin, was significantly improved by L-arginine infusion in obese subjects and those with Type 2 diabetes, while the infusions had no observable effect on healthy subjects.

An excellent food source of L-arginine is brewer's yeast, which contains as much as 750 mg. of L-arginine per tablespoon. Other sources of L-arginine include raw cereals, chocolate, and nuts.

Taurine

Taurine, another amino acid, is sometimes depleted in people with diabetes, particularly people with Type 1 diabetes. There is no vegetable source of taurine. A potent antioxidant, taurine is good for the heart. Among its other effects, it helps the body excrete cholesterol by converting it into bile acid.

A year-long study published in 1995 compared groups of diabetic rats treated with either ultralente insulin, Vitamin E, or taurine in their drinking water. Rats that received taurine had levels of protein in their urine 50 percent lower than others, and also showed improvements in liver function. In the same study, Vitamin E supplementation produced a negative result in animals.

The Benefits of Broth

For people who are deficient in amino acids, Dr. C. Norman Shealy recommends the amino acids be replenished naturally, in the form of a animal-based broth, rather than as amino acid supplements.

To make a broth containing all the essential amino acids, put a quart of water in a crock pot or cooking pot and add 8 ounces of either meat, chicken, turkey, fish, or beef. Add an onion, a carrot, a stick of celery, and a tablespoon each of vinegar and of soy sauce, then let cook on low heat for twelve hours. The broth you create contains all the essential amino acids.

Dr. Shealy recommends the consumption of a quart of this broth per day for a month, then slowly tapering down to a cup a day, which can be consumed as a maintenance dose.

Another animal study, published in the *American Journal of Clinical Nutrition* in 2000, concluded that taurine supplementation reduced abdominal fat accumulation, lowered blood sugar, and lowered insulin resistance in research animals, apparently because of its effects on reducing the production and increasing the excretion of cholesterol.

Taurine is primarily found in meat and fish.

Coenzyme Q_{10}

Coenzyme Q_{10} is a protein molecule found in every cell in the body, but is most plentiful in the heart and the liver. Coenzyme Q_{10} is important for energy production, particularly in the mitochondria, which are the power plants of individual cells. It beefs up the immune system, and it's also a powerful antioxidant that protects against free radical damage. It has been estimated that perhaps 12 million people in Japan use it in commercial formulations to help manage cardiovascular problems. Some studies indicate that Coenzyme Q_{10} may help protect against the tissue damage of heart disease and may slow the aging process by sup-

Supplement Combinations

A great number of commercial supplements contain different combinations of vitamins, minerals, herbs, and other substances believed to be helpful to people with diabetes. These are marketed as aids to lowering blood sugar and raising insulin resistance. Theoretically, these products provide something of value to people with diabetes. Here are a few commercial products currently on the market:

- *Pancreas Tonic*, sold by U.S. Botanicals, showed a blood sugar lowering effect when fed to diabetic rats for three months, compared with rats who ate rat chow. Trumpeted on a few TV shows as a "cure for diabetes," it is the most notorious of these supplements. Pancreas Tonic contains Indian herbs that have been shown to reduce blood sugar in studies, including gymnema, pterocarpus masupium, bitter melon, and fenugreek. The company has overseen one small test using this product on human subjects, and says larger tests are under way.

- *Atkins Nutritional's Blood Sugar Formula*, sold by the Atkins Center for Complementary Medicine, contains 15 ingredients including chromium, magnesium, niacinamide, vanadium, zinc, alpha lipoic acid, Vitamin C, maganese, Vitamin E, folic acid, and bioperine.

- *Blood Sugar with Gymnema*, sold by Nature's Way, contains gymnema extract, bilberry leaf, bitter melon, Vitamin A, chromium, fenugreek extract, and nopal.

- *Diabetic Nutrition RX*, sold by Progressive Research Labs, contains chromium, L-carnitine, L-glutamine, vanadium, calcium, magnesium, potassium, amylase, betaine, copper, maganese, huckleberry, lipase, pancreatin, papain, selenium, niacinamide, Vitamin A, Vitamin B_1, Vitamin B_6, and zinc.

Although many of the nutrients and herbs these products list have some potential benefit for those with diabetes, little research has been done on most. As with many herbal products, some of the labels probably don't accurately list the substances they contain.

Precautions: Use at least the same care in evaluating these combination products as you would use on particular vitamins, minerals, and herbs. Consumers should carefully read the labels, consider the ingredients chosen, and find out something about the integrity of the manufacturer. Check with your doctor before trying any product such as this, and carefully monitor your blood sugar thereafter, making adjustments in medications as prodent and necessary.

porting the functioning of the immune system. Coenzyme Q_{10} also may help stimulate the production of insulin, and could have an effect on blood sugar.

A study in Japan in 1966 with a very similar substance to Coenzyme Q_{10} produced lower blood sugar levels in people with diabetes.

A 1993 Italian study concluded that supplementation with Coenzyme Q_{10} resulted in improved heart and lung function in patients who had suffered congestive heart failure. Two small trials in 1995 also showed it improved physical performance in patients with muscular and nerve atrophy problems.

In 1999 a double-blind trial conducted in India matched two groups of patients with heart problems who were taking blood pressure medication. In addition to their medication, for two months one group took Coenzyme Q_{10} (60 mg. twice a day), while a second group of patients took Vitamin B complex. At the conclusion of the study, subjects who took Coenzyme Q_{10} had lower blood pressure, lower fasting insulin, lower blood sugar, and lower levels of triglycerides. Subjects also had higher levels of HDL cholesterol, Vitamin A, Vitamin C, Vitamin E, and beta carotene than the control group. Subjects who took only B vitamins showed increased levels of Vitamin C and beta carotene.

Several studies have shown that supplementation with Coenzyme Q_{10} for several months reduces blood pressure in people with hypertension. One double-blind study showed that supplementation with Coenzyme Q_{10} had a beneficial effect on periodontal disease, which requires an increased production of energy for healing.

According to Dr. Robert Atkins, a study conducted in Belgium found that among a group of overweight patients, half were deficient in Coenzyme Q_{10}. This group lost more weight on a standard diet when they received supplements of 100 mg. per day of Coenzyme Q_{10}.

The amount of Coenzyme Q_{10} required by the body is not known. No doses have been established for any human disorder. Ordinary diets supply a small amount.

Coenzyme Q_{10} production may be inhibited by some diabetes drugs such as glyburide and tolazamide. According to Dr. Anderson, anyone taking cholesterol-lowering drugs from the *statin* family should probably supplement with 30 to 60 mg. of Coenzyme Q_{10} daily, since these drugs lower levels of Coenzyme Q_{10} in LDL cholesterol.

Some practitioners recommend supplements of 90 to 120 mg. of Coenzyme Q_{10} per day for people with heart problems. Therapeutic doses are sometimes recommended up to the level of 200 to 400 mg. per day. Beneficial effects do not show up for a few months.

Good natural sources of Coenzyme Q_{10} include meat, spinach, sardines, and peanuts.

Precautions: No serious side effects have yet been reported with the use of Coenzyme Q_{10}, but it is not recommended for pregnant or lactating women, or for people who have demonstrated a hypersensitivity to its use. Loss of appetite, bowel discomfort, nausea, or diarrhea are occasional side effects, affecting less than 1 percent of subjects in one large study.

DHEA

First identified in 1934, dehydroepiandrosterone, or DHEA, is the most plentiful steroid hormone in the human body. It converts into estrogen, testosterone, and other steroid hormones in men and women. DHEA production is known to peak about age thirty, then fall gradually. Levels of DHEA also drop during illness. DHEA's true significance in the body is something of a mystery. It was once considered almost a panacea for many physical ailments, but that view is now more problematic.

A 1994 study of adult males with Type 1 diabetes found lower than normal DHEA levels. A study in 1991 found that people with lower levels of DHEA in their blood had increased body mass and impaired glucose tolerance.

A study at the University of California at San Diego found increased physical and psychological well-being reported after supplementation with DHEA. Animal research published in 1996 found that overweight animals lost weight when given DHEA along with their regular diets. Chillingly, one study found that DHEA supplements led to greater insulin resistance and a drop in "good" HDL cholesterol.

DHEA probably should not be used as a supplement unless levels are tested and found to be low, and then its use should be supervised by a medical doctor. A deficiency of DHEA is less than 180 nanograms per deciliter in men and 130 nanograms per deciliter in women.

Fats in the meal will block absorption of DHEA. Some people let supplements dissolve under the tongue, although the taste is not particularly pleasant. If you must use this supplement, low doses are probably safest, perhaps between 1 and 5 mg. per day, until additional studies are completed.

Precautions: Since DHEA converts to steroid hormones, some scientists speculate that it may exacerbate hormone-dependent cancers such as breast cancer and prostate cancer. Some doctors recommend that blood serum levels of steroid hormones, and liver enzymes, be monitored while DHEA supplementation is under way. Researchers are debating whether oral doses of DHEA can even be useful, since it may be destroyed in the liver before it has any effect.

A natural source of chemicals that may convert to DHEA in the body is said to be the Mexican wild yam, which is sold in supplements as "natural DHEA," a claim that is hotly debated.

Additional Supplements

Some other supplements that may be of interest include protein and amino acid-laden *bee pollen* or flower pollen, which speeds up the metabolism and helps curb the appetite. Raw honey is a natural source, as are edible flowers, but these contain only small amounts of pollen. People who are allergic to bee stings or who have hay fever may suffer allergic reactions.

L-Phenylalanine, an essential amino acid, may be of use in weight-loss efforts and sometimes alleviates depression. Natural sources include cheese, almonds, peanuts, sesame seeds, and soybeans. It should be taken before retiring, on an empty stomach, and in particular should not be taken with protein. In fact, if you have high blood pressure, L-phenylalanine should be taken only under a doctor's supervision. It isn't suitable for pregnant women or people taking antidepressants such as MAO inhibitors.

Cod liver oil supplementation improves albumin excretion levels in people with Type 2 diabetes with nephrophy for at least a year, according to research conducted at Gunma University School of Medicine in Japan and published in *Diabetes Residential Clinical Practice* in 1995. Cod liver oil is rich in the same essential fatty acids as fish oil, but it has extremely high levels of Vitamin A and should be used carefully, and for only a few days at a time.

Tea tree oil may help people with periodontal problems. In one study, tea tree oil was also as effective as some medicines in the treatment of fungal infections of the toenails. A sesame oil rinse after brushing the teeth is an Ayurvedic remedy that may help with periodontal problems, along with regular visits to a dental practitioner.

Chapter 6

Herbal Medicines

Many herbs included in this chapter may be helpful for people with diabetes. Herbal medicines made from plants have been used in treating diabetes for centuries, and more than 400 traditional plant treatments or folk remedies for diabetes mellitus have been recorded. The oldest surviving herbal medicines have stood the test of time, with research that documents their efficacy.

Nutritionally oriented doctors, and practitioners of naturopathy, traditional Chinese medicine, and Ayurvedic medicine, and other herbalists, sometimes use herbs to treat diabetes. These practitioners often use different herbs, in different ways. Western herbal medicine uses herbs more or less as medicines: one herbal preparation is usually selected to treat a particular complaint on a short-term basis. In Asia, combinations of herbs are often used for broad-spectrum effects. Herbal treatments may take effect slowly, but usually show benefit within one to three months.

In European countries such as Germany, physicians are required to study the use of herbs as part of their medical training. In North America, nutritionally oriented physicians, naturopaths, Ayurvedic practitioners, herbalists, and other practitioners can be consulted for a comprehensive treatment plan involving herbs. Two of the best sources of information on medicinal herbs are *The Complete German Commission E Monographs*, an extensive and scientific review of particular herbs conducted by the German government, and *The Lawrence Review of Natural Products*, a reference book published in the United States.

Perhaps one-fourth of all pharmacological drugs have been produced from the active ingredients in herbs. This includes the diabetes medication metformin, which utilizes the active ingredient in French lilac or goat's rue, an old European folk remedy for diabetes.

At this writing, some 1,500 different herbs are being sold commercially in the United States, and it's estimated that perhaps one-third of adults in the U.S. population use them. Many herbs have a documented effect on blood sugar, blood pressure, and other symptoms of diabetes. However, there is no herbal substitute for insulin. Herbs listed here include aloe vera, alfalfa, astralagus, bilberry, bitter melon, burdock, cayenne, dandelion, fenugreek, gingko biloba, ginseng, glucomannan, Gosha-jinki-gan, guar, gymnema, hawthorn, milk thistle, neem, petrocarpus, psyllium, saltbush, St. John's wort, and valerian.

Precautions: Always notify your medical doctor of herbs you wish to take before you take them, since many affect blood sugar levels. Doses of medications or insulin may have to be lowered or adjusted at an appropriate time. More frequent testing of blood sugars is a reasonable precaution against plunges in blood sugar. Careful testing for a week should give you an idea if the supplement is having a bad effect on you. *If you experience a strong reaction* within an hour or two of taking a particular herb, by all means *stop taking it.* Breathing problems, skin rashes, diarrhea, or headaches are symptoms of an allergic reaction to the herb or to an additive or impurity. Many herbs also affect the liver—adults over the age of 65 with diminished liver function should be extremely cautious when using either herbs or supplements, to avoid liver toxicity. Liver function should be tested periodically for all people with diabetes, including those using herbals, supplements, and pharmaceutical drugs. Before taking herbal supplements, ask your doctor or pharmacist about adverse reactions with medications you are currently taking.

Aloe Vera

The spiny, pale green desert plant, aloe vera, may help lower blood sugar levels. The dried sap is a traditional remedy for diabetes on the Arabian peninsula, and the plant itself has a rich history. Called the "plant of immortality," aloe vera was a traditional funeral gift for Egyptian pharaohs. Alexander the Great is said to have conquered the island of Socotra to have an adequate supply for his soldiers.

Aloe comes in two forms. "Aloe" is a solid residue obtained from drying the bitter yellow latex just beneath the skin; it is a powerful laxative, and the only part of the plant approved for internal medical use. "Aloe vera gel extract," the form commonly sold in health food stores and used in cosmetics, is composed of pulverized whole aloe leaves, and despite the label, it is not actually an extract at all.

Researchers at the Department of Complementary Medicine at the University of Exeter, England, examined ten controlled clinical trials of aloe vera. The studies suggested that oral administration of aloe vera "might be a useful adjunct for lowering blood glucose in diabetic patients as well as for reducing blood lipid levels," according to the authors of an analysis published in 1999 in the *British Journal of General Practice.*

One study found that newly diagnosed people with diabetes who were given aloe vera juice experienced lowered blood sugar and triglyceride levels. In 1996 the same authors conducted research on people with diabetes whose blood sugar was not being controlled by the drug glibenclamide. Research subjects were given a juice containing 80 percent aloe vera—one tablespoonful in the morning and at bedtime, along with two 5 mg. tablets of glibenclamide. In this group, blood sugar dropped significantly within two weeks, triglyceride levels dropped within four weeks, and both continued to fall. However, even after 42 days of treatment, blood sugar levels of research subjects were not normal.

In a small study conducted in 1986, five patients with Type 2 diabetes were given half a teaspoonful of aloe vera per day for four to fourteen weeks. Subjects experienced a fall in fasting blood sugar, from an average of 273 to 151 mg./dl. Mice with induced diabetes also benefit.

According to the *Review of Natural Products,* a small study in China also found that parenteral administration of aloe extract protected the liver from chemical injury, resulting in some improvements in patients with hepatitis.

Precautions: Extracts including significant amounts of chemicals such as anthraquinones (concentrated in the aloe latex) may cause severe gastric cramping when consumed, and should not be used by pregnant women and children. Although aloe is a folk remedy for minor skin problems, skin rashes from related plant species and a burning sensation in some people with dermabraded skin have been reported.

Alfalfa

Originating in southwest Asia, alfalfa, or *Medicago sativa*, is a folk remedy for diabetes that may strengthen the constitution. Arabs in the Old World fed their horses alfalfa to increase their endurance and strength in battle, and Chinese herbalists once prescribed it as a digestive aid. Alfalfa alkalizes and detoxifies the body, cleanses the liver, and reduces fluid retention. It is recommended in Ayurvedic medicine for diabetes, anemia, arthritis, and other conditions, including poor digestion.

Alfalfa contains antifungal agents and is said to promote pituitary gland health. It is high in nutrients, including beta carotene and calcium. It contains protein and Vitamins A, B_1, B_6, C, E, and K, as well as saponins—chemicals that, in animal studies, block the absorption of cholesterol and prevent the formation of plaque.

No relevant human studies involving alfalfa were located, but animal studies show some blood sugar lowering effects. In a European study of mice that were diabetic, published in *Diabetologia* in 1990, alfalfa retarded the onset of diabetes by lowering blood sugar and reducing *polydipsia*, or excessive thirst. A study published in the *British Journal of Nutrition* in 1997 found that alfalfa lowered blood sugar and stimulated the release of insulin in diabetic mice.

The *Encyclopedia of Natural Remedies* recommends alfalfa for diabetes, taken daily. The sprouts, leaves, petals, and flowers of the slightly bitter-tasting plant may be eaten. Leaves are ground into a powder or tablets for use as a supplement. Alfalfa tea may be made using two teaspoons of alfalfa to a cup of boiling water, steeped fifteen minutes. Up to three cups of tea per day may be consumed. No therapeutic dosage has been established.

Precautions: Large quantities of alfalfa seeds should not be eaten, since they contain high levels of a toxic amino acid, L-canavanine, which disappears as plants germinate and mature. Over time, L-canavanine can affect the functioning of platelets and white blood cells. Pregnant women should consult their doctors before using alfalfa.

Astragalus

Astragalus is a small, thorny shrub native to the mountains of the Middle East that may strengthen the immune system. Astragalus is also called goat's thorn, green dragon, gum dragon, gum tragacanth, hog gum, Syrian tragacanth, and tragacanth. In Chinese herbal medicine, the dried root of a plant four to seven years old is sold as Huang Qi, or "yellow leader," an important tonic herb also used to prepare stock for soup said to enhance the immune system. A water soluble gum is obtained by tapping the branches and tap roots of the astragalus plant.

Some studies have shown that ingesting astragalus with a meal high in sugar can moderate blood sugar levels, like other soluble fibers, although other studies have shown no blood sugar lowering effect. Unlike other soluble fibers, Astragalus showed no apparent effect on cholesterol or triglyceride levels after a three-week period of supplementation.

Textbooks of Chinese medicine recommend 9 to 15 grams of crude herb per day. A decoction may be made by boiling the root in water for a few minutes and brewing a tea. Supplements and tinctures containing astralagus are also available. Among the 2,000 varieties of astralagus, the Chinese plant *Astragalus membranaceus* is most extensively studied.

Astralagus is a food ingredient widely used in foods and dressings, and as an additive is used to thicken ice cream. It is labeled as generally recognized as safe (GRAS) in the United States.

Bilberry

Bilberry has been used with positive results in the treatment of diabetic retinopathy, macular degeneration, and other problems. Also known as European blueberry or *Vaccinium myrtillus*, bilberry is a shrub that grows in the meadows and forests of northern Europe, Canada, and the

United States, bearing blue-black berries. Bilberry is a close cousin to the American blueberry or huckleberry, and a folk remedy for diabetes. During World War II it was said that Royal Air Force pilots could see better during night bombing raids after eating bilberry jam. Bilberry extracts have been prescribed for diabetic retinopathy for more than fifty years. Bilberry may also help prevent cataracts. According to Time-Life's *Medical Advisor*, bilberry may also slightly lower blood sugar and help maintain the vascular system.

Bilberry contains potent flavonoids. Anthocyanosides, the most potent, are antioxidants that strengthen the capillaries and connective tissues and help restore circulation to the retina of the eye.

Berries or leaves are used medicinally. Berries are eaten at the rate of 20 to 60 grams per day. To make tea, steep two or three handfuls of leaves in four cups of hot water for half an hour; drink up to three cups a day. The extract, standardized to provide 25 percent anthocyanosides, may be more potent. The standard dose of extract is 80 to 60 mg. three times per day.

American and Canadian blueberries probably have similar properties to bilberry, although not much scientific research has been done on them as yet.

Precautions: There are no known contraindications to bilberry, which has no known side effects in recommended amounts.

Bitter Melon

Bitter melon, or *Momordica charantia*, also called bitter gourd, karella, or balsam pear, is an Indian folk remedy for diabetes in the unripe form. A staple of Chinese and Indian cuisine, it is somewhat expensive in North America, but can be found in Asian grocery stores and some health food stores. As befits its name, the taste of this fruit is quite bitter. Bitter melon may lower blood sugar and improve glucose tolerance, and also has antibiotic, antimicrobial, and antiviral properties.

Active ingredients are believed to be oleanolic acid glycosides such as charantin, which prevent absorption of sugar from the intestine. Polypeptide-P, an insulin-like chemical that lowers blood sugar when administered subcutaneously, was isolated from the fruit and seeds in 1981.

In a 1993 study, subjects who received an extract of bitter melon for three weeks experienced a 25 percent drop in blood sugars. A study published in 1986 found that bitter melon juice "significantly improved" the glucose tolerance of 73 percent of 18 research subjects with Type 2 diabetes.

A study with mice recorded improvements in blood sugar after ingestion of bitter melon extract, and a small improvement in glucose tolerance when fruits were consumed as a daily dietary supplement. Another animal study with rats using extract of bitter melon saw a retardation of diabetic retinopathy.

The extract of the unripe fruit or fresh juice can improve glucose tolerance. Practitioners recommend a two-ounce shot of the juice daily, or 50 to 60 ml., the amount used in clinical trials, which is generally considered a safe dose. However, most over-the-counter herbal products are not standardized in terms of active ingredients. The term "bitter principals" used on labels is quite general and isn't useful in comparing products.

The melon may be eaten as food, although it is so bitter some people cannot tolerate it. Fruits and seeds are believed to be the most useful; not considered useful are products made from leaves or other parts of the vine.

Precautions: Bitter melon is generally considered to have a low toxicity, with some possible side effects in the gastrointestinal tract if large amounts are consumed. However, bitter melon does have an antifertility effect, and it is not recommended for pregnant women since it can induce contractions, bleeding, or spontaneous abortion. The red arils around the seeds of bitter melon are toxic to children. One child died from drinking the juice; additionally, two children experienced a coma caused by low blood sugar from drinking tea made from the plant, although both children recovered. For adults, given a normal oral dose of 50 ml., there are no reports of serious side effects

Burdock

Burdock, or *Articum lappa*, is cultivated in parts of Eastern Europe such as Yugoslavia and Poland. Described as a "blood purifier," the root pieces as well as fruits and leaves are used in teas as folk remedies for various health problems. Burdock root is commonly used as a food in Asia, and health food stores in the United States occasionally carry it and market it as a medical food. It is a diuretic that removes water from the body.

Burdock root contains up to 50 percent inulin, and the fruit is about one-third inulin, a substance that can lower blood glucose levels. Consuming the root or fruit may mildly lower blood sugar. In one study, people with diabetes who ate crackers made from powdered burdock after consuming a meal containing starches had lower blood sugar after the meal than a control group who didn't eat the crackers. In studies with rats with diabetes, burdock lowers blood sugar.

Precautions: Allergic skin reactions have been experienced by some people. There have been reports of poisoning by Burdock root teas, but these were due to adulteration of product rather than the Burdock itself.

Cayenne

A plant native to South America, cayenne, or *Capsicum annuum*, is used in herbal medicine as a tonic to improve blood circulation. Cayenne is closely related to red bell pepper, paprika, jalapenos, and similar peppers. The active ingredient, *capsaicin*, can provide some relief of pain and other discomforts associated with peripheral neuropathy when it is applied as a cream or a hot oil.

In 1992 a study conducted at twelve sites by the Capsaicin Study Group studied a cream containing 0.075 percent capsaicin. The cream produced a temporary but significant reduction in peripheral neuropathy in 277 patients with diabetes, according to research results published in the professional journal *Diabetes Care*. Statistically significant improvements were recorded in overall pain status, as well as improvements in walking, working, sleeping, and recreational activities.

Added to herbal medicines, or used as a kitchen spice, cayenne also may slightly improve blood circulation.

Precautions: Use creams or oils topically. Capsaicin cream should be applied only to small areas of skin and then rubbed in thoroughly. Use only small amounts of cream; wear protective gloves when applying to the body or wash hands immediately afterward. Avoid getting cream in your eyes or on areas that are inflamed. Topical application often creates some discomfort in the beginning but typically goes away. Commercial preparations come in two strengths; try the weaker strength first.

Dandelion

Dandelion, or *Taraxacum officinale*, is a folk remedy for diabetes and for liver disorders. Ingestion of dandelion is sometimes recommended for people seeking to lose weight, and as a laxative and a tonic. Leaves are used as greens or in wine; long taproots are sometimes roasted for a beverage similar to coffee, which is said to have a tonic effect on the pancreas and spleen. Dandelion may help flush the kidneys, speed up the metabolism, and dampen the craving for sweets.

Dandelion root detoxifies the liver, helping to remove wastes, and stimulates the production of bile. Dandelion leaves stimulate digestion, and are one of the richest sources of beta carotene, containing even more than carrots. It is a mild laxative. Dandelion may have a slight beneficial effect on blood sugar—studies show it lowers blood sugar in rabbits but has no effect on blood sugar in mice. Inulin, one of its chemical constituents, may produce the blood sugar effect. The sugars in the plant are not believed to aggravate diabetes.

Leaves may be eaten as part of a salad. A beverage may be made by boiling 2 or 3 teaspoons of roasted, slightly burnt root chunks in hot water for 10 to 15 minutes, then drinking as often as three times per day.

Precaution: Toxicity is low, but dandelion plants may cause contact dermatitis in sensitive individuals. According to *The Natural Pharmacy*, people with an obstruction of the bile ducts should avoid dandelion, which should also be used very cautiously by people with ulcers or gallstones since it may cause an overproduction of stomach acid.

Fenugreek

Fenugreek, or *Trigonella foenum-graecum*, is an Asian folk remedy for diabetes, boils, and tuberculosis. The seeds of fenugreek, or *methica*, are used as a digestive aid in Indian and Chinese medicine. Fenugreek is consumed as a food or a spice in India and southeastern Europe. Several studies have shown it reduces blood sugar and lowers LDL cholesterol. Fenugreek has anti-inflammatory, antiseptic, and laxative effects.

Most blood sugar lowering effects are attributed to fenugreek's high fiber content, but an amino acid that increases the release of insulin, 4-hydroxyisoleucine, has also been extracted from seeds.

A study on people with Type 2 diabetes who consumed 15 grams of powdered fenugreek seeds soaked in water, published in the *European Journal of Clinical Nutrition*, found lowered blood sugar levels after eating, and slightly lowered insulin levels.

In another study, 2.5 grams of fenugreek per day given to patients with mild Type 2 diabetes for three months significantly reduced the patient's after-dinner blood sugar. However, in the same study, fenugreek only slightly reduced blood sugar levels in patients with severe Type 2 diabetes.

A ten-day study of people with Type 1 diabetes who ingested 100 grams of defatted fenugreek seed powder divided in half at lunch and dinner found the subjects had lower fasting blood sugar and improved results on glucose tolerance tests. Subjects excreted less glucose and had reductions in cholesterol and triglyceride levels.

Seeds and leaves of fenugreek are rich in protein and fiber. Fiber is believed to prevent absorption of sugar from the intestine. Fenugreek is typically used in the form of seeds or defatted seed powder, which is 54 percent fiber.

Doses of about 15 grams of seeds per day are traditional. Whole seeds soaked in water for eight hours are prescribed in Ayurvedic medicine. Fenugreek may also be taken as a spice, a tea, or an inhalant, or used in massage oil, poultices, or plasters. The *Illustrated Encyclopedia of Natural Remedies* recommends daily drinking of fenugreek decoction.

Fenugreek is listed as an ingredient in many combination supplements sold to people with diabetes.

Precautions: Fenugreek is safe when used in culinary quantities, but low blood sugar can result from large doses. Because it stimulates the flow of urine, it should not be taken by women who are pregnant, or given to children under two years of age. It can also promote water retention and weight gain.

Ginkgo Biloba

The world's oldest deciduous tree, the *Gingko biloba*, or maidenhair tree, survived the Ice Age in a corner of northern China. One of the most frequently prescribed herbs in Europe, ginkgo may help prevent some nervous disorders associated with aging. It improves mental function, increases blood flow to the brain, and increases circulation and blood flow to the arms and legs. Ginkgo may reduce the risk of heart disease, lower blood pressure, and reduce cholesterol. It may also be useful for eye problems such as macular degeneration and diabetic retinopathy.

Ginkgo leaves are used to make an extract that contains two important groups of chemicals: ginkgo flavone glycosides and terpene lactones. These are bioflavonoids and antioxidants, which inhibit stickiness of blood platelets, thus improving blood circulation.

A 1988 study in Paris on people with early stages of diabetic retinopathy found a statistically significant improvement in subjects who took ginkgo. Ginkgo prevents retinopathy in rats with diabetes, and supplements may have a protective effect for humans.

Germany's Commission E approved gingko for pain on walking due to insufficient blood flow to the extremities or intermittent claudication, as well as concentration problems and depression. According to the Commission E monograph, one study showed that it increased sexual response in women and men.

Standardized ginkgo extract, designated Egb 761, should contain 24 percent ginkgo flavone glycosides. The dosage for most individuals is 40 mg. taken three times per day; doses between 120 and 240 mg. per day have gotten results in studies. The authors of an article on ginkgo in *Archives of Family Medicine* suggest limiting intake to 120 mg. per day. Typically, between one and three months are required before the full effects are felt.

Precautions: Ginkgo is generally safe, but in a few cases it has been linked with strokes. It may also enhance the action of blood-thinning

Dangerous Herbs

Serious health problems have been reported with a few herbal products used by people with diabetes, according to "Illnesses and Injuries Associated with the Use of Selected Dietary Supplements," published in 1993 by the U.S. Food and Drug Administration Center for Food Safety and Applied Nutrition. Other sources have also reported problems with particular herbs or herbal products.

Ackee fruit, in its unripe form, contains two very potent active ingredients that can drastically lower blood sugar. Although cooked Ackee fruit is sometimes used in Jamaican cuisine, more than 5,000 deaths have been attributed to the ingestion of raw Ackee fruit in Jamaica. Ackee fruit is too toxic to be used in attempting to lower blood sugar, warned the authors of a survey of herbs published in *The Diabetes Educator*.

Chaparral, or creosote bush, is a common desert shrub used by Native Americans as a medicine. Sold as a tea, tablet, or capsule, it is sometimes included in dietary supplements. Promoted as a "blood purifier" and natural antioxidant, the FDA says chaparral is associated with several cases of acute nonviral hepatitis or rapidly developing liver damage in the United States, and one in Canada.

Comfrey has a benign reputation in the United States, but it does contain toxic compounds known as pyrrolizidine alkaloids. These substances are more concentrated in the roots, but even consumption of the leaves can lead to cirrhosis, liver cancer, or damage to other organs. Worldwide, according to the FDA, these substances have been repeatedly associated with a particular type of liver disease in humans, and additional health problems such as pulmonary and kidney pathologies and even cancer in research animals. Comfrey is available only by prescription in the United Kingdom, Canada, Australia, and Germany.

Ephedra, or *Ma huang*, sold as a weight control product and energy booster, contains amphetamine-like chemical stimulants, including the alkaloids ephedrine and pseudoephedrine. High blood pressure, rapid heart rate, neuropathy, psychosis, muscle injury, stroke, and memory loss after use of these products has been reported to the

FDA. Some fifteen deaths and hundreds of adverse reactions to ephedra have been reported, mostly from very large doses.

Lobelia, or Indian tobacco, contains alkaloids that have a pharmacological action weaker than but similar to nicotine. As an ingredient in dietary supplements, lobelia can cause stimulation of the autonomic nervous system or depression. Low doses can cause dilation of the bronchia and quickened breathing. Higher doses can cause depression of breathing, and also sweating, racing heart, hypertension, and even coma and death.

Germander is marketed as an aid to weight loss, in tea, elixir, capsule, or tablet form, either alone or with other ingredients. In France, commercial products containing germander have resulted in at least 27 cases of acute nonviral hepatitis, including one death.

Germanium, promoted as an immune system modulator or stimulant, is a nonessential element sometimes marketed as inorganic germanium salts in compounds such as elixirs. Some twenty cases of acute renal failure have been reported, including two deaths. None of the patients recovered completely normal kidney function.

A Chinese herbal preparation containing stephania and magnolia, sold as an aid to weight loss, was implicated as the cause of severe kidney injury in 48 women in Belgium, 18 of whom experienced terminal kidney failure.

Yohimbe, a product made from the bark of the African yohimbe tree, is marketed as an antidote to male impotence and as a supplement for bodybuilders. Yohimbe has risks and benefits.

Yohimbe dilates blood vessels and stimulates the central nervous system; it has a history of use as an aphrodisiac. One study published in the *New England Journal of Medicine* suggested it could be effective for the treatment of psychogenic erectile dysfunction in men with diabetes. A meta-analysis of several studies published in the *Journal of Urology* in 1998 concluded that the benefits of yohimbine medication for erectile dysfunction outweighed the risks, with serious adverse reactions uncommon and reversible.

However, a few incidences of renal failure, seizures, and death have been reported from the use of yohimbe. The FDA says yohimbe

Continued

should be avoided by people with diabetes, low blood pressure, and heart, liver, or kidney disease. Yohimbe dilates blood vessels at least partially through the alkaloid yohimbine, a prescription drug in the United States. It is a monoamine oxidase (MAO) inhibitor, and can cause serious side effects when eaten with foods containing tyramine, such as liver, cheese, red wine, or with over-the-counter medicines containing phenylpropanolamine such as nasal decongestants and diet aids. Yohimbe is toxic in large doses and should only be taken under the supervision of a physician. Symptoms of an overdose include weakness and fatigue, nervous stimulation followed by paralysis, stomach disorders, and possibly death.

medications, including aspirin; people who take such medications should consult with their medical doctors before taking gingko. The product sheet for Egb 761 says the 120 mg. dose should not be used in children under twelve.

Ginseng

One of the most widely used herbs in the world, ginseng comes from the root of the genus *Panax*, which grows wild in Asia and also in North America, producing Asian and American ginseng, which are believed to be different in their effects. Ginseng is used in traditional Chinese medicine as a tonic that has prophylactic, restorative, and even aphrodisiac properties. Ginseng is an *adaptogen*, said to help the body adapt to all forms of stress and change, and to promote longevity. It is also said to prevent toxicity of the liver. Ginseng's blood sugar lowering effects are also beneficial.

Siberian ginseng, or *Eleutherococcus senticosus*, is a similar but not identical plant that is sometimes substituted for ginseng.

A Canadian study published in the year 2000 in *Annals of Internal Medicine* found that American ginseng lowered blood sugar levels by approximately 20 percent in subjects with Type 2 diabetes, when compared with placebo. About ten subjects were given 3 grams of

American ginseng forty minutes before and during an oral glucose challenge test, and their blood sugar levels compared with those of a control group who did not receive ginseng. According to Dr. Andrew Weil, this study was "one of the first to test an herbal product scientifically."

An earlier study published in *Diabetes Care* found that ginseng lowered fasting blood sugar and glycosylated hemoglobin HbA1c levels in people with Type 2 diabetes relative to placebo. A study in 1995 showed people with diabetes experienced mood improvements, strength improvements, and reduced fasting blood sugar while taking ginseng. Previous small trials in Eastern Europe and Asia also reported blood sugar lowering effects. Therapeutic dosage is 100 to 200 mg. per day.

Precautions: Ginseng is believed to be quite safe, but a few adverse reactions have been reported. Most common side effects are nervousness, irritability, and excitation, which usually diminish after a few days of use or with reduction in dose. Like many of the herbs listed here, ginseng can enhance blood sugar lowering effects of diabetes medications, resulting in low blood sugar. It can also *raise* blood pressure when taken with certain antidepressant drugs such as monoamine oxidase inhibitors. Problems with concentration have been reported after long-term use, according to *The Lawrence Review of Natural Products*. Best suited to older people, ginseng should be avoided by pregnant women and children. Some researchers say that ginseng has an estrogen-like effect in women.

Siberian ginseng is contraindicated in patients with high blood pressure. The German Commission E monograph recommends limiting the use of Siberian ginseng to three months.

Glucomannan

Glucomannan, konjac-mannan or *Amorphophallus konjac*, is a fiber that delays the absorption of glucose from the intestine. Research shows it can lower blood sugar and cholesterol, and reduce the need for hypoglycemic medications. Known as *konnyaku* in Japan, where it is a commonly used food, this fiber is also an ingredient in "grapefruit diet" tablets, and a mild laxative.

A patent on file at the U.S. patent office claims that glucomannan can produce weight loss without appetite changes, presumably because

Medication and Herbs

Some herbs can lower blood sugar, and significant reductions may require adjustments in any medications you take for diabetes, including either diabetes pills or insulin—this should definitely be done in consultation with your medical doctor.

Precautions with Insulin: The following herbs and supplements are among those that might improve blood sugar control, and therefore may require you to reduce the amount of insulin you take: bitter melon, burdock, chromium, coccinia indica, dandelion, fenugreek, garlic, ginseng, gymnema, onion, pterocarpus, saltbush, and vanadium.

Precautions with Diabetes Pills: The following herbs and supplements might require a reduction in medication for people taking pills to control Type 2 diabetes: bitter melon, bilberry leaf, burdock, L-carnitine, chromium, Coenzyme Q10, dandelion, fenugreek, garlic, ginseng, gymnema, alpha lipoic acid, onion, ptreocarpus, saltbush, and vanadium.

the fiber blows up in the digestive system and produces a "full" feeling. However, not all research substantiates glucomannan's benefits as an aid to weight loss. It is a hydrophilic gum, which is generally considered to be of marginal effectiveness for weight loss.

According to a study published in *Diabetes Care*, June 1999, glucomannan lowered blood sugar, blood pressure, and lipid levels in patients with Type 2 diabetes who were judged to be at risk of coronary heart disease. In a crossover trial conducted at St. Michael's Hospital in Ontario, Canada, research subjects who continued diabetes medications while eating glucomannan-enriched biscuits for three weeks saw significant blood sugar reductions. Subjects also had reduced cholesterol and systolic blood pressure levels. The authors suggested that glucomannan fiber added to conventional medical treatments might improve their effectiveness.

In a 1979 trial, thirteen people with diabetes who received 3.6 or 7.2 grams of glucomannan per day for 90 days saw fasting blood sugar levels fall an average of 29 percent. Most participants were able to reduce their insulin or medication requirements, according to results published in *The Lancet*. A 1990 study involving 72 people with Type 2 diabetes showed significant reductions in both fasting and after meal blood sugar after consuming glucomannan in food for a month or two.

In addition, a study published in the *American Journal of Clinical Nutrition* in 1995 showed a 10 percent decrease in cholesterol levels in 63 men given 3.9 grams of glucomannan daily for a month. In another study, the administration of 100 mg. of 1 percent glucomannan solution to ten overweight patients for almost three months resulted in a mean decrease of 18 percent in serum cholesterol.

Glucomannan, or konjac flour, is often available at health food stores. It is classified as "Generally Recognized as Safe."

Precautions: Glucomannan fiber absorbs water very quickly. Four people who took diet tablets composed of glucomannan suffered severe obstructions of their esophagus when the tablets swelled before they could completely swallow them. In Australia, tablets containing glucomannan are banned because of seven such cases reported in 1984–85, although encapsulated tablets and powdered glucomannan are still available.

Gosha-jinki-gan

Gosha-jinki-gan, or GJG, is a *kampo*, or Japanese folk medicine. Basically a mixture of ten different herbs, Gosha-jinki-gan is used in Japan to treat the subjective symptoms of neuropathy.

A study published in *Diabetes Research and Clinical Practice* found that administering 7.5 grams of gosha-jinki-gan per day for three months improved symptoms of perceived numbness, cold, and sensitivity to vibrations in nine of thirteen people with peripheral neuropathy. When treatments were discontinued for two months, subjective symptoms worsened in seven of the thirteen.

A medical journal in Japan reported the case of a 65-year-old woman with a cataract in her eye that was resistant to treatment. When gosha-jinki-gan was added to her treatment regimen, which included eye drops, her eyesight stabilized ten days after the herbal treatment began and did not deteriorate further, according to a case study published in 1991.

A study using rats with diabetes at Hoshi University in Tokyo concluded that gosha-jinki-gan increased blood flow in peripheral tissues.

Guar

Guar is a traditional Ayurvedic remedy for diabetes; similar to fennel, it is also sometimes used to treat obesity. Also known as cluster bean, galactomannan, Jaguar gum, or *Cyamopsis tetragonolobus*, guar is a legume that grows in Pakistan, India, and in the southwestern United States. It has been studied as a supplement and food additive to determine what role it might play in managing insulin resistance, as have other soluble fibers such as oat bran and psyllium. Results for guar gum are promising but inconclusive. Guar does reduce serum cholesterol when used over long periods of time. Some studies have shown improved blood sugar and HbA1c levels with the ingestion of guar, but other studies have found no difference.

Guar gum is very high in soluble fiber, and flour is also produced from guar.

One small study published in 1985 added a fairly low dose of 4 grams of guar gum twice a day to the diets of people with Type 2 diabetes. Subjects experienced a decrease in insulin resistance and fasting insulin levels at the end of the treatment period, as well as a decrease in HbA1c levels from an average of 8.5 to 7.9.

A study at the Royal Postgraduate Medical School in London of people with Type 2 diabetes used 5 grams of guar sprinkled over food at main meals for a month, and found significantly lower glycosylated hemoglobin and fasting blood sugar levels after treatment. Another double-blind study of healthy middle-age men who were given 10 grams of guar gum three times a day for six weeks found lower blood sugar and increased insulin sensitivity.

At Sahlgrenska Hospital in Sweden, a study of 25 healthy middle-age men given 10 grams of guar three times a day for six weeks found increases in insulin sensitivity and decreases in blood sugar, cholesterol, triglycerides, and systolic and diastolic blood pressure. Another study found that supplementation with guar for two weeks yielded a 9 percent reduction in blood pressure in men who were moderately overweight.

Not all studies involving people with Type 2 diabetes have found a benefit with guar. A study published in *Diabetes Care* in 1987 looked at people with Type 2 diabetes with nearly normal levels of fasting plasma glucose, and concluded there were no benefits in ingesting 5 grams of guar with main meals for two months. Another study of people more than 50 percent overweight who were given from 8 to 16 grams of guar gum per day found no improvement in insulin resistance or blood sugar.

Studies using large amounts of guar, that is, 20 grams per day or so, have identified patients with side effects so troublesome they dropped out of the studies. These side effects included excessive farting, increased defecation, and feelings of being overly full. Smaller amounts taken more frequently seem to be better tolerated.

Precautions: Guar gum and guar flour are classified as "Generally Recognized as Safe." Guar has been used for more than a century as a thickening agent in foods and pharmaceuticals. However, ingestion may affect the absorption of medicines that are taken at the same time. Like other fibers, guar should always be taken with large amounts of liquid. As a weight loss product, guar gum has resulted in esophageal obstructions in patients taking large doses—since it swells up 10 to 20 times in size when absorbing water.

Gymnema

Gymnema sylvestre is a climbing tropical plant native to India and Africa. The Hindi name of the plant, *gurmar*, means "sugar destroyer." Gymnema has been used in Ayurvedic medicine as a treatment for Type 2 diabetes for several thousand years. Gymnema apparently lowers blood sugar in people who have high blood sugar but has no affect on normal people. It increases the secretion of insulin in both Type 1 and Type 2 diabetics and may increase the number of beta cells in the pancreas. It is also a diuretic, an astringent, and a tonic. Dabbed onto the tongue, gymnema inhibits the ability to taste sweet or bitter flavors.

The blood sugar lowering effects of gymnema were first documented more than eighty years ago. The root and leaves of gymnema are rich in gymnemic acids, which contain a mix of acidic plant sugars known as glycosides.

In one study in India, lasting eighteen to twenty months, gymnema extract was given to 22 people with Type 2 diabetes along with oral diabetes medications. In this study, 21 out of 22 were able to reduce their dosage of diabetes medications, and five subjects stopped taking medication altogether and maintained control using only gymnema extract at the rate of 400 mg. per day. Increased levels of insulin production suggested to researchers that beta cells could have been regenerated or repaired by gymnema.

In a 1990 study, water soluble extracts of gymnema increased serum insulin and returned blood sugars to normal in diabetic rats. Gymnema extracts *doubled* the number of Islet of Langerhans cells and beta cells in test animals, indicating either repair or regeneration of the pancreas.

In an interesting 1983 study, subjects were offered sweets one hour after a drop of gymnema extract was dabbed on the tongue. Researchers concluded that extracts of gymnema leaves reduced the taste for sweets.

Gymnema lowers blood sugar gradually. The leaves are generally used to lower blood sugar, often at the rate of 2 to 4 grams of leaf powder per day. Most studies in India have used a water soluble acidic fraction of leaves, at a rate of 400 mg. per day.

Gymnema is listed as an ingredient in many herbal products sold to people with diabetes.

Precautions: The safety of gymnema has not been established, but it's probably safe. Its purchase may require a prescription in the United Kingdom.

Hawthorn

Hawthorn, or *Crataegus laevigata*, is a medicinal shrub native to Europe. Hawthorn berries, leaves, and flowers are European folk remedies to strengthen the heart and invigorate blood circulation. Long touted as an extender of longevity in China, hawthorn is believed to dilate blood vessels and reduce blood pressure, while also moderating the heart rate. Hawthorn is prescribed in Europe for many circulatory disorders. It may mildly reduce blood pressure. It is said to be the plant medicine of choice in Europe to regulate heart functions.

Hawthorn is believed to work by dilating the larger blood vessels, increasing the functional capacity of the heart. It also has a diuretic action. Hawthorn contains many bioflavinoid complexes that are strong antioxidants. These include quercetin, believed to block the accumulation of sorbitol.

As a treatment, hawthorn berries may be consumed at the rate of 4 to 5 grams per day. A hawthorn tea can also be prepared by steeping dried flowers and berries in hot water for ten to fifteen minutes.

Hawthorn extracts made from leaves and flowers are used in Europe to reduce blood pressure. Standardized extracts are preferred, containing 2.2 percent total bioflavonoid content, or 18.75 percent oligomeric procyanidins. Doses of extract range from 80 to 300 mg. per day, taken two or three times per day. Hawthorn takes at least two weeks to begin working and can take as long as two months to have maximum effect.

Precautions: Germany's Commission E has found no adverse side effects. While several studies in Germany have documented Hawthorn's positive effects in the treatment of heart disease, healthy people in the United States are beginning to use it as a tonic, to prevent heart problems. Dr. Pelletier advises caution in self-medicating for heart problems, which should be dealt with by a medical doctor. Hawthorn is not an across-the-board substitute for cardiac medication.

Milk Thistle

Used as a folk remedy since the time of ancient Greece for liver problems, milk thistle, or *Silybum marianum*, is a protectant of the liver and an antioxidant. It is indicated for liver problems due to cirrhosis, alcohol abuse, or damage due to toxins such as pesticides, environmental pollution, or heavy metals. Widely used as a liver tonic in Europe, milk thistle alters the outer membrane of the liver to block the entrance of toxins, and stimulates the growth of new liver cells.

Studies published in the *Journal of the American Medical Association* estimate that perhaps 75 percent of American adults have low-level or subclinical liver damage. More than 200 studies have shown that milk thistle can prevent and reverse liver damage. Strengthening the liver strengthens the internal environment of the body, because the liver protects the body against many toxins.

In Italy, a study of Italian subjects with diabetes who also had alcoholic cirrhosis found treatment with 600 mg. of silymarin per day significantly lowered blood sugar levels and HbA1c levels, reduced the excretion of sugar in the urine, and reduced insulin requirements after four months of treatment. Insulin is typically required in this group because of insulin resistance, but insulin requirements were lowered in the group treated with milk thistle. The group that did not receive milk thistle showed higher fasting insulin levels and stable insulin requirements. Researchers concluded that the treatment may reduce oxidation damage to cell membranes and insulin resistance.

Commercial extracts of milk thistle are standardized to 70 to 80 percent silymarin, a bioflavonoid complex found in milk thistle, which actually consists of three active ingredients. Germany's Commission E recommends doses of 200 to 400 mg. silymarin per day as a supportive treatment for toxic liver damage and chronic inflammatory liver disease.

Precautions: Milk thistle is quite safe, even in large doses, but extracts may have a mild laxative effect on some people that usually goes away after two to three days.

Neem Oil

In India and other parts of Asia, the large evergreen neem tree's spreading canopy is used medicinally in many ways. Neem, or *Azadirachta indica*, is a folk remedy and almost a panacea for many health problems, including diabetes, heart problems, skin problems, malaria, and worms. It is a natural pesticide and contraceptive.

Neem seeds yield a yellow, bitter oil that smells a little like garlic. Administered to normal and diabetic rats, neem oil reduced glucose up to 48 percent after administration.

Neem is an ingredient in some commercial supplements for diabetes.

Precautions: Neem oil is safe for adults, but the seeds of neem are poisonous in large doses. Neem oil has resulted in an illness similar to Reyes syndrome, toxicity, and even death in infants and children.

Psyllium

The seeds and husks of psyllium add fiber to the diet. Native to Iran and India, and also known as *Plantago ovata* or *Plantago ispaghula*, psyllium seeds contain more mucilage than do the husks, and are less irritating to the bowels, but either can be helpful to people with diabetes. Mixed in with food, fibers are said to reduce the emptying of the stomach, and thereby decrease the rate of sugar absorption and lower blood sugar, while also lowering levels of fat in the blood.

In a 1991 study, psyllium reduced blood sugar levels only when sprinkled on cereal, but not when taken without food. Several studies have shown that psyllium can lower total cholesterol without adversely affecting HDL cholesterol.

Research studies have used 5 to 15 grams per day, mixed with food. A couple of teaspoons per day of psyllium seeds is sometimes recommended. One spoonful of husks is sufficient for laxative purposes.

Precautions: The Commission E Monographs state that people with diabetes who have difficulty regulating their disease should not use psyllium. Psyllium should be taken under the supervision of a health care professional, and medications adjusted as necessary. Any high-fiber product should be taken with additional water. Very high doses can result in bowel irritation or diarrhea. Products that contain other laxatives mixed with psyllium should not be used. Since products such as regular Metamucil contain sugar, Sugar Free Metamucil is a better laxative if you have diabetes.

Pterocarpus

A tree that grows in India, *Pterocarpus marsupium*, has a bark used in Indian folk medicine as a treatment for diabetes. One flavonoid that can be extracted from the bark of this plant, epicatechin, which is also found in green tea, prevents damage to beta cells in rats. A study published in *The Lancet* found that epicatechin regenerates beta cell function in rats with induced diabetes.

Saltbush

Saltbush, sea orach, or *Atriplex halimus* is a shrub that apparently has some blood sugar lowering effect. It grows around the Mediterranean Sea, especially in the Jordan Valley. Saltbush is a primary food of the sand rat, which fattens up and develops the equivalent of Type 2 diabetes when saltbush is withdrawn from the diet and replaced with standard rat chow. Saltbush contains fiber, protein, and trace minerals such as chromium.

One study in Israel on human subjects with Type 2 diabetes showed an improvement in blood sugar levels and glucose tolerance when they consumed 3 grams of saltbush per day.

St. John's Wort

St. John's wort, or *Hypericum perforatum*, is a popular herbal remedy for mild to moderate depression. It is said to be prescribed by German doctors more frequently than Prozac. Several studies have found that it works in a significant number of cases, although like most herbs, it takes a few weeks to take effect.

The standard recommendation for mild to moderate depression is 300 mg. of standardized extract per day. As an alternative, the Commission E monograph also recommends 2 to 4 grams of whole herb per day.

Precautions: St. John's wort may cause sensitivity to sunlight in humans, similar to effects caused in animals who eat the plant, when it is taken with tetracycline antibiotics or Retin-A used for skin problems. St. John's wort may react with other antidepressant drugs such as selective serotonin reuptake inhibitors, causing a condition known as "serotonin syndrome."

Valerian

Compounds in the root of valerian, or *Valeriana officinalis*, are believed to act against stress and to relax you. A large perennial that grows in Asia, Europe, and North America, valerian has been used in Asian medicine for more than a thousand years as a treatment for nervousness and insomnia. It was widely used in North America before World War II when faster-acting pharmacological drugs appeared. Valerian may be useful for people with high stress levels, insomnia, and anxiety. Approved by Germany's Commission E as a treatment for restlessness and sleep disorders that are based on nervous conditions, valerian is a mild sedative and an aid to sleep. Unlike most drugs used for insomnia, valerian does not interact unfavorably with alcohol. It does not extend sleeping time, but makes it easier to go to sleep, and apparently makes sleep more restful.

In a study involving more than 11,000 people in Germany, 94 percent of subjects who took valerian saw their sleep improved. Of these, 72 percent who had trouble falling asleep reported a resolution of the problem, and another 22 percent reported improvement. Results occurred in about two days on average, in the ten-day trial. Other studies have found that valerian increases deep sleep and relieves mild anxiety.

Valerian root extracts are standardized at 0.5 percent essential oils. For insomnia, 300 to 500 mg. of extract 30 to 60 minutes before bedtime is usually recommended. Smaller doses between 50 to 100 mg. may benefit people with performance anxiety or those under stress. However, it often takes two to three weeks before the full effects are felt. In Germany, valerian is often combined with other herbs, such as hops, lemon balm, passionflower, or skullcap, which have produced good results.

Valerian is classified as "Generally Recognized As Safe" in the United States. The Commission E indicates no side effects or contraindications. Research indicates valerian does not impair the ability to drive or operate machinery.

Precautions: Valerian can increase sedation when taken with monoamine oxidase inhibitors. Although Valerian is safe, it should be used only when needed for anxiety and stress.

Be Careful with Herbs

Herbs are considered safer than pharmaceutical drugs, since there are many fewer complaints of adverse reactions reported to the FDA—approximately 1,000 reports for herbal products, versus 160,000 reports regarding over-the-counter and pharmaceutical drugs from 1993–1998, according to FDA statistics. Patients with Type 2 diabetes should use caution because serious potential risks exist with herbal medicines, as the following sections describe.

Taking the Wrong Herb

If you are trying to treat yourself, don't take an herb just because you heard people gossiping about it on a talk show. A herb that is not right for your condition may actually harm you. Remember that with many herbs and folk remedies, research with human subjects who have diabetes is skimpy or nonexistent. Nutritionally oriented doctors or reputable herbalists can provide guidance.

Taking the Wrong Dose

Supplement labels typically recommend a small dose, since manufacturers are conservative and fear lawsuits. These are often below what a practitioner might recommend. However, taking more than recommended by a practitioner or a nutritionally oriented doctor is also unwise, as herbs can have adverse side effects. More is not always better.

Bad or Adulterated Herbs

Unfortunately, many herbal supplements are adulterated or contaminated. The herb industry is not regulated like the pharmaceutical industry, and shoddy mixing and mislabeling occurs with some frequency. Some ginseng capsules, for instance, have been found to contain no ginseng and large quantities of caffeine. According to the publication *Herbal Gram*, a 1998 check of traditional Chinese medicines in Taiwan, where they are widely used, found that about a fourth of samples taken were adulterated, most commonly with synthetic substances such as nonsteroidal anti-inflammatory drugs or steroids. Some Ayurvedic herbal mixtures have been analyzed and found to contain high levels of lead, which is obviously toxic, and Indian formulations have a reputation of being contaminated with feces, insects, and other contaminants. Herbs manufactured in the United States are believed to be much safer and less likely to be contaminated with heavy metals such as arsenic, lead, or mercury.

Inaccurate Labeling

Herbal products are not subject to the same government scrutiny as pharmacological drugs. Herbal formulations may contain varying amounts of active ingredients, making their effects less predictable than standard drugs. For instance, when the *Los Angeles Times* tested ten over-the-counter bottles of the antidepressant herbal remedy St. John's wort, it found that 70 percent contained between 75 to 135 percent of what was stated on the label, and 30 percent contained half or less of the labeled ingredients. Similar spot checks have been run on other herbs and supplements with similar distressing results. The FDA periodically tests ten to twelve herbal products off the shelf, according to Dr. Pelletier, and usually only about one-third contain what is listed on their labels. Typically, one-third contains more of the herb than stated, and about one-third contains none at all. The word *standardized* on the label of commercial herb products should mean you are receiving a particular amount of the herb in each tablet or capsule or tincture.

Interactions of Herbs with Prescription Medications

Herbs may react adversely with medications you are taking. Garlic, ginkgo, ginger, and feverfew may increase the action of some prescription drugs, such as *warfarin sodium*. Valerian may cause too much sedation if taken in combination with barbiturates. Hawthorn and ginseng may interfere with the action or monitoring of *digoxin*. Immunostimulants such as zinc and Enchinacea can interact with immunosuppressants such as corticosteroids. Even kelp, as a source of iron, may interfere with thyroid replacement therapies. Check with your doctor before you begin taking herbs.

Lost Potency

Storing herbs someplace like the bathroom, where you put medications, can expose them to moisture and cause them to lose their potency. Herbs should usually be stored in a dark, cool, dry place.

While medicinal herbs indirectly strengthen the body, exercise, the topic of the next chapter, directly lowers blood sugar.

Chapter 7

Exercise

Regular, moderate exercise is part of good diabetes care in all systems of medicine. Conventional doctors who treat diabetes regularly are expected to write and recommend "exercise prescriptions," which help stabilize blood sugar, blood pressure, and weight. Exercise is also highly recommended in alternative treatment systems such as naturopathy, traditional Chinese medicine, and Ayurvedic medicine.

Pick something you like, and exercise can be a lot of fun. It can lower blood sugar, increase muscle tone, strengthen the heart, lower blood pressure, and combat anxiety and depression. Many benefits of exercise are also incorporated into some of the movement-oriented mind/body therapies, including yoga, tai chi, chi gong, progressive muscle relaxation, and music therapy when combined with dance therapy.

"Exercise is very important," observes Dr. Allen Neiswander, an Alhambra, California, homeopathic physician. "If you sit around all day, you'll kill yourself."

It goes without saying that any exercise program should be undertaken in consultation with a medical doctor. Your medical doctor should completely check out the status of your heart, blood pressure, eyes, and feet. You should monitor your blood sugar levels as advised by your doctor, before and after exercising. If blood glucose levels are too high, perhaps above 200 mg./dl., your doctor may advise you not to exercise that

Aerobic Exercise

Aerobic exercise strengthens the heart and lungs, and burns calories. About three half-hour sessions a week are recommended for cardiovascular benefits. The chart below estimates the calories a 150-pound woman might burn in thirty minutes of aerobic exercise. If you weigh more, you will burn more calories than listed.

Workout	Calories Burned	Other Health Benefits
Light aerobics	210	Strengthens legs, improves flexibility, improves bone density
Ballroom dancing	105	Improves balance, strengthens legs
Bicycling (moderate)	132	Strengthens legs
Cross-country skiing	231	Strengthens torso, arms, and legs; improves coordination and balance
Golf w/out cart	174	Improves upper body flexibility, torso and leg strength
Ice skating	192	Improves coordination and balance, strengthens legs
Jumping rope	330	Improves coordination and strength of legs
Racquetball	363	Improves speed, flexibility, strength, and bone density

Workout	Calories Burned	Other Health Benefits
Running (11–12-minute mile)	276	Improves leg strength, bone density
Stair climbing	206	Strengthens legs, bone density
Swimming (slowly)	261	Improves flexibility and strength
Walking (briskly)	260	Improves leg strength

day. The first few minutes of exercise sometimes raises blood sugar levels, but a decent period of exercise will lower them. Exercise is essential, so your doctor will be able to help you find a suitable program.

It's no secret that the human body was made to *move*. Until we created the artificial paradise of civilization, man walked, squatted, lunged, ran, plucked, bent over, grabbed, groped, grubbed, and leaped high to secure his meals. The invention of agriculture enabled us to become a less transient species, but even life on the farm was extraordinarily hard physical work until farm machinery was invented. Even the cleaning and cooking of food once involved a lot of lifting, mixing, and moving around.

The modern concept of exercise is a relatively new idea, an imperfect replacement for the efforts our ancestors exerted hunting and gathering real food in the wild kingdom. Although our bodies haven't actually evolved much since we became civilized, we are programmed to eat about the same amount of calories our ancestors consumed in their vigorous pursuit of natural, nutritious meals. We now must be creative and diligent to burn off all the calories we still consume, calories no longer needed to power our daily activities. Instead of being necessary for life, exercise is often now viewed as recreation, or as hard work.

Unfortunately, between 25 to 31 percent of adult men and women in the United States are *completely* sedentary. Among people seeking to lose weight, two out of three are exercising a little, but less than half this number follow the federal guidelines of exercising thirty minutes per day, five days a week, according to the U.S. Centers for Disease Control.

Regular, sensible, appropriate exercise reduces the effects of almost every chronic illness, including high blood pressure and diabetes. For this reason, the U.S. Surgeon General recommended in 1996 that Americans engage in a minimum of thirty minutes of moderately intense physical activity most, if not all, days of the week. Exercise greatly lowers the possibility of diabetes, especially among those at highest risk for contracting it, according to research published in the *New England Journal of Medicine* in 1991.

A study of alumni of the University of Pennsylvania found that physical activity was *inversely* related to the incidence of Type 2 diabetes. Exercise's protective effects were actually *highest* among those at highest risk of contracting the disease, that is, people with a high body-mass index, a history of high blood pressure, or diabetes in the family.

A study of Finnish men at high risk for Type 2 diabetes found that those who engaged in moderately intense physical activity for at least forty minutes per week had 64 percent less chance of being diagnosed with diabetes than men who didn't exercise. Finnish men with good cardiorespiratory fitness also had less diabetes.

Regular exercise is one of the best predictors of success at dieting or weight maintenance. People who exercise lose weight faster than people who do not exercise. Exercise also improves long-term weight control. Interestingly enough, improved physical fitness also lowers the risk of heart disease and *increases* life expectancy even if the person exercising remains overweight.

It is increasingly recognized that exercise helps maintain good mental health and combats depression. Several hundred research studies have been conducted in this area. Many studies have shown that exercise can help treat clinical as well as mild to moderate depression. Exercising can help relieve related feelings such as anxiety. It improves your perception of yourself, and your self-esteem. Both aerobic and resistance training exercise enhance mood states, according to research.

Among the well-documented benefits of exercise are:

- Helps you lose or control weight

- Lowers insulin resistance

- Reduces stress

- Reduces muscle tension

- Improves mental function

- Improves muscle mass

- Combats depression

- Improves mental outlook

- Improves sleep

Several studies have also concluded that regular, moderate exercise extends life expectancy and improves quality of life.

Insulin Sensitivity

Exercise lowers blood sugar by improving the body's sensitivity to insulin, or lowering insulin resistance. Moving the body moves the muscles, which utilize 95 percent of the glucose consumed below the neck. As a rule of thumb, it is estimated that exercising for about half an hour lowers blood sugar approximately 20 to 25 percent. Exercise also causes the smallest blood vessels, called capillaries, to open and allow more blood to circulate, thereby lowering blood pressure.

Exercise that is rhythmic and continuous or *aerobic* is frequently recommended by doctors, since this has the most obvious cardiovascular benefits. Walking, running, swimming, and aerobics exercise classes are examples of aerobic exercise. Other forms of exercise such as resistance training can also be beneficial. Resistance training involves pushing against a weight, as with many exercise machines. An analysis published in *Sports Medicine* in November 2000 noted that improvements in insulin sensitivity can be achieved with either aerobic exercise or resistance training.

From a scientific point of view, exercise equivalent to a one hour walk triggers the release of fat-burning enzymes, called *hormone sensitive lipase*, for about twelve hours. Walking twice a day, or once every twelve hours, will keep the natural fat burners on all day and slowly help clear away fat deposits from the body.

The best time to exercise is after eating, because this is when blood sugar levels are highest. Research at the Quebec Heart Institute at Laval Hospital in Sainte Foy, Canada, found that exercise had no effect on blood sugar levels on men with Type 2 diabetes when performed in a fasting state. However, exercise produced a *significant* decrease in blood sugar when done after meals.

Walking is the most commonly reported leisure-time activity in the United States. It is an excellent exercise that is relatively common even among groups that are normally not active, such as older people. It is pleasant and inexpensive. Los Angeles exercise physiologist Dr. Claudia Graham recommends a fifteen- to twenty-minute walk about an hour after meals for blood sugar control. In areas where the weather is bad during the winter, sports clubs or mall-walking clubs may be an alternative. For more information on exercise and diabetes, see *The Type 2 Diabetes Sourcebook*.

Of course, as exercise is undertaken, adequate water should be consumed to replace fluids lost during exercise, and to prevent dehydration. Most authorities recommend six to eight 8-ounce glasses of water per day. Good, well-fitting, comfortable shoes should also be worn, and reasonable checks and precautions taken as suggested by your doctor.

If you seek to lose or even to maintain your weight, of course, exercise should go hand in hand with a good diet. Many people enjoy the benefits of bodywork or massage, the topic of the next chapter.

Chapter 8

Bodywork

"The physician must be experienced in many things, but most assuredly in rubbing," said the Greek physician Hippocrates. Massage was a recommended treatment for diabetes in Victorian times, and it still has a number of wonderful if temporary effects on people with diabetes. Once performed by doctors, medical massage (now called physical therapy) was abandoned in the middle of the 20th century because it was considered too time-consuming for doctors to perform. Being massaged by a bodyworker or massage therapist, or even a friend or loved one, can relieve a great deal of physical, emotional, and mental stress.

Massage temporarily increases the flow of energy through the body. It enhances blood and lymph circulation, increasing the blood's capacity to carry oxygen and nutrients to all the cells. Massage increases the removal of waste products and toxins from the body, reducing inflammation and speeding up healing. It often lowers blood pressure. It reduces muscular tension and anxiety that may contribute to pain. A study published in 1989 concluded that connective tissue massage stimulates the production of pain-relieving endorphins. Massage allows for greater range of movement, and also boosts athletic performance.

Bodywork is a newer name for massage, implying an integration of body and mind that benefits health. The skin is the body's largest organ, with a vast network of direct connections to the brain. In addition to its physically rejuvenating effects, bodywork can be an effective complement to psychotherapy. A few practitioners even incorporate aspects of talk therapy into therapeutic massage.

It's common sense *not* to massage parts of the body that are infected or inflamed, or the sites of recent injuries. However, if you inject insulin, massaging the injection site for fifteen minutes after the injection will increase the supply of free insulin and lower blood sugar more than 8 percent a half hour after the massage, according to research published in 1983.

There are many types of bodywork, including Swedish massage, shiatsu, reflexology, the Rosen method, Rolfing, Hellerwork, the Feldenkrais method, osteopathic manipulation, and chiropractic manipulation.

Swedish Massage

Swedish massage, developed by the Swedish physician Per Henrik Ling, is relaxing and reduces stress. This massage treats the whole body, rubbing in circular and sweeping motions with the hands. These include long, full body strokes called *effleurage*, usually at the start and finish of a treatment. Various muscles and sets of muscles are kneaded, shaken, rubbed, and sometimes tapped with fists, the edge of the hand, or fingertips, as the therapist works. Oils may be used to facilitate the movement of the therapist's hand, including aromatic oils that are most fragrant and may yield better therapeutic results.

While Swedish massage is entirely focused on the body, Esalen massage is a slower, gentler, dreamier variation focused on both mind and body, and it is often incorporated into Swedish massage.

Shiatsu

Shiatsu massage, a form of Japanese therapeutic massage similar to acupressure, works on special points called *tsubos* on the skin. Pressure applied for a few seconds on these points by a Shiatsu practitioner relieves stress and unblocks energy channels. Shiatsu is more curative than Swedish massage, since it seeks to discover a cause of illness or discomfort and then rebalance the body's center of gravity by gentle stretching. Pressure is applied to tsubos by the therapist's fingertips, hands, elbows, or even toes; each point is held for a few seconds. For best results, the breathing of the therapist should be in sync with the breathing of the client.

Reflexology

Reflexology sessions begin and end with a foot massage, but it works by applying pressure to points on the feet that are believed to correspond to different areas of the body. A sensitivity or tender area on the foot is said to indicate a problem associated with that part of the body, while pressure on the tender spot is believed to release energy that is blocked. Since the feet are hard places to reach, and treatment takes a half hour or more of identifying and then applying pressure to particular reflex points, this therapy is best done by a professional reflexologist, although it can be self-administered by flexible people once contact points and techniques are properly learned. After thirty days of treatment, Chinese research published in 1993 concluded that foot reflexotherapy plus medication lowered blood glucose more in people with Type 2 diabetes than the use of medication alone. In this study, peroxidation of blood fats and platelet aggregation were also greatly improved in the reflexotherapy group.

Rosen Method

Physical therapist Marion Rosen developed a method that might be called mind/body massage. The Rosen method concentrates on releasing the emotional blockages *read* by a therapist in tense muscles. Psychiatrist Wilhelm Reich long ago theorized that patterns of muscle tension he called *armoring* directly corresponded with particular emotional problems. First developed in the 1930s, Rosen's method uses a combination of light touch and verbal questions by the therapist to the patient. The therapist attends to the breath, as expressed or not expressed in the muscles. This process is intended to reveal and draw attention to parts of the body where tension is being held, and the association with emotional issues. Raising the awareness of the patient allows tension to be released. Diabetes educator Diana Guthrie observes that Rosen therapy could be of assistance to people just diagnosed with diabetes, since strong feelings often surface and need to be worked through at this time. The same might hold true of any other particularly stressful time.

Feldenkrais Method

The Feldenkrais method was developed by a Russian-born Israeli physicist, Moshe Feldenkrais, to heal himself. This method is a form of guided movement that corrects posture and also strengthens self-awareness. Not massage in the traditional sense, it focuses attention on the point where thought and action join. Rhythmic sequences of very sophisticated movements, sometimes guided by a therapist, are followed by imagining of similar, smoother, or stronger movements of the same type. It aims to create new patterns of movement, feeling, and thinking.

Trager Approach

The Trager approach, developed by a physician, Milton Trager, is another postural correction system that aims at developing a sense of lightness and freedom in the client. Trager sessions first involve passive movement, and then instruction in movement sequences to re-create and enhance movements performed by the therapist.

Rolfing

Rolfing, the creation of biophysicist Ida Rolf, is a form of deep tissue massage that Rolf performed on celebrities such as Buckminster Fuller and Georgia O'Keeffe. Rolf also did work at the Esalen Institute in the 1960s. Several research studies have been done on Rolfing. They show decreases in anxiety levels in people who were treated over five weeks, increases in muscular efficiency, and improved heart rate functions that correspond with a reduction in stress. Rolfing aims to reorder the body

Hydrotherapy

Hydrotherapy is not therapy with water, but rather, an old naturopathic healing technique. Towels dipped in hot or cold water and then wrung out are placed on the body, providing therapeutic doses of heat and cold on the skin. Hydrotherapy is said to reduce the toxic load on the body and to stimulate the immune system.

According to William Collinge, author of *American Holistic Health Association Complete Guide to Alternative Medicine*, the fluctuations in temperature created by hydrotherapy have an antitoxic effect, stimulating blood circulation, digestion, and the elimination of waste products from the body. Blood circulation to the kidneys, liver, stomach, and intestine is said to improve after hydrotherapy.

to bring head, shoulders, pelvis, and legs into more ideal vertical alignment by loosening the *fascia*, or tissue, that folds muscles together. Fascia is believed to harden from injury or chronic stress, restricting full range of movement. Treatment usually takes place over ten sessions that focus on different parts of the body.

Hellerwork was designed by Joseph Heller, a former Rolf therapist who created a variation on Rolfing. It incorporates a movement reeducation process and exercises involving everyday movements such as walking and sitting into its eleven sessions.

Osteopathic Manipulation

Osteopathic manipulation is more a system of restoring blood and lymph circulation than a massage technique, although it does involve some gentle manipulation by the hands of an osteopathic physician. A study of a hundred patients with high blood pressure, published in 1961 in the *Journal of the American Osteopathic Association*, found that osteopathic manipulation lowered this group's blood pressure from an average of 199/123 to 166/114.

Chiropractic Treatment

Chiropractic treatment is usually not useful for diabetes, but a few chiropractors are experimenting with it as an adjunct treatment. In one case, an eighty-year-old man with diabetes, low back pain, and burning pains in the lower extremities from polyneuropathy, as well as poor balance, was treated with manipulation and myofascial therapy eighteen times in four months. According to a report in the *Journal of Manipulative Therapy*, a dramatic improvement in symptoms and clinical signs of nerve function was the result.

Many forms of massage or bodywork can relieve physical and mental stress. Massage increases blood circulation and helps relax and strengthen the body in people with diabetes. Chelation therapy and DMSO, two controversial treatments covered in the next chapter, may also be of benefit for some symptoms of diabetes.

Chapter 9

Chelation Therapy and DMSO

Chelation therapy is an intravenous treatment, a controversial alternative to heart surgery said to rejuvenate blood vessels and blood circulation, prevent hardening of the arteries, and lower blood pressure. Chelation therapy may be of use in healing gross gangrene. DMSO is a topically applied chemical that may speed healing of ulcers and other problems involving the feet. Many of the same doctors utilize them both in medical treatment.

Chelation Therapy

Chelation therapy consists of a lengthy series of intravenous infusions of a synthetic amino acid known as ethylene diamine tetra-acetic acid, or EDTA. Infusions of EDTA are an accepted conventional medical treatment for lead poisoning. EDTA is also a fairly common food additive. As a medical treatment for cardiovascular problems, chelation therapy lost ground after an early surge of popularity during the 1950s and 1960s in the United States, perhaps because the patent held by its manufacturer expired.

For improved cardiovascular health, EDTA infusions are said to remove minerals such as lead, mercury, copper, iron, aluminum, and calcium from deposits of plaque along the walls of veins and arteries and from the bloodstream. These minerals are believed to block blood flow in the circulatory system, muscles, and other areas. EDTA is said to "bind" or chelate with these minerals, allowing them to be excreted. Chelation therapy is said to make arteries and veins more flexible, to lower blood pressure, and to improve circulation.

Twenty to thirty chelation infusions are said to be a minimum for most conditions, but some require many more. Treatments are often given twice a week, with each infusion lasting several hours. Costs of chelation therapy are rarely covered by health insurance.

According to Morton Walker, DPM, the author of several books on chelation therapy, physicians who give chelation therapy treat people with diabetes with supplements including chromium in the form of glucose tolerance factor, a low fat, high fiber diet, and an exercise program before chelation therapy actually begins. Doctors who give chelation therapy are members of the American College of Advancement in Medicine, or ACAM, located in Laguna Hills, California. Dr. Walker's book, *The Chelation Answer*, examined ACAM files to report that 197 patients out of 200 who took chelation therapy for gross gangrene were able to save their legs, apparently because the therapy increased blood circulation to the infected areas.

Chelation therapy is controversial. A review of research on chelation therapy, published in the *American Heart Journal*, found an "almost total lack of convincing evidence for efficacy."

However, two FDA-approved studies conducted in Sao Paulo, Brazil, using sodium-magnesium EDTA infusions concluded that chelation therapy was beneficial. One of these, a small, randomized, double-blind pilot study, studied male patients with peripheral vascular disease. After ten of twenty planned infusions, some patients had such obvious benefit that the "blind" code was broken early and showed that the EDTA group had improved. All participants then received EDTA, according to results published in 1990.

The second Brazilian study, conducted at the Hyperbaric Oxygen Clinic in Sao Paulo, was a retrospective analysis of 2,870 patients with various diseases who had been treated with sodium-magnesium EDTA chelation therapy. Researchers found "marked improvement" in 76 percent of patients with ischemic heart disease, 91 percent of patients with peripheral vascular disease, 24 percent in patients with cerebrovascular and other degenerative cerebral diseases, and three out of four patients with scleroderma. The authors of this study, published in 1988, recommended renewed study of EDTA chelation therapy to rule out what they called a "tomato effect"—a condition in which a drug actually works but physicians believe it doesn't work.

Chelation therapy treatments are long but usually uneventful. Standard and extensive laboratory tests given before chelation infusion begin involve hair, urine, blood, and sometimes saliva and feces tests, plus a diet analysis. Vitamin and mineral deficiencies are expected and must be addressed before and during treatment, usually with large doses of supplemental vitamins and minerals. The main side effect that has been reported is pain at the infusion site. Other rare side effects include temporary tingling or numb sensations around the mouth, fever, nausea, diarrhea, headache, low blood sugar, and insulin shock.

Garlic, onions, and high fiber foods, particularly those containing Vitamin C, Vitamin E, Vitamins B_3 and B_6, magnesium, manganese, and bromelain also have a natural chelating effect.

Precautions: Contraindications for chelation therapy are people with serious kidney problems, pregnant women, or patients with gross vitamin or mineral deficiencies. Chelation therapy binds and removes some of the B vitamins, particularly B_6 or pyridoxine, as well as zinc and chromium, so appropriate supplements must be taken. Periodic checks of vitamin and mineral status are prudent and necessary during treatment. Medical doctors or doctors of osteopathy licensed for the intravenous administration of drugs are the only health practitioners who may legally perform chelation therapy.

DMSO

Under the supervision of a medical doctor, the topical application of dimethyl sulfoxide, or DMSO, may speed healing of diabetic ulcers that are stubborn to heal. It is also used to reduce pain and increase mobility by people with arthritis, and to help heal sports injuries.

DMSO is a chemical solvent that easily penetrates human tissue. A chemical by-product of the paper-making process that looks a bit like mineral oil, DMSO produces a powerful, fishlike smell in the person using it. The reason is because DMSO contains a great deal of sulfur, a component of amino acids.

The potential usefulness of DMSO for people with Type 2 diabetes comes mainly from its ability to accelerate healing in skin ulcers on the legs, feet, and other parts of the body. Ulcers are very slow to heal in people with diabetes. This is particularly true in people with peripheral neuropathy who have poor blood circulation and a lack of nerve sensation in extremities such as the feet. Neuropathy also makes it easy to acquire small wounds or sores on the feet, since sensation is less than normal.

In a study reported in the *Journal of the American Geriatrics Society* in January 1985, 14 of 20 patients with chronic and perforated foot ulcers treated daily with DMSO achieved complete healing in four to fifteen weeks. Another four patients achieved a partial resolution of the ulcers, although with two patients the treatment had no effect. Complete healing was achieved in only two patients in the control group, which was equal in size to the group that used DMSO. "Local DMSO is effective, simple, devoid of systemic side effects, and inexpensive," the authors wrote. "It should be employed for diabetic foot ulcers prior to the consideration of surgical measures."

Ten years earlier, Dr. Rene Miranda Tirado, an assistant professor of nutrition and dietetics at the University of Chile, used a medicinal DMSO spray or direct application of DMSO on more than 1,300 patients with ulcers, skin lesions, and second-degree burns. At a DMSO symposium held under the auspices of the New York Academy of Sciences in 1974, Dr. Tirado reported that approximately 95 percent of patients were reported completely healed after twenty days of treatment. In some patients this healing was considered miraculous, since some ulcers were cured that had been in existence for as long as fifteen years. According to the Chilean study, pain associated with the lesions disappeared after the first few applications.

However, an overview of clinical trials for peripheral neuropathic pain published in the magazine *Pain* in November 1997 cited only limited research support for the effectiveness of DMSO as a pain relieving treatment.

Morton Walker, a podiatrist and the author of *DMSO: Nature's Healer*, cites anecdotal evidence that DMSO may be useful in the treatment of other foot problems experienced by people with diabetes. These include bunions, hammertoes, hard and soft corns, calluses, plantar warts, ingrown toenails, club nails, fungus toenails, and athlete's foot.

DMSO is a controversial substance, not used by most medical doctors. It suffers from the fact that it is an industrial by-product that is widely available, and therefore cannot be patented or easily controlled by the Food and Drug Administration. It is also difficult to design good double-blind experiments with DMSO, since its pungent, fishy odor cannot be disguised.

Methysulfonylmethane (MSM) another potentially useful supplement, is chemically similar to DMSO. MSM may have some similar effects, but it produces no odor. MSM "can be helpful for diabetic neuropathy of the extremities and gastrointestinal tract," according to *The Miracle of MSM*, a 1999 book by Dr. Stanley W. Jacob, Dr. Ronald M. Lawrence, and Martin Zucker. Dr. Jacob is the director of the DMSO Clinic at Oregon Health Sciences University in Portland, Oregon.

Members of the American College of Advancement in Medicine often know DMSO since they give it as a part of chelation therapy.

Precautions: Only *medical grade* DMSO should be used—industrial grade DMSO contains acids and acetones that can cause liver damage. Both the hands and the application site must be scrupulously clean before DMSO is applied, since anything that touches the surface of the skin will also be absorbed. Side effects of DMSO include a reddening of the skin, which usually disappears after repeated applications. About one-third of those who use DMSO report a burning sensation at the area of contact. Other skin problems, such as itching, mild blistering, and roughness have been reported.

In 1965, changes in the lens of the eyes in several species of research mammals were reported in experiments that involved the application of DMSO. Rabbits, dogs, and pigs became slightly nearsighted as a result of DMSO treatment. Eye changes of this type have not been found in studies involving humans, or in primates such as monkeys. A three-month study of DMSO on 65 volunteers at an institution in Vacaville, California, used DMSO at between three to thirty times the usual treatment dose in humans and produced no lens changes, according to Dr. Walker.

EDTA chelation therapy infusions may be useful in improving blood circulation, reducing the effects of hardening of the arteries, and in speeding the healing of diabetic foot ulcers. A good diet, exercise, and appropriate vitamin and mineral supplements are necessary when receiving chelation therapy. DMSO, also controversial, may speed the healing of foot ulcers and minor problems involving the foot when applied topically.

While treatments that target the physical body may greatly improve health status, a group of therapies known as mind/body therapies, which are covered in the next section, may have equally impressive health benefits.

Part II

MIND/BODY THERAPIES

"The greatest revolution of our generation is the discovery that human beings, by changing the inner attitudes of their minds, can change the outer aspects of their lives." —William James

IF YOU HAVE DIABETES, the regular practice of mind/body techniques may help lower blood sugar and pressure, increase blood circulation to extremities, combat depression, and even assist in efforts to lose or maintain weight.

Mind/body therapies are intimately involved with the concept of stress and stress relief. Stress is relieved by a number of well-researched mind/body therapies, including meditation, hypnosis, biofeedback, imagery, and yoga or other movement therapies. Social support and even humor therapy also relieve stress. Music therapy and aromatherapy are two very sensual modalities which connect the mind with the body, lower stress, and improve mood. Most mind/body therapies also combat depression and help decrease physical pain.

Over time, the practice of mind/body therapies may help you lower the amount of medications you take, or to discontinue medication entirely in partnership with your doctor. Choosing to embark on the regular practice of a mind/body therapy may give you a welcome feeling of personal power and control.

Chapter 10

Stress

In 1879, a Prussian military officer returned from the Franco-Prussian war to find that his beloved wife had been unfaithful to him during his absence. The officer developed diabetes within a few days, according to Henry Maudsley, a doctor who was one of the founders of modern psychiatry. This is one of several incidents of diabetes being diagnosed after a time of great emotional stress that have been documented in medical literature.

Certainly, stress can trigger the onset of Type 2 diabetes. It can also be a crucial factor in how quickly diabetes progresses. Chronic, negative stress grinds away at the body, the mind, the emotions, and the spirit. In our hyperactive, achievement-oriented society, every person alive has times of feeling stressed-out. Stress is ubiquitous in our society. It may be physical, mental, or even emotional. While certain people seem to thrive on certain types of stress, chronic negative stress is quite harmful to your health. Some doctors believe that stress is the root cause of all disease.

Stress is one of the more expansive concepts in Western medicine, which is generally reductionistic in its search for symptoms and root causes of disease. Stress may be compared with the grand Eastern concepts of *prana* or *chi*. More than 2,000 years ago the Greek physician Hippocrates defined "health" as mind and body in harmony. Hippocrates defined "disease" as mind and body out of harmony. Dr. Hans

Selye, the father of stress medicine, summed up this line of thought when he stated: "Life is stress and stress is life."

Certainly we live in stressful times. Many studies have shown that modern life is becoming more and more stressful. Driven by unstoppable technological advances, like cellular phones, computers, fax machines, and E-mail, the pace of life itself seems to be accelerating. A well-known survey of life's most stressful events, first taken more than thirty years ago, was repeated in 1997. The authors concluded that American life had become 45 percent more stressful in the past three decades.

Extreme negative stress, or *distress*, can make diabetes worse, most obviously by sending blood sugars and blood pressure soaring. Carrying a burden of constant, excessive stress can affect health behaviors, making it more difficult to take care of yourself day after day. Since stress may often be managed, it makes sense to understand its effects and then to take action to control it however you can.

Fight or Flight

Acute stress triggers the "fight or flight response," named almost a hundred years ago by esteemed Harvard University physiologist Walter Cannon. This response prepares body and mind for a primal emergency, such as the presence of a beast in the jungle.

Stress causes the immediate release of several hormones, including adrenaline and cortisol. These break down stored carbohydrate in the liver, converting it into glucose for energy. Other stress hormones break down fat and protein stores and convert them to glucose. Blood sugar increases. The heartbeat quickens. Blood pressure soars. The digestive system shuts down, and blood rushes to the muscles. The eyes dilate, the field of vision narrows, hearing intensifies, the sex organs shrink. The immune response is dampened. In the twinkling of an eye the entire body sings with nervous energy. The mind sharpens, preparing to make a fast choice between combat or flight.

Years ago the fight or flight reflex kept human beings alive in a hostile dog-eat-dog world. The response to stress had to be intensely focused, purposeful movement. With only a few exceptions, we have eliminated physical danger and direct physical action responses from our daily lives. But the fight or flight reflex remains. As stress builds upon stress, our blood sugar remains elevated, our blood pressure soars, our muscles remain tense and prepared for combat.

The stresses we experience these days are not the acute "fight or flight" type that call for an immediate physical response. Emotional and chronic stress to which we cannot respond physically has a continuing affect on our bodies and minds, and it is more debilitating. A number of bad things happen when chronic stress cannot be released. Emotional stress, for instance, mobilizes energy by raising blood sugar and releasing free fatty acids into the blood. This results in higher cholesterol, triglycerides, and ketone levels that can't be easily regulated by a person with diabetes. The responsibility of dealing with the ups and downs of any chronic illness, and all the measuring, worrying, and record-keeping the management of diabetes can entail, creates an additional overlay of physical and emotional stress. Having no release from this physical and mental state of tension is unnatural, and ultimately harmful.

Research

One experiment dramatically demonstrated the effects of stress on a strain of obese laboratory mice with the genetic potential to become diabetic. One group of mice was restrained for an hour in a small restraining device, another group was not restrained. At the end of the study, the restrained mice had blood sugar levels *twice* high as the group of similar mice that were not restrained. Furthermore, mice without the genetic potential to develop diabetes did not show this elevated blood sugar effect even when put under the same stress. Evidence of the adverse effects of stress on glucose metabolism are more consistent in animal models of Type 2 diabetes than in Type 1 diabetes, according to an 1993 analysis published in *Psychosomatic Medicine*, although the reason for this is not clear.

The Pima Indian tribe has one of the highest known incidences of Type 2 diabetes in the world. In one study, 75 percent of Pima Indians experienced high blood sugar levels two hours after eating when they were given a stressful computer-driven math test. Research subjects without the Indian tribe's predilection for diabetes had normal blood sugar after taking the test and eating. This experiment suggests that stress might trigger high blood sugar in individuals who are predisposed.

In Germany, a study of 410 people with either Type 1 or Type 2 diabetes, published in the year 2000, concluded that 17 percent suffered from "extreme psychosocial stress." The effects of this stress showed up as depression, fears, and various physical complaints. German researchers observed that psychosocial stress was often associated with poor blood sugar control.

Research at the University of Helsinki in Finland, published in 1996, examined 90 middle-age subjects for stress-related variables such as Type A behavior, hostility, anger, and feelings of excessive fatigue. The study concluded that high levels of these variables correlated with high levels of insulin, high blood sugar, high fat levels, high blood pressure, and increased abdominal obesity. In Denmark, a study of middle-age men found that psychosocial stress was associated with premature aging and increased insulin resistance.

According to Dr. Paul Rosch, a psychiatrist who is president of the American Institute of Stress in Yonkers, New York, stress has both direct and indirect effects on blood sugar levels of people with diabetes. Emotional stress in particular is associated with increased secretions of adrenaline and hydrocortisone, hormones that directly raise blood sugar.

Lately, it's also been recognized that stress affects many people's ability to hold to a diet. Stress can trigger eating binges that are themselves a reaction to stress. Eating binges knock you off a diet designed to help control blood sugar, thus indirectly raising blood sugar. Blood sugars can bounce up and down as a result of stress and eating problems, creating more emotional upheaval in the form of anxiety, nervousness, tiredness, and fatigue.

Mind and Body

Mind/body therapies directly counter the effects of stress. Such therapies begin with the knowledge that mind and body are intertwined in sickness and also in healing. They may take the participant into a special zone, a place where mind and body work in gentle, healing tandem. This may be seen as a very comforting place, an enchanted place, a place

Nutritional Support

Stress puts great pressure on the adrenal glands, which secrete several stress hormones. The adrenals can become "exhausted" by chronic stress. A good diet and exercise are crucial in keeping these glands functioning well, since both strengthen the body and help relieve stress. Vitamin and mineral supplements can also be helpful, if levels are depleted.

Nutritional support for the adrenals involves adequate levels of Vitamin C, pantothenic acid, Vitamin B6, zinc, and magnesium.

Ginseng and Siberian ginseng are among the "adaptogenic" herbs known to support adrenal gland function, directly countering the effects of stress.

of change, a place where physical stabilization, rejuvenation, and deep relaxation can occur. For many people in the West, visiting this enchanted spiritual island is difficult but possible. Visiting this place regularly, by practicing mind/body therapies, helps us rest, rejuvenate, and heal.

Mind/body therapies may help you control particular symptoms of diabetes such as high blood pressure and high blood sugar, and provide some benefit for emotional symptoms such as depression and anxiety, which often accompany chronic illness.

According to Dr. Kenneth Pelletier, director of the Complementary and Alternative Medicine Program at Stanford University, mind/body therapies have the highest level of research support of all forms of alternative therapy. Dr. Pelletier, who participated in some of the first research on these therapies, has noted that people must *change* if they practice mind/body therapies, an aspect that may have slowed their rapid acceptance into mainstream medical treatment. In his book, *The Best Alternative Therapies*, Dr. Pelletier states that among the 600-odd recognized alternative therapies, mind/body therapies are applicable to the greatest number of health conditions, including diabetes. This area holds such promise for people with diabetes that the American Diabetes Association has formed a Council on Behavioral Medicine and Psy-

Overeating and Stress

Dr. Pamela Peeke, a stress researcher at the National Institutes of Health and the author of *Fight Fat Over 40*, believes that stress is a prime factor in weight gain, particularly in the middle and later years.

Stress causes the body to release adrenaline and cortisol. Adrenaline dissipates quickly, but cortisol triggers the release of glucose and fat from stores in the body, particularly from the abdominal region, which is easiest to access by the body. The presence of cortisol actually *stimulates* the appetite for food, particularly carbohydrates, which convert into what Dr. Peeke calls "stress fat."

Continuing high levels of cortisol impair liver function and create ongoing high blood sugar, high cholesterol, and high blood pressure, and make blood more predisposed to clot. People under chronic stress cannot think clearly, which also may affect their food choices, Dr. Peeke notes.

Obesity doesn't necessarily *cause* insulin resistance, but it can precede it or aggravate it, Dr. Rosch says. In particular, he says, stress probably contributes to the "apple-shaped" figure with lots of central body fat that is statistically associated with insulin resistance, heart problems, certain cancers, and Type 2 diabetes.

Sex hormones could also play a role in the tendency to gain weight later in life, according to Dr. Rosch. Although male and female sex hormones protect against abdominal fat deposits, Dr. Rosch notes that levels of these hormones decline after menopause and later in life.

Dr. Peeke believes that reducing your stress level is fundamental to an effective weight-loss strategy, particularly after the age of forty when less calories are needed due to a normal slowdown of metabolism.

chology to coordinate activities of people working on mind/body techniques.

The brain is not separate from the body. The nervous system is a physical extension of the brain, which reaches into every corner of the body and every type of body tissue. Through the nervous system, the brain is connected to everything under the skin, including the bones, all the endocrine glands and lymph nodes, the internal organs, the heart, the lungs, and the skin, and other sense organs. The brain is tied to the immune system; some nerves end right in the bone marrow which produces white blood cells. The brain is also a gland that manufactures a cornucopia of useful chemicals and releases them into the bloodstream. Obviously, the brain has a primary role in physical and mental health. Even the placebo effect, in which healing occurs as a result of medical treatments known to have no effect, is probably all mental. Mind/body therapies such as meditation work very effectively, benefiting people with diabetes by harnessing the great untapped power of the human mind.

Chapter 11

Meditation

Meditation is an important mind/body therapy, and one of the most thoroughly researched. The practice of meditation directly counters harmful stress and improves many symptoms of diabetes. The relaxation response, a form of meditation, as well as transcendental meditation and mindfulness meditation, are examined in this chapter.

Meditation is an Eastern practice, widely practiced in India and some other countries. What we call meditation occurs almost entirely in the mind, but it affects the body in many ways. Meditation has been called the other side of prayer because it involves passive acceptance of the universe as it is, and letting that universe flow through the mind, rather than attempting any sort of active dialogue with a higher power. This applies to transcendental meditation, which is linked to Eastern spiritual practices, as well as other forms of meditation that are becoming more popular in the West.

Relaxation Response

Dr. Herbert Benson, an associate professor of medicine at Harvard Medical School and founder of the Mind/Body Institute at Deaconess Hospital, was one of the first to extensively measure the physical effects of meditation. Dr. Benson developed a generic form of meditation he calls the *relaxation response*. The relaxation response involves finding a quiet place, relaxing, breathing deeply, and focusing passively on one meaningful word or phrase for a few minutes. Rather than focusing on a particular mystic word or sound called a *mantra*, as in transcendental meditation, Dr. Benson originally suggested that the relaxation response be called forth by focusing on something neutral such as the word *one*. Later, Dr. Benson determined that the relaxation response became more effective and beneficial if the person who was meditating used a word or phrase of spiritual significance to them.

The physical body changes in good ways as we meditate or practice other mind/body therapies. Brain waves slow down and rhythms become more constant. Changes occur in the two parts of the autonomic or "self-ruling" nervous system. The *sympathetic* nervous system, located mostly below the neck, is activated by the stress response. The *parasympathetic* nervous system, located mostly above the neck, takes over during the relaxation response. The parasympathetic system restores, repairs, and maintains the body, functions that occur when the body is relaxed.

Here are a series of measurable physical responses, the opposite of the body's response to stress, which collectively constitute what may be called the relaxation response:

Stress Response	Relaxation Response
Raises blood sugar	Normalizes blood sugar
Raises blood pressure	Lowers blood pressure
Raises rate of breathing	Lowers rate of breathing
Increases the heart rate	Lowers heart rate
Increases oxygen consumption	Lowers oxygen consumption
More blood flow to skeletal muscles	Less blood flow to skeletal muscles
Less blood flow to digestive system	More blood flow to digestive system
Increases perspiration	Decreases perspiration

You may avoid quick rises in blood sugar and blood pressure triggered by stress by regularly practicing mind/body exercises that elicit the relaxation response. In *The Relaxation Response*, Dr. Benson reported that two 20-minute deep relaxation sessions per day could decrease insulin requirements and lower the production of stress hormones such as catechloamine for up to 24 hours.

In his book, *Timeless Healing*, written with Marg Stark, Dr. Benson states that from 60 to 90 percent of visits to doctors' offices are a result of stress. He lists some of the other research done with the relaxation response, which shows its beneficial effects:

- Followed for three years, people with high blood pressure who practiced the relaxation response needed lower doses of medicine or no medication at all to control their blood pressure.

- People with mild to moderate depressions, or anxiety, were less hostile, angry, depressed, and anxious after practicing the relaxation response

- Among subjects with sleep-onset insomnia, 75 percent were cured and the remaining 25 percent had improved sleep, mostly with fewer medications

- Working people had fewer sick days, improved performance on the job, and lower blood pressure after practicing the relaxation response for a period of time

To the extent that any medical condition is caused or made worse by stress, Dr. Benson states, the relaxation response can cure or improve it. Although meditation may be learned at home, it is probably best learned from a teacher of the technique.

Transcendental Meditation

Transcendental meditation, a practice originating in India, was introduced into the United States in the 1970s by Maharishi Mahesh Yogi. Practicing transcendental meditation allows the meditator to move into a state of passive but blissful coexistence with a higher power. More than 500 research studies have been done on transcendental meditation. Studies show it has a positive effect on blood pressure, heart rate, blood sugar, and numerous other physical functions. Its many documented health benefits include lowering levels of stress hormones in the body. Qualified teachers of transcendental meditation may be found at transcendental meditation centers in many communities. Learning from expert teachers is the best way to master this technique, although they typically will charge a significant fee.

It's interesting to note that the practice of transcendental meditation was dropped by most Ayurvedic practitioners in India many years ago. However, meditation has been reincorporated into a system Ayurvedic medicine by Marahishi's followers, called Maharishi Ayur-Veda, taught at the Maharishi College of Vedic Medicine in Albuquerque, New Mexico. Proponents of this combined system say they've restored meditation, a lost tradition, to its place of historic importance in health care.

Ayurvedic medicine sees all people as having one of three body and personality types, called *doshas*. People are treated according to their dosha. For many practitioners of Ayurvedic medicine, an imbalance of the *vata* dosha, which governs the nervous system, is seen to be widespread in the West. Life in our stress-riddled society results in, among other things, dietary behavior that leads us to eat too much refined sugar, fat, and salt. A traditional antidote to vata imbalance is meditation, which strengthens the immune system and relieves stress.

Research studies involving transcendental meditation have found that people over the age of forty who meditate have less medical problems than average for their age group when compared with people who don't meditate. Meditators have lower levels of stress hormones such as cortisol in their blood. Studies of transcendental meditation show that regular meditators have an improved immune response, lower blood pressure, and decreased muscle tension. Other published studies show that it helps stabilize the autonomic nervous system, helps ward off depression, assists in the normalization of weight, results in better sleep patterns, and even results in measurably less gum disease. A couple of very small studies, one a pilot study conducted in Singapore and the other an unpublished doctoral thesis completed in Italy, concluded that transcendental meditation helps normalize blood sugars as measured by an oral glucose tolerance test.

Type 2 diabetes and high blood pressure were two of the ten chronic diseases treated by Maharishi Ayur-Veda during research in the Netherlands. A three-month pilot study involving a total of 126 people concluded that for the ten chronic diseases studied, participants benefited from the use of Maharishi Ayur-Veda. Subjects were drawn from a list of people who had shown an interest in transcendental meditation in the past. All subjects received nutritional programs tailored to them, herbal preparations specific to their disease, and simple lifestyle guidelines. On a voluntary basis, subjects were permitted to utilize yoga, massage, cleansing, or purification therapies, as well as transcendental meditation. Of the four subjects with Type 2 diabetes in the Netherlands study, three reported improvement and one was unchanged. Improvement was verified by recent glucose tolerance tests or all-day curves of blood sugar tests supplied by the patient, which were compared with previous data. Two subjects who brought day curves of blood glucose showed normal and high-normal values after treatment. One of the four was able to cut his dose of oral medication in half. The third patient who improved had a greatly improved glucose tolerance test—moving from four "clearly pathological" values to one slightly raised value.

Of the nine subjects with high blood pressure in the Dutch study, three were able to reduce or discontinue their blood pressure medication. After three months, five of nine people were rated as improved. Criteria for improvement was the lowering of diastolic blood pressure of at least 10 mmHG when medications were reduced by half or more, or diastolic reductions of 15 mmHG with medication continuing at the same level.

Mindfulness Meditation

Mindfulness meditation, a third form of meditation, has also shown benefits in reducing stress. Rather than focusing on a word or sound, mindfulness meditation trains people to focus completely on the activity at hand—be it eating, walking, yoga, or whatever. This meditative technique, actually an old Buddhist practice called *vipassana*, or insight meditation, is taught at the Stress Reduction Clinic at the University of Massachusetts Medical Center, where it has been extensively studied.

The Art of Breathing

Meditation involves special breathing techniques that produce slow, rhythmic breathing and decrease the body's use of oxygen. Dr. Herbert Benson calls this decrease in the body's use of oxygen a hallmark of the relaxation response. He observes that the use of oxygen decreases 10 to 17 percent within the first three minutes of eliciting the relaxation response, a faster decline even than when sleeping.

Most people actually breathe quite shallowly and much too quickly when under stress. Breathing slowly and properly helps relieve stress and focus the mind.

The average person takes between 16 to 20 breaths per minute, or one breath every three or four seconds. Slowing this to approximately four breaths per minute, or one full breath every fifteen seconds or so, is extraordinarily relaxing. Deep abdominal breaths are particularly useful in alleviating stress.

In the book *Full Catastrophe Living*, Dr. Jon Kabat-Zinn has stated that mindfulness meditation allows people to develop an inner balance of mind to face and respond to life situations with clarity, stability, understanding, and wisdom. Patients with chronic pain, diabetes, high blood pressure, and other conditions may benefit from it, he has stated.

In general, the benefits of learning and practicing mindfulness meditation involve a greater body and mind awareness, which allows people to cope with physical or mental problems that are stress related. Decreased physical and emotional symptoms, more energy, greater self-esteem, an increased enthusiasm for life, and a heightened ability to cope with pain and stressful situations are said to be the major benefits of mindfulness meditation.

Several forms of meditation deliver obvious and important health benefits for people with diabetes. The relaxation response, transcendental meditation, and mindfulness meditation all counter the harmful effects of stress, and their practice may help lower blood sugar or blood pressure. The next chapter focuses on one of the more controversial of the mind/body therapies, hypnotherapy. Hypnotherapy provides a unique type of mind/body support for people with diabetes.

Chapter 12

Hypnosis

Hypnotherapy probably began with the mesmerizing gaze of the shaman. Hypnosis as we know it was invented and popularized in the 18th century by the charismatic European physician Franz Mesmer, who is considered the father of medical hypnosis. William James, Sigmund Freud, and Milton Erikson studied hypnosis, which was recognized as a valid treatment in 1958 by the American Medical Association. Mind/body therapies such as hypnosis, autogenic training, or even reciting affirmations may deeply relax you and help you manage diabetes.

Basics of Hypnosis

Like other mind/body therapies, hypnosis provides greater stability of heart rate and blood pressure and other functions controlled by the autonomic nervous system. Brain waves slow when you are under hypnosis. Hypnosis may help stabilize blood sugar, the most crucial marker of diabetic control. Hypnotherapy can be useful in relaxing the mind and body, and in confronting emotional issues such as fear and anger, which can stand in the way of good self-management, attempts to lose weight, and optimum mental health. Insights generated during hypnosis can help reduce depression, fear, and anxiety, and lead to a positive acceptance of the disease. Hypnosis can help people overcome highly personal obstacles to keeping themselves healthy. Hypnosis can help you deal with bad habits such as smoking. Self-hypnosis can provide an enhanced sense of personal control.

Hypnosis is usually an easy process. Almost all people can be hypnotized, although some catch on more quickly than others. Experts estimate that between 20 to 30 percent of people are easily hypnotized and completely responsive to hypnotic suggestion. People who like to take personal responsibility for their health, people who believe they have a good imagination, and people who have a clear goal or outcome in mind are most likely to have success with hypnotherapy, according to Dr. Karen Olness, a pediatrician, hypnotist, and professor at Case Western Reserve University School of Medicine. Hypnosis can be enhanced with the aid of biofeedback, another mind/body technique, which provides constant progress reports on changes within the body.

Images or sensory thoughts called *imagery*, or *visualization*, are among the techniques used in hypnosis and other mind/body therapies. Visualization is a daunting concept to some people, but it is quite simple to do. Dr. Kenneth Pelletier suggests closing your eyes for a minute, and opening them when you can say how many windows are in your living room. To count windows with your eyes closed, he observes, you must visualize.

Contrary to popular myth, hypnosis does not involve being under the complete control of the hypnotherapist. While in a hypnotic trance, you may be aware of what is going on around you if you choose to focus on it. *Self-hypnosis* may be learned with the aid of a hypnotherapist, and practiced at home as needed. Self-hypnosis can be useful in the management of chronic illnesses such as diabetes, or even cancer, and it may be used as needed. Of course, it's also necessary to put in sufficient time to acquire and utilize the skill. Note that hypnosis is an individual experience—what works for one may not work for another.

Learning self-hypnosis from a coach or teacher allows you to master it more quickly, to correct errors that may occur, and to receive useful encouragement and advice. Dr. Olness recommends matching your health problem to the background and training of the hypnotist. In other words, try to find a hypnotherapist who knows something about diabetes. A good hypnotist will get to know you as an individual, and match a hypnotic method to your needs.

Susan's Story

Susan Shaw is a Tarzana, California, certified clinical hypnotist who knows from personal experience that hypnotism can be beneficial for people with diabetes. She has dealt with Type 1 diabetes for thirty years. Some years ago, a doctor told Susan that her blood sugars had become brittle—and could not be medically controlled. She turned to hypnotism, more or less as a last resort.

Her response to hypnotism was extraordinarily good—her HbA1c test results fell to 6 percent, which is almost perfect. Her personal success encouraged her to study hypnotism. As a certified clinical hypnotherapist, Shaw's clients now include many people with both Type 1 and Type 2 diabetes. Many of her clients have reduced their blood sugar levels, reduced the level of medications they take, reduced their weight, or overcome personal obstacles to doing beneficial things such as exercising as a result of hypnotherapy, she says.

"People will often only see a hypnotist as a last resort, when they are desperate to modify their behavior," Shaw says. "When medical practitioners give the patient orders, they also tell patients to just accept their disease. Acceptance is a big thing, almost as crucial as diet or medications. Many people with diabetes have problems in simply accepting their diabetes. This is one place where hypnosis can help people."

Hypnosis is similar to other mind/body therapies in that brain waves slow to a more relaxed state, Susan says. The right brain, which is intuitive and creative, can be accessed with imagery.

"The dialogue between the mind and body is composed of images," she believes. "It's like the subconscious. People can enter into this dialogue between the mind and body with imagery. Sometimes you don't even need to change what's going on in other areas. If you can just open it up with imagery, people can see where they are. Then they can deal with it in a loving, relatively fearless state."

Hypnosis relaxes you, she says, and simply relaxing can improve your blood sugars. Blood sugar levels are linked to levels of stress hormones. Like other mind/body therapies, hypnosis reduces stress.

Shaw believes the fear that accompanies a diagnosis of diabetes is just as strong as the fear that accompanies a diagnosis of cancer, except that the fear is buried. Fear of complications is often an issue. Paradoxically, she adds, not dealing with the fear of complications can stop people from practicing good self-care.

"Doctors warn people with diabetes that their life expectancy may be less, but this is so far out in the future, it doesn't really motivate people," she says. "Some people are depressed because they feel they have a death sentence hanging over their heads, but for many others there is no sense of urgency. In addition to this buried fear, people often have a lot of rage, which can also stop them from practicing good self-management. A lot of people diagnosed with diabetes have no avenue to express their feelings because it's not socially acceptable."

Diabetes is a chronic, long haul disease. But Susan observes that many of her clients feel that medical professionals expect them to make all the lifestyle changes immediately, not a bit at a time.

"It's useful to show people they're about more than their diabetes, that life isn't just about doing all these things perfectly," she says. "Some people actually use eating and the tools of diabetes management against themselves, almost as instruments of torture. And then again, some doctors start looking for reasons to blame the patient if their recommendations aren't achieving the desired result."

People with diabetes sometimes experience tremendous fear, she notes, including questions about how long they will live. Some are afraid they might pass out from low blood sugar. Some experience anger and guilt, and wonder what they did to deserve their illness. Fear, Shaw notes, is not an incentive to change, it's rather an obstacle. Sometimes people need to just overcome the panic they feel, she says, and learn to take it slow, and to achieve peace with themselves.

As a clinical hypnotherapist, Shaw makes liberal use of imagery. She gently guides the patient to access images they themselves generate while under hypnosis. The imagery generated by the patient is more powerful than any that may be supplied by the therapist, she believes. As proof of the power of images, she points to a 1978 study by Jean Achterberg in which people with diabetes drew and described their pancreas and the action of insulin. Those who had the most positive images were predicted to have greater stress reduction and better blood sugar control. Hypnosis is helpful in itself, but it is the imagery process that confronts the underlying issues and generates the self-knowledge that truly changes people.

To demonstrate how imagery can work, Shaw might put a particular patient into a trance. The patient would sit in a black chair, close their eyes, and listen to her soothing, suggestive voice until they are "under." The patient, Shaw knows, has a great problem testing their blood sugars as recommended. As the session continues, she might gently suggest that the patient visualize three doors, and to visualize what's behind each door, one door at a time. Behind the first door, she might suggest to the patient, is the self who doesn't test their blood sugars. Behind the second is the self who wants to test. Behind the third, the sacred or spiritual self.

When some people look behind the first door, she says, they find a self who's fat, angry, and depressed. Behind the second door might be a self with unrealistic expectations, a slim, perfect self who tests every two hours. And behind the third door is often an "inner guide," she says, a person who always knows what to do for this patient. This inner guide often tells the patient to take it one step at a time, she observes, to treat yourself in a loving manner, and to give yourself some kind and loving attention.

For instance, one of her clients was a teenage girl who wasn't testing. The girl was skipping insulin shots. Obviously depressed, the girl also needed to get her blood sugars under control. Under hypnosis, she put the girl in touch with part of her that didn't test her blood sugar. This was a moment of discovery. This encounter made the girl aware of how depressed she actually was. Not only that, but hypnosis put the girl in touch with her higher self, who told her about the importance of loving herself, of appreciating herself for the things she did do, and of making changes one step at a time. Hypnosis made a significant difference in this girl's life.

As another example of the use of imagery, Shaw says, she sometimes has the patient talk to their diabetes while under hypnosis. People are encouraged to allow an image to come out of their idea of diabetes. Sometimes the person visualizes diabetes as a monster, or as a black hole sucking the person in. Susan gained insights into her own disease through this technique: she visualized her diabetes as a thing chasing her and trying to kill her. During her treatment, she turned her own thinking around by changing the negative image into a positive one, the image of a tiger.

Guided Imagery

Guided imagery may be used to relieve anxiety, to prepare people for medical procedures, and as a therapeutic intervention. Imagery can strengthen the immune system, reduce pain, and lower blood pressure. Guided imagery can put patients into an altered state of consciousness similar to hypnosis that can measurably lower the rate of heart and reduce stress reactions that show up in the sympathetic nervous system activity.

Radiation oncologist Dr. O. Carl Simonton and Stephanie Simonton, a psychologist who was his wife, began this form of imagery as an adjunct to cancer therapy in the early 1970s, and found that it extended the life spans of cancer patients who utilized it. Patients were encouraged to visualize active responses to their illness—such as an army of chemotherapy drugs destroying cancer cells. Imagery may also use gentler images, perhaps a globe of healing white light descending into the body, with equally good effect.

At the University of Wisconsin in Green Bay, the Professional Program in Nursing developed an imagery script to help people with diabetes adhere to their routine. Participants indicated that the motivational script they used was effective. Blood sugar testing, exercise, weight management, and diet were positively affected by guided imagery, researchers concluded in 1999.

Commercial products have also been developed to assist people with diabetes in this process. Belleruth Naperstak, the author of a series of popular wellness tapes, has created a guided imagery and affirmation tape entitled "Affirmations for Diabetes," which is specific to diabetes. One diabetes educator, Dr. Susan Michael, calls the Naperstak tapes "excellent," and says they have been useful to a number of her clients with diabetes.

When imagery is incorporated into weight-loss treatment, it helps make people aware of how their body feels at a particular moment. She says people who are overweight often lose an awareness of their body.

This awareness can be reestablished with the help of hypnosis, and used to achieve a goal such as weight loss. For instance, she notes, in visualizing the act of eating, a person might have an image of a stomach, they might notice how full it is, whether it's hungry or not. This visualization can be useful if people are eating for lots of reasons other than hunger, and can make them aware if they're actually hungry or if their eating springs from another source.

Shaw believes many people with diabetes can benefit from hypnosis. But she adds that the person has to want to change, and to truly confront and deal with the issues they have with diabetes. People who benefit most, she says, are people motivated to take charge of their own care, who benefit from proactive techniques.

"Hypnosis is not necessarily a passive project," she says. "It requires some effort to look at yourself. It takes some courage to look at these things, and change."

Research on Hypnosis

In January 1990 the *American Journal of Clinical Hypnosis* reported a study of seven people with Type 1 diabetes at the State University of New York's Downstate Medical Center. Research subjects all had poor blood sugar control for the previous six months, as evidenced by standard test results. However, when hypnotism was added to their treatment, their average HbA1c levels dropped from 13.2 to 9.7, and average blood sugar plummeted from 426 mg./dl. to 149 mg./dl. In this study, patients were also encouraged to set long-term goals and to be "the boss of their disease." For instance, under hypnosis, one young man was allowed to experience his dream of becoming a fireman, to experience riding on the fire truck. Experiences like these resulted in greater knowledge and self-awareness, and led to superior symptom control.

There is good evidence that the use of hypnosis can strengthen the immune system, and possibly extend life. One well-known randomized, double-blind study of women with terminal breast cancer, conducted at Stanford University, found that women who were taught to use self-hypnosis and who participated in support groups lived twice as long as a group of women who did not. Dr. Olness has conducted research with children and adolescents showing that self-hypnosis improves measures of immune system function, in addition to reducing stress.

Hypnotists can be board-certified by either the American Board of Medical Hypnosis, the American Board of Dental Hypnosis, or the American Board of Psychological Hypnosis. Professional organizations such as the American Society of Clinical Hypnosis or the Society for Clinical and Experimental Hypnosis can refer to local clinicians who are practitioners of hypnosis. More than 4,000 licensed health professionals are certified as hypnotists by the American Society of Clinical Hypnosis. Books and tapes that teach self-hypnosis are the least expensive method but probably not as useful as they claim to be, according to Dr. Olness.

Precautions: Hypnosis is safe, but people with serious psychiatric problems are not good candidates for this or any mind/body therapy. Older people and people with neurological disorders seem to be less easily hypnotized than most.

Autogenic Training

Autogenic training is the most widely practiced form of self-hypnosis in the world. More than 2,500 papers have been published attesting to the effectiveness of autogenic training on particular health conditions.

In the early 20th century, French pharmacist Emile Coué taught what he called "conscious auto-suggestions" in his free clinic. Coué used this basic affirmation: "Every day in every way, I am getting better and better." He suggested this affirmation be repeated twenty times a day, beginning first thing every morning, and that the words be spoken in a calm, relaxed, and confident manner. Many Frenchmen who tried this in Coué's free clinic began to feel better.

Around 1932, German doctor Johannes Schultz was studying the medical uses of hypnosis, and what he called autogenic training sprang from that. Like Coué, Schultz used repeated affirmations to great effect. Schultz's Canadian collaborator, Wolfgang Luthe, compared autogenic training to transcendental meditation, yoga, Zen meditation, progressive relaxation, self-hypnosis, biofeedback, and some behavioral therapy in that it elicits an antistress "relaxation response." Dr. Schultz's manual, *Introduction to the Methods of Autogenic Therapy,* translated into English by Luthe in 1977, offers some instruction in applying this method to particular medical problems.

According to Luthe, autogenic therapy is quite safe for most cases of diabetes. The regular practice of autogenic exercises for endocrine and metabolic disorders is said to decrease blood and urinary glucose levels, decrease insulin requirements, increase protein-bound iodine, and lower cortisol levels. However, he wrote, the exercises should be discontinued if medication or blood sugar levels are troublesome, if blood sugar levels are too low, or if exercises cannot be practiced at an adequate level.

In basic autogenic training, passive exercises revolve around the spoken words *heavy* and *warm*. The mental idea of "heaviness" is said to elicit a subjective experience of muscles relaxing, while "warmth" elicits increased blood flow to parts of the body such as the hands and feet. In addition to linking mind with body, focusing on heaviness and warmth puts you in contact with the voluntary muscle system of the body as well as the involuntary muscles in the circulatory system.

People with diabetes may use the Fifth Standard exercise in autogenic training. This focuses attention on the solar plexus area, behind the stomach and in front of the backbone, which is the location of the pancreas, the adrenal glands, and the digestive system.

Somewhat like progressive muscle relaxation, a sequence of autogenic exercises might all begin with the line, "My left arm is heavy," repeated three times. To this first phrase would be added more phrases—"my right arm is heavy, both arms are heavy, my right leg is heavy, my left leg is heavy, both legs are heavy, my arms and legs are heavy," adding each to the first and repeating three times, then summarized by repeating only once: "My right arm is heavy, my arms and legs are heavy."

Next, always beginning with the right arm, autogenic exercises might move into the idea of warmth. This sequence might end with the statement: "My right arm is heavy, my arms and legs are heavy and warm, my heartbeat is calm and regular, it breathes me, my solar plexus is warm."

A variation of autogenic training called biogenics, developed by Dr. C. Norman Shealy, combines autogenic training with biofeedback. Dr. Shealy recommends the practice of biogenics for people with diabetes and attributes a few miraculous healings to its use.

Affirmations

Affirmations are a quick, simplified form of autogenic training. Prayers or positive thoughts that are repeated may be seen as verbal affirmations. Louise Hay, a metaphysical author, has published a long series of affirmations for dealing with particular illnesses. Hay thinks illnesses are associated with particular unhealthy thought patterns that can be broken by repeated good thoughts. One of these is her affirmation to release fear:

"I love and approve of myself. I love and approve of my body. I feed it nourishing foods and beverages. I exercise it in ways that are fun. I recognize my body as a wondrous and magnificent machine and I feel privileged to live in it."

Like Emile Coué's simple phrases, Hay's affirmations are designed to be repeated many times per day.

You may also write an affirmation for yourself, which addresses your particular medical condition in a positive way. This may be the most effective form of affirmation of all. When used for health purposes, affirmations do need an expectation of success on the part of the person using them, to be effective, according to Dr. Richard Gerber. Experts suggest incorporating simple, childlike rhythms and rhymes into the phrases to reinforce the idea and make them easier to remember. Statements should contain all positives and no negatives. Repetition is absolutely crucial to this therapy—repeat each phrase at least three times, perhaps several times per day.

Hypnosis, autogenic therapy, and affirmations are mind/body therapies that may help your health. They may help you control blood sugars, blood pressure, and strengthen immune function while reducing the harmful effects of emotional and physical stress. Biofeedback, another important mind/body therapy, is discussed in the next chapter.

Chapter 13

Biofeedback

For people with diabetes, biological feedback, or *biofeedback*, can help increase blood circulation and lower blood pressure. Some studies have shown improvements in blood sugar levels with biofeedback. Using biofeedback, people with diabetes may be able to learn to open up their own blood vessels in vulnerable physical extremities, such as the hands and feet, to help prevent or alleviate problems associated with neuropathy. Like other mind/body techniques, biofeedback relieves physical and emotional stress.

Biofeedback teaches you to use simple machines and sensors that help you regulate functions such as your heartbeat, skin temperature, or blood pressure. These functions, controlled by the autonomic, or *self-ruling*, nervous system, were once considered beyond the influence of the individual. Once learned from a biofeedback technician, biofeedback offers you a uniquely tangible way to see and influence your body, and also to relieve stress. A few people are put off by the hand held biofeedback devices, but many enjoy tinkering with them.

There are several kinds of biofeedback, so select the form appropriate for what you are trying to do. While some people master and benefit from biofeedback quickly, others may require two or three months to see significant changes.

Types of Biofeedback

There are several types of biofeedback that may be useful to people with diabetes including:

- *Electrothermal* biofeedback measures the temperature of the skin, and is usually done at extremities such as the hands and feet to measure changes in blood flow, with higher temperatures indicating more blood in the area.

- *Electrodermal*, or EDR, biofeedback measures changes in perspiration on the skin, a measure of anxiety.

- *Electromyographic*, or EMG, biofeedback measures the action of muscles as fibers fire off during exertion, contracting or expanding a muscle group.

- *Electroencephalographic*, or EEG, biofeedback measures brain wave activity, which reflects the effects of stress and other variables such as sleep.

Research

In 1992, a study for the National Institutes of Health found biofeedback useful for more than 150 different medical conditions.

The same year, research at the University of Wisconsin in La Crosse found biofeedback helpful in regulating the blood volume pulse of subjects with diabetes. Treatment included four weeks of a self-selected relaxation method and four weeks of thermal biofeedback, which measures changes in skin temperature. With a relaxation method alone, average toe temperature increased 9 percent, and blood volume in the toe increased 2 percent. When biofeedback was added, toe temperature increased 31 percent and blood volume increased 22 percent, according to results published in *Diabetes Care*.

At Duke University, researchers studied a dozen patients with Type 2 diabetes who complained of high stress levels. Both groups followed a standard diet and exercise regimen, but the second group also received training in progressive muscle relaxation and electromyographic, or EMG, biofeedback. At the end of the study, subjects taught the relaxation techniques achieved better blood sugar control. However, a second study did not replicate these positive results.

In another study at Duke University, a group of forty people with Type 2 diabetes was divided in half. One group received relaxation training. Although the two groups had about the same level of metabolic control, subjects who reported significant anxiety at that time in their lives did show the most significant improvements in blood sugar control from relaxation, according to Richard S. Surwit, Ph.D., a professor of medical psychology at Duke University Medical Center.

In 1996, a study at the Medical College of Ohio in Toledo, Ohio, found that patients with Type 1 diabetes improved the stability of their blood sugar levels with the aid of biofeedback. Lead researcher Angele McGrady noted that stress raises blood glucose and that the use of biofeedback therapy lowered both stress and blood sugar levels.

Another study, at the Veterans Administration Outpatient Clinic in Los Angeles, examined the effects of progressive relaxation training and EMG biofeedback on twenty adults with Type 2 diabetes. Results published in 1997 showed that stress reduction and relaxation were achieved, but no significant changes in glucose tolerance or other measures of diabetic control were found.

With the aid of biofeedback, patients with high blood pressure can be taught how to reduce increases in blood pressure caused by stress, according to a 1997 study. Other studies using biofeedback have shown significant improvements in levels of depression, anxiety, insomnia, and chronic pain. Where biofeedback is applicable and appropriate, about 80 percent of users usually benefit.

Biofeedback may be practiced at home, but it must be learned from an experienced practitioner, preferably one who has had some experience working with people with diabetes. There are approximately 10,000 biofeedback practitioners in the United States, about 2,000 of whom are certified. The Association for Applied Psychophysiology and Biofeedback, listed in Appendix A, can provide a list of local clinicians.

Biological feedback provides a relaxing antidote to stress. The use of simple, handheld machines may help improve the symptoms of diabetes, such as high blood pressure. Blood sugar and other symptoms may improve. Social support, an important but often overlooked form of stress relief, is covered in the next chapter.

Chapter 14

Social Support

Loving, positive, supportive interactions with family, friends, and other people in your life are a form of mind/body therapy, since they counteract stress and keep you healthy. Many studies have shown that social, emotional, and practical support can bolster your spirits and help you manage diabetes. Your ability to control blood sugar, blood pressure, and other symptoms may improve when you give or receive social support. Recent research shows you may live a bit longer too.

How Support Networks Help

We all have social support networks, consisting of groups of people and individuals who populate our lives. In addition to personal relationships with family and friends, social support may include friends at work or professional relationships, or participating in organized religion, social clubs, exercise classes, and volunteer activities. Even looking after pets or taking care of plants lowers blood pressure and increases life satisfaction, according to some studies. As a practical matter, people with a higher level of social support take better care of themselves and manage chronic illnesses such as diabetes and heart disease more effectively. A large body of research shows that people with good social support have lower rates of illness, live longer, and have a superior level of satisfaction with their own lives.

According to the authors of *Why We Get Sick: The New Science of Darwinian Medicine*, our primitive ancestors roamed the earth for millions of years in groups of 35–100 people, in humanity's so-called hunter-gatherer stage. In these small groups, with their division of labor and sharing of resources, our unshakeable need for community surely developed. Although we no longer live like Paleolithic man, many of us feel a distinct need for what may be called social support.

Family is often the bedrock of social support. Research at the University of Arizona School of Medicine found that people who described their parents in positive, affectionate terms during their middle years were less likely to suffer from chronic medical conditions such as high blood pressure. Friends can be quite supportive, sometimes just by listening, sometimes by extending sympathy or practical advice in ways in which family members are not able or willing to do. Talking and listening to another person can divert you from your own worries and cares, and remind you that you are an entirely unique human being and not just a person with diabetes.

Diabetes support groups can also be quite helpful. Local affiliates of the American Diabetes Association maintain lists of support groups, which are usually free. Support groups may be composed entirely of people with diabetes, but they are sometimes led by a professional facilitator who can make sure that everyone who wishes to speak has a chance to do so. Support groups can be comforting, stress-relieving environments, providing sympathy and solace. They can be a forum to discuss issues related to diabetes that you may not be able to talk about in any other place. People who attend support groups are often up on some of latest research and treatments for diabetes, and so might indirectly help you learn more about managing certain aspects of your disease. However, support groups are not for everybody. Experts in this area advise attending a group three times before deciding if participation is for you.

Unlike people (who can be judgmental), pets can give and accept unconditional love, which is extremely important to all of us. Cats, birds, monkeys, fish, and other pets can keep you company. Dogs can be good exercise companions, if you enjoy walking. A 1988 study of heart attack patients found that those who kept a pet or pets were most likely to completely recover, even more so than people with spouses, supportive families, and friends. Many recent studies have concluded that people with social support have lower rates of heart attacks, take better care of their health, and handle stress and diabetes in a markedly superior way.

A landmark study in this area was concluded a few years ago by Dr. Stewart Wolf and medical students from the University of Pennsylvania. Dr. Wolf and his colleagues tracked the rate of heart attacks among the Italian-American residents of Roseto, Pennsylvania, over a period of more than twenty years. Interestingly, inhabitants of Roseto all hailed from the same part of rural Italy and had unusually close family and social ties when compared with their Pennsylvania neighbors. At a time when heart attack rates were soaring elsewhere in the United States, researchers were amazed to find that the residents of Roseto had an amazingly low rate of heart disease—only *one-third* as many heart attacks as residents of similar nearby small towns. This proved to be a tangible benefit of Roseto's close-knit, supportive community, which apparently provided a huge buffer against stress. Low rates of heart disease in Roseto were independent of all known risk factors for heart disease such as smoking, alcohol consumption, high cholesterol, and even obesity.

Under stressful conditions, social support may help people with diabetes control blood sugar. A study at the Washington University School of Medicine in St. Louis, Missouri, found that HbA1c levels were about the same between people with either good or poor social support under normal conditions. However, under conditions of high stress, social support made a *significant* difference in long-term blood sugar control. The authors concluded: "These data suggest that during stressful times social support may insulate patients with diabetes from the adverse physiologic and behavioral consequences of stress and thereby foster better glucose control."

A 1998 study at the Tokyo Institute of Psychiatry in Japan, found that HbA1c levels were lower for people who perceived and utilized social supports, similar to levels of people who were educated about how to manage diabetes and care for themselves. A study published in the *American Journal of Public Health* in 1987 concluded that both education and peer support helped elderly people with Type 2 diabetes lose weight and control blood sugars.

Good Communication

Working on your communication skills can help you deal more effectively with family members, friends, or medical professionals, and lower levels of interpersonal stress. One key to communication is effective, active, empathetic listening. This may help you cultivate social support.

Experts say the best way to communicate with other people is with what is called an *assertive* communications style. Directly state what you want, without being overly aggressive or overly passive. Assertive communication often begins sentences with the words "I feel" or "I think," showing ownership of feelings. Assertive communicators look you in the eye, politely ask for what they want, and assert or repeat themselves as necessary. They accept their right to answer yes or no to questions from another person. Assertive communicators tend to create "win-win" exchanges, in which no one goes away hurt or angry.

People using an *aggressive* communications style often interrupt and intimidate others, making demands rather than requests, leaving a residue of resentment, hostility, or anger in their wake. They often begin sentences with the word "You," which tends to place blame and responsibility on another person and make them defensive. *Passive* communicators try to manipulate others without directly stating what they want. They often wind up passively allowing others to choose what they do, and when they do this, it's at personal cost to themselves. Aggressive or passive communications styles, accompanied by aggressive or passive body language, often result in "win-lose" exchanges between family members and friends.

Assertively asking questions of your medical doctor may also help you control diabetes. Researchers at the New England Medical Center in Boston helped people with diabetes formulate questions for their doctors, using twenty-minute coaching sessions prior to doctors' visits. The study concluded that coached patients had lower glucose levels during follow-up visits and experienced fewer limitations on their lifestyles because of diabetes.

People with higher levels of social support practice better health behaviors. In 1996, a study of people with Type 2 diabetes conducted at the University of Hawaii found that people with a higher level of social support, such as a supportive spouse, family, friend, or support group, were better at taking care of their general health, and also in following health recommendations for controlling diabetes. A 1995 study of people with Type 2 diabetes at the Universidad de Guanajuato in Leon, Mexico, agreed that adherence to dietary recommendations and medications was *greater* in people with social support.

Although women are generally regarded as more social than men, men may derive at least as much benefit from social support. A 1993 study of people newly diagnosed with Type 2 diabetes at Stockholm University in Sweden found that men with high levels of emotional, informative, or practical social support had better blood sugar control than women with a similar level of support.

Support groups may actually bolster your health. A study of older people with diabetes at a U.S. Veterans Affairs Center looked at two groups of patients eighteen months after an education program. One group had attended support group sessions, another had not. Quality of life, knowledge about diabetes, and psychological and social functioning were greatest in the people who attended support groups. People who attended support groups also were less depressed.

Counseling

Many people find counseling helpful during hard times. Meeting for a while with a good psychologist or lay counselor can help you sort out life issues and work through hard times. Seeing a therapist is an acceptable health behavior, even after you are first diagnosed. The acceptance of chronic disease, and the attendant fear of complications, are big, stressful issues to many people with diabetes. Chronic disease sets off a shower of fears and worries, and some people need a safe, nonjudgmental place to discuss these issues.

Psychological counseling may be useful in dealing with issues such as fear, anger, anxiety, depression, resentment. Simply having your thoughts heard often relieves stress. Talking to another person cuts your burden in half, goes an old saying. Speaking to a psychologist or lay counselor about things that trouble you combats the depressing notion that you are alone with your problems and that no one in the world wants to hear what you have to say. Family counseling is an alternative if you are having problems with a spouse, or an individual within your family circle. Communication skills can almost always be improved.

However, if your personal situation seems overwhelming, if you have a serious depression that won't go away, or you are thinking of suicide, you should consult a psychiatrist—a medical doctor with an expertise in psychology who can prescribe medication, if necessary.

Even group therapy has shown some promise in helping people sort out emotional issues related to diabetes. At the Max Planck Institute of Psychiatry in Munich, Germany, people with Type 1 and Type 2 diabetes showed significant improvement after a seven-session group therapy treatment and educational program that directly addressed the issues of acceptance and fear. The German study combined progressive muscle relaxation training and exercises in imagination with an analysis of dysfunctional health beliefs. During group therapy sessions, people were urged to articulate and confront their fears. They were then asked to put their fears into perspective and to develop plans for making positive changes in their lives, such as developing social networks and improving diabetes control. Both traditional therapy and cognitive therapies were used. At the end of the seven sessions, research subjects reported measurably less fear, and greater acceptance of diabetes. Some of the patients also showed a significant improvement in metabolic control in the course of the program.

Organized Religion

If you are of a religious bent, participating in organized religion and attending religious services can be a healthy form of social support. Of more than a thousand formal research studies on this topic, approximately two-thirds have concluded that people who are involved in their religion are healthier than those who are not. Many studies report lower rates of cancer, heart disease, and other medical problems as well as greater longevity among those who are religiously committed.

Prayer

Prayer, a focal point of all religions, probably extends back to the dim beginnings of human history in pagan times. Petitionary prayers for oneself or intercessory prayers for other people who may not be present are among the many forms of prayer, which is also a form of meditation. Among other things, prayer can have the effect of making the individual feel connected to something larger and more powerful than himself, or herself, and listened to, or supported. Prayer directly relieves emotional stress.

The Serenity Prayer, written by theologian Reinhold Niebuhr, is used by many 12-step programs. It may be helpful in reminding you to sort out things that are not important to you from things that are important, and in accepting what you must accept.

The Serenity Prayer

God grant me the Serenity

To accept the things I cannot change

The courage to change the things that I can

And the wisdom to know the difference.

A 1996 study examined the spiritual well-being among people with diabetes. The study concluded that those who were religious experienced less uncertainty and a greater sense of psychological and social well-being than those who were not.

A study of 4,000 Canadians over the age of 65 found that those persons who participated in religious activities were 40 percent less likely to have high blood pressure than those who had no religious involvement. In the United States, a six-year study of 2,000 older people funded by the National Institutes of Health found that people who attended religious services at least once a week were 40 percent less likely to have high blood pressure than those who didn't attend or attended less frequently. A study at Yale University of 3,000 people over the age of sixty found that those who rarely went to church had twice as many strokes as those who attended regularly.

A study conducted in 1995 at the Georgetown University School of Medicine found that religion was beneficial to healing 81 percent of the time, harmful 4 percent of the time, and the rest of the time was neutral.

Attending religious services puts one in touch with moral and ethical teachings, sacred music and chants, ancient and familiar rituals and more, in the context of a supportive group of like-minded people. Moral and ethical concepts such as forgiveness, faith, hope, and love, taught by most religions, are powerful and important factors in mental and physical health. A 1997 study at Stanford University looked at 55 college students who were trained to forgive a person who had hurt them. After six weeks, the students who were trained were measurably less angry, had more self-confidence and more emotional restraint, and were more hopeful than the other students in the control group. These gains in mental health status were maintained when the students were tested again more than two months later.

Even though many people get along just fine without organized religion, others benefit greatly from this form of social support.

Helping

Helping other people actually increases life expectancy, according to a study published in 1992, conducted at the University of Michigan. Giving emotional or practical support to others certainly relieves stress, and diverts us from our own obsessions. It's good for your health to interact with people in a positive, helpful way.

One of the world's keenest observers, the biologist Charles Darwin, saw that people are naturally inclined to help each other. Darwin also recognized that helping acts are most likely to be performed when they involve reciprocal action that benefits the helper as well as the person helped.

Dr. Hans Selye, a pioneer in the field of stress research, believed that harmful stress could be interrupted when people *act* to help themselves or others. What Dr. Selye called *altruistic egoism* is a lifestyle designed to quiet the stress response. Practicing altruistic egoism, he said, would create feelings of "accomplishment and security through the inspiration in others of love, goodwill and gratitude for what we have done or are likely to do in the future."

In *Adaptation to Life*, psychiatrist George Valliant reported on a thirty-year study of Harvard graduates. He concluded that graduates who coped poorly with stress became ill four times more often than people who coped well. After examining the number and quality of the subjects' relationships at middle age, Dr. Valliant concluded that an altruistic lifestyle was an absolutely crucial factor in mental health.

Boston University psychologist David McClelland has studied a number of successful healers and tried to identify the reasons for their success. McClelland has stated that some kind of tender loving care seems to be a crucial ingredient in the healers' abilities to heal. Caring about others apparently strengthens the immune system. In one experiment, McClelland showed research subjects a film on Mother Teresa's work with the poor in India, and found that the immune systems of research subjects motivated to help others, *without regard for the outcome*, were strengthened the most.

Helping other people may also be seen as a form of mindfulness meditation, in which the other person is the focus of the meditation. According to Allan Luks and Peggy Payne, authors of *The Healing Power of Doing Good*, helping other people resembles mindfulness meditation in that you focus all your energy on the present and what's in front of you. This produces a heightened awareness of emotions, thoughts, and sensations. Helping other people distracts you from your own thoughts and gives you a break from constant worries about your own problems.

One study showed that the health of more than 98 percent of those who volunteered actually improved. In this survey, people who did volunteer work increased their sense of usefulness by 97 percent, their sense of companionship 91 percent, their sense of self-satisfaction 84 percent, and their sense of independence 52 percent. In another survey, of several thousand volunteers, approximately 95 percent reported that helping another person on a regular basis made them feel physically good. This loving, rejuvenating, calmed-down feeling almost always returned when the helping act was remembered. The benefits of helping spring most frequently from helping strangers, not just family or friends, according to Luks.

Humor

As the late Norman Cousins demonstrated, laughing is good for your health. In partnership with his medical doctor, Cousins cured himself of a serious illness by regularly and frequently viewing humorous movies and films, and taking large doses of Vitamin C. He documented his victory over alkylosing spondylitis in the best-selling book, *Anatomy of an Illness*.

The laughing author was living proof that the act of laughing makes us healthier. Laughing lifts us out of our mundane daily existence, allows us to soar like sparrows over our problems, dropping our cares as we fly. Laughter gives us a healthy perspective on our own lives.

Laughter-loving physician Hunter "Patch" Adams believes that a good sense of humor is the bedrock of good mental health, and an effective social lubricant that enhances communication between individuals and groups. Among the physical responses to laughter are muscle relaxation, increased oxygenation of the blood, and lower heart rate and blood pressure. Laughter antidotes stress, since it lowers the secretion of the stress hormone, cortisol, Dr. Adams reports.

You already know what might amuse you, and what tickles your fancy. Seek out all the things that make you roar, snort, or chuckle. Visit comedy clubs, see humorous movies, watch funny TV shows, read laughable books, hunt down pungent political cartoons, and more. Seek out an old friend or acquaintance with a sense of humor, and try to get that person to tell you a good joke, or tell them one. Spend more time in the company of people or things that amuse you.

Laughing clubs, popular in India, in which groups of people get together to laugh together, have recently begun to appear in the United States.

The Humor Project, headquartered in Saratoga Springs, New York, holds humorous conferences and sells funny books and tapes. The American Association for Therapeutic Humor, in St. Louis, Missouri, recommends specific books to read.

Robert Coles, a Harvard Medical School psychiatrist, observed that as we age we become more likely to seek our satisfactions in daily deeds involving other people, rather than in grand metaphysical designs.

Social support enhances your sense of well-being, your management of diabetes, and your general health. Support groups and other forms of social support may help you manage high blood sugar and high blood pressure, and improve the way you take care of yourself. Counseling may help during hard times. Even giving time to help other people can help you. The next chapter examines the most physical mind/body therapies, including the Eastern discipline of yoga, which has become very popular in the United States.

Chapter 15

Yoga and More

Ancient and exotic mind/body therapies from India and China such as yoga, tai chi, and chi gong combine concentration, disciplined physical movement, and careful breathing. These are the only mind/body therapies that resemble exercise and share some of its beneficial effects. Practiced under the eye of an instructor, or even at home, these therapies can help normalize heart rate, improve blood circulation, strengthen the body, and may help you control blood sugar and blood pressure by evoking a relaxation response.

Yoga, or *union*, an aspect of Ayurvedic medicine, is believed to be the oldest system of natural healing in the world. The Chinese fitness exercises of tai chi and chi gong also have roots in ancient times. These activities are not quite exercise, since they have a mental and almost spiritual focus. Yoga, for instance, is sometimes practiced in India as preparation for meditation. Mindfulness meditation incorporates yoga into the meditation itself.

Hatha Yoga

Classical, or *hatha*, yoga teaches you to use physical exercises called poses, or *asanas*, interspersed with periods of controlled breathing and deeper relaxation. Hatha yoga is a mentally focused exercise. Although it is only one of the forms of yoga, it's the most suitable for people with diabetes. Hatha yoga is meant to be performed rhythmically and slowly, with moments of discomfort and exertion broken by periods of deep breathing and deep relaxation.

Among its many benefits, yoga strengthens the body, builds physical endurance, and increases balance and flexibility. It helps regulate weight, strengthens resistance to illness, and helps train and focus the mind. The practice of yoga improves blood flow, aligns the spine with the head, and energizes glands and organs. And, of course, it relieves stress.

The controlled breathing techniques used in yoga are believed to balance the flow of life energy, or *prana*, in the body. Prana is a nebulous concept, more spiritual than biological, since it is invisible and cannot be identified and measured. According to Dr. Richard Gerber, prana may be seen as the energy from sunlight, which charges the oxygen we breathe. This energy is subsequently taken in and moved through the body's seven energy centers, called *chakras*. In yogic theory, stress, bad diet, or toxins can all interrupt the flow of prana and therefore impact mental, spiritual, or physical health.

The regular practice of yoga may help blood sugar control, according to a study conducted at the Central Research Institute for Yoga in Delhi, India, published in *Diabetes Residential Clinical Practice* in 1993. This study involved almost 150 people with Type 2 diabetes. After forty days of practicing yoga, 104 patients showed a "fair to good response" based on reductions of blood sugar and glucose tolerance, which were measured by oral glucose tolerance tests. During the study, subjects were also given a vegetarian diet. Many participants were able to decrease their doses of oral hypoglycemic drugs.

An hour of yoga each day is an important part of Dr. Dean Ornish's program in San Francisco to reverse heart disease without drugs and surgery. In this program, yoga is the modality that has the highest correlation with success. People who practiced yoga two hours or more a day are said to derive the greatest benefits from Dr. Ornish's multidisciplinary program, which includes a rigorous diet, support groups, and education in communication and stress management techniques.

Several years ago, Dr. Chandra Patel, a London heart specialist, used a combination of yoga and biofeedback therapy to treat twenty patients with high blood pressure; five of the patients were able to stop their heart medications, and another seven reduced their dosages of antihypertensive drugs from 33 to 60 percent, according to research published in 1973.

Thousands of research studies of yoga have been conducted in India, cataloging its health benefits. However, most of these studies are said to have been poorly designed, and they are not given much credence in the West. According to Dr. Gerber, some research suggests that the regular practice of particular yoga postures believed to assist pancreas function may stimulate the endocrine system and help with overall metabolism. In some research, he adds, particular yoga postures are being applied to specific medical conditions.

Yoga classes are offered at many schools, YMCAs, sports clubs, or through private salons. In the United States, the American Yoga Association can refer local practitioners. Books and tapes that teach yoga postures are also available, but learning and practicing yoga in a class is probably best. Most people do better in a class, where the finer points of each pose may be explained by an experienced instructor, and where the rest periods execution, timing, and duration of postures, and the rate of breathing, are all controlled.

Good Postures

The American Yoga Association's Wellness Book recommends a particular sequence of yoga postures for people with diabetes. Practicing these postures is said to increase blood circulation, especially to peripheral areas. Daily practice is recommended. However, if you don't have time to do the full routine, the authors suggest you do warm-up exercises plus three from the list, followed by a full relaxation procedure and a few minutes of meditation. Exercises should always begin with a warm-ups and be concluded with relaxation and meditation.

Recommended Postures and Benefits

- *Alternate Triangle.* Compresses organs, stimulating metabolism

- *Twisting Triangle.* Flexibility and circulation in hips and back

- *Standing Sun Pose.* Improves digestion and circulatory system function.

- *Cobra V-Raise.* Strengthens legs, back, and shoulders; improves organ function; reduces body fat and strengthens heart

- *Baby Pose.* Improves circulation to brain and pelvis, and improves digestion

- *Spine Twist.* Strengthens heart; improves digestion

- *Seated Sun Pose.* Massages internal organs

- *Tortoise Stretch.* Improves pelvic circulation; also stretches nerves and muscles in legs and ankles

- *Floor Stretch.* Releases tight muscles along spine and back of the leg

- *Shoulder Stand.* Stimulates thyroid and parathyroid

- *Easy Bridge.* Improves thyroid functioning; eases back pain and fatigue

- *Bow Pose.* Improves functioning of digestive system; enhances vitality

Remember that yoga postures work best if done properly. In attempting these postures, take care to try to place your hands and feet in the proper positions, since this will enhance blood circulation, particularly to the extremities of the body. Yoga instructors usually provide guidance on the finer points of postures during yoga sessions. Attention to proper breathing is crucial, since it brings forth the greatest benefits from yoga. The most relaxing yoga breathing involves slow, deep belly breaths, in which your abdomen is extended on the inhalation breath. Benefits of proper breathing include greater oxygenation of the blood, a flushing out of toxins from the muscles, and an increased supply of nutrients to the brain.

Precautions: Most hatha yoga postures are relaxing and safe for most people with diabetes. However, for people with complications such as diabetic retinopathy, some postures recommended above, such as the Shoulder Stand, may not be advised. Also not recommended for people

Progressive Muscle Relaxation

Progressive muscle relaxation is a mind/body therapy often recommended to relieve stress and muscular tension. It was originally developed by a cardiologist as a form of exercise for patients who were in bed, recovering from heart surgery, but has become widely accepted. Muscle relaxation techniques are similar to some breathing and relaxation techniques practiced in hatha yoga, and they are easily learned.

Progressive muscle relaxation is best practiced in a relaxed, quiet place, following instructions on cassette tapes that are widely available in bookstores, health food stores, and other outlets. Basically, it involves flexing and relaxing groups of muscles, one group at a time, in conjunction with deep, controlled breathing. One sequence is flexing and relaxing muscles in the feet, followed by flexing and relaxing the calves, thighs, buttocks, lower abdomen, upper abdomen, hands, arms, back and shoulders, neck, and face. This is followed by a period of slow, deep, steady breathing.

Progressive muscle relaxation evokes the relaxation response, relieves muscle tension, and helps relieve stress.

with retinopathy is the posture known as the Plow, and similar postures which elevate the feet over the head, thereby increasing blood pressure on the blood vessels of the eye. Always check with your medical doctor before beginning any exercise program. Also keep in mind that yoga postures should be done to the point of discomfort, not pain. If you find a particular class too strenuous, seek a slower, lower-level class. Some forms of yoga, such as "power yoga," are quite strenuous and should be avoided by novices.

Tai Chi

The ancient Chinese exercise systems of *tai chi* and *chi gong* also combine exercise with disciplined breathing and controlled movement. Although not as widely researched as yoga, they have many similar health benefits. Either may be a useful antidote to stress and help control blood pressure.

Tai chi is a form of slow, gentle exercise that originated in China. It follows a particular set of moves to which various meanings are attached. Tai chi is actually a form of meditation, originating in the martial arts, which is believed to balance mind and body. The most popular form of exercise in China, tai chi is practiced primary for its benefits to health. The exercises take from fifteen to twenty minutes to perform, and ideally are practiced twice a day.

A study at LaTrobe University in Australia in 1992 concluded that tai chi had beneficial effects on heart rate and blood pressure, equivalent to brisk walking. Tai chi improves balance and posture, and can prevent injuries from falling down. A study of elderly people at the University of Connecticut found that those who practiced tai chi gained more strength than those who practiced standard balance training, strength training, or a combination of the two.

Chi Gong

Chi gong in its internal form is another Chinese system of exercises with spiritual elements. Its movements somewhat resemble the movements of tai chi and are intended to encourage the flow of energy through the body. Chi gong exercises are said to cleanse and refine the natural, invisible flowing universal energy called *chi*.

Chi gong is practiced in China as preventive medicine. Chinese research concludes that it reduces high blood pressure, heart disease, gastrointestinal ailments, and other health problems in elderly people. One study extended for twenty years, and when completed in 1993, researchers concluded that subjects who practiced chi gong had lower blood pressure and 50 percent less illness and death from strokes.

In the United States, a study at Columbia University showed that people who practiced chi gong experienced an average drop in blood pressure of 10 percent.

While internal chi gong is quite popular as an exercise, external chi gong is an aspect of traditional Chinese medicine that is practiced only by highly trained chi gong masters. An energy therapy covered in later chapters, external chi gong involves projecting chi energy from the hands of the healer to the subject.

Yoga, tai chi, and chi gong all combine controlled breathing and mild, moderate exercise. They deliver a sustained stress-relieving effect. Practiced on a regular basis, these therapies may help lower blood sugar or blood pressure. The next chapter examines music therapy, a mind/body therapy that harnesses the sensual and natural rhythmic energy of music.

Chapter 16

Music Therapy

$\mathbf{M}$usic has been used therapeutically at least since biblical times, when David the shepherd and future king strummed his harp to soothe the emotionally troubled Israeli monarch, King Saul. Music therapy got started as a profession after World War II, when it was used to rehabilitate soldiers who were emotionally disturbed. A great deal of research shows that music is a pleasant and useful mind/body therapy for people with diabetes and other chronic illnesses.

Healing Power of Music

Music lifts the spirits, hence its integration into most forms of organized religion. Music influences endocrine and immune system function and lowers the level of stress hormones. As our bodies become entranced in musical rhythm, and we tap our fingers or feet in time to the music, it induces relaxation and reduces stress, anxiety, feelings of depression and social isolation. Music may decrease blood pressure, lower the heart rate, lower the respiratory rate, and even slow down intestinal contractions. It is useful in managing pain, increasing workplace satisfaction, and reducing aggressive behavior. Research conducted by French otolaryngoloist Dr. Alfred Tomatis shows that music recharges and retunes the brain, dispels tension, and increases enthusi-

Musical Beds

Musical beds or musical chairs may help relieve stress. Furniture that bathes you in pleasant musical sounds and gentle vibration as you sleep is already on the market. Musical beds retail for several thousand dollars each, but handy people can build one themselves. In a musical bed, built-in speakers placed under the bed pipe music up through the mattress. Sound waves vibrate through the body as music is heard. This form of music therapy becomes subliminal once you fall asleep in the musical bed or chair.

Sleeping in a musical bed is said to combat stress and to help sleepers relax and release conflicts that are buried. Holistic physician C. Norman Shealy says musical beds help move energy, or chi, through the body.

Of course, sleepers need appropriate music to sleep or relax. Many people find classical music relaxing. Another possibility is David Ison's "TheraSound," a music designed for therapeutic purposes, to affect particular chakras or energy centers. A study by the National Institutes of Health published in March 1999 found that Ison's Thera-Sound Psychoacoustic Method helped research subjects cope with stress.

asm for life. If you enjoy it, music can increase the quality of life and well-being in general. As sense organs, our ears are directly connected to our brains.

Listening to music can be therapeutic and relaxing. The same is true when you play an instrument, sing, chant, or dance. Music may be listened to passively, as during an exercise class or in a doctor's office. It may be actively selected, when you choose music you like to hear in your home, your office, or even your bedroom. Music distracts us from our cares, but it also has an entraining effect, with its regularity of rhythm. This may help bring body rhythms such as heartbeat, and daily circadian rhythms such as sleep and wakefulness, into greater harmony with the world. Many studies have shown that music enhances creativity and the ability to learn and promotes self-awareness.

It's not completely understood how music works as therapy, but speculation is that it may improve the communication between the right and left hemispheres of the brain. Musical rhythms may cause the body to release endorphins or other chemicals that affect mood and the sensitivity to pain.

Music may be combined with other healing modalities, yielding good results. For instance, an unusual program at the Mt. Sinai Health Care System in Cleveland, Ohio, combines gospel music, low impact aerobics, and tai chi with educational and blood sugar testing sessions. Developed by Eva Bradley, a registered nurse and diabetes educator with Mt. Sinai's diabetes education department, participants in the "Spiritualcise" program are basically encouraged to exercise in a pleasant, active, supportive musical environment. Participants in the program have improved self-esteem, self-image, and self-motivation, Bradley reports.

A new type of rehabilitative music from Germany, called Medical Resonance Therapy Music, has shown some usefulness for people with diabetes. In experiments in Russia, this music was measurably superior to a basic rehabilitative music program, inducing a more pronounced relaxation in subjects, as shown by heart function, mood improvement, muscle tension, and alpha rhythm brain wave increases. When light therapy in the form of dynamic color exposure was added to this music therapy, Russian researchers observed that the relaxing effect was even more pronounced.

Music picks many people up when they're blue, and brings them into contact with a kind of uplifting spiritual emotion. At the Stanford School of Medicine, a study of older adults who were depressed compared three groups. One group learned music listening stress-reduction techniques in their home, taught by a music therapist. Another group received a self-administered program of music. The third group of patients, on the waiting list, received no music therapy. Participants in both groups using music scored "significantly better" than the control group on standard tests measuring depression, stress levels, self-esteem, and mood. More impressively, these improvements were maintained over a nine-month follow-up period, according to results published in the *Journal of Gerontology* in 1994.

Music reduces stress and anxiety. A study at Orlando Regional Healthcare System, Florida, found that patients recovering from cardiac surgery had lower heart rate and blood pressure when exposed to music,

Medical Resonance Therapy Music

Medical Resonance Therapy Music, a therapeutic music written and designed by German medical music composer Peter Huebner, is proving to benefit a number of medical conditions, including diabetes, heart problems, and excessive stress.

Some research shows Huebner's musical therapy system to be helpful to people with diabetes. Medical Resonance Therapy Music resulted in faster insulin processing, reduced irritability, and improved composure in a group of children with Type 1 diabetes. A reduction in sleeping disorders and headaches in a group of female patients with diabetes was also observed in a research study.

Huebner's music relieves stress in groups of people with various medical complaints. In one study of mentally overburdened women, 22 percent achieved a complete normalization of mental function, and 44 percent saw significant improvement in mental function when exposed to musical resonance therapy. In the control group, none of the women achieved normalization, and only 23 percent experienced significant improvement. Another research study found Medical Resonance Therapy Music stimulated the imaginations of older and middle-age people.

regardless of whether or not the ambient hospital noise bothered them. Studies of people recovering from heart attacks and people receiving chemotherapy for the first time also show decreased anxiety levels with music.

Another study of 108 anxious female college students found that three sessions of relaxing music relieved as much anxiety as three sessions of progressive muscle relaxation. Even animals respond to music. In a study in San Antonio, Texas, baboons exposed to radio music had lower heart rates than baboons that were not exposed to music for two weeks.

There are now approximately 5,000 registered music therapists in the United States and Canada. Organizations such as the American Music Therapy Association can refer people to a local music therapist.

Music can be an enormously pleasant form of therapy, helping bring mind and body into greater harmony with life, and increasing relaxation. People who love music, and people who are depressed or recovering from acute medical problems, are among those who may benefit from its relaxing effects. Music is at once both physical and spiritual; it reduces stress in people with diabetes, and may therefore improve self-management and satisfaction with life.

Chapter 17

Aromatherapy

Sensual, fragrant aromatic plant oils can be a relaxing and helpful mind/body therapy for people with diabetes. Before the birth of Christ, Hippocrates used aromatic fumigations to rid Athens of a plague. More recently, French army surgeon Dr. Jean Valnet discovered that aromatic oils could be used to treat soldiers who were wounded in battle and patients in psychiatric hospitals. He published *Aromatherapie* in 1964, a classic book in this field. Aromatherapy is one of the gentlest of all therapies, most popular in France.

Essential oils can rejuvenate and relax you, combating the ill effects of stress. Some oils may slightly lower blood sugar or blood pressure, or have a hormonal balancing effect. Aromatherapy can include a therapeutic massage by a professional aromatherapist, or self-treatment at home with aromas you like and select.

Treatment with Essential Oils

Over 150 different essential oils have been extracted from plants, trees, fruit, flowers, herbs, and spices. Since these oils are inhaled as gases or diluted and worked into the skin, their effects are quite subtle. The aromas produced by each pleasant, pungent essential oil are distinctive. Fragrances may be used individually or blended.

From a scientific point of view, aromatic oils activate the 5 million cells of the nasal cavity to relieve stress and improve mood. Aromatherapy is believed to act by soothing the limbic system in the brain, which controls emotions, memory, and levels of particular hormones.

Regular aromatherapy treatments involving massages with essential oils are said to rebalance bodily systems, although aromatherapists say it takes time to establish any benefit beyond short-lived relaxing and rejuvenating effects. For a problem such as stress or anxiety, insomnia or depression, some aromatherapists say that several weeks of treatment could be needed to show any results.

At home, essential oils may be added to bathwater in small amounts, inhaled from vaporizers, or used in compresses. Absorption through the skin is greatest when added to a bath; add a few drops of oil just before you enter. Regular massages by a professional aromatherapist are a preferred method of treatment. Massage of hands and feet may be substituted for full body massage with about the same effects. Oils used in massage should be greatly diluted. Valerie Ann Worwood, author of *The Complete Book of Essential Oils & Aromatherapy*, recommends a ratio of five drops of essential oil per one teaspoon of vegetable oil such as almond oil or sunflower oil.

Aromatherapy is not a primary treatment for diabetes. In June 2000 the *British Journal of General Practice* looked at more than a dozen randomized trials of aromatherapy conducted with either oils combined with massage or as a single modality. Several studies showed a mild, measurable, pain-relieving or relaxing effect from essential oils. While these effects were not strong enough to merit treatment of a problem like anxiety by aromatherapy alone, the authors conclude that aromatherapy may be useful as an adjunct treatment.

When exploring aromatherapy, choose essential oils that have a pleasant smell, advises Nicola Salter, a Los Angeles aromatherapist. If you mix your own, select oils that complement each other in your own mind, using smaller amounts of the most strongly scented. Each oil has a slightly different effect.

For people with Type 2 diabetes, Salter recommends a mix of regulatory oils such as rosewood, germanium, frankincense, and thyme, perhaps mixing three of the oils you like into a blend. For individuals with diabetes, she might recommend other oils selected to address emo-

Oils to Avoid

Angelica, sometimes used for colds, fever, or flatulence, is an essential oil that should be avoided if you have diabetes, according to the *Encyclopedia of Natural Remedies*.

tional factors of the individual person, which she believes are as important as the physical symptoms in treatment with aromatherapy. For anxiety, for instance, she might recommend a mix of rose, geranium, and melissa. For grieving, she might suggest a mixture of rose, geranium, lavender, and bergamot, to take the stress off the immune system. For people with high blood pressure, she would avoid stimulating oils such as clove, thyme, and black pepper. Other practitioners suggest marjoram, lavender, and ylang ylang for their beneficial effects.

Essential oils can be purchased over the counter and used at home. The best should be labeled "pure essential oil" or "100 percent certified organic," according to Salter. Cosmetics companies often market synthetic essential oils, but natural oils from natural sources are highly preferred. The Aura Cacia company markets an essential oil mixture said to be tailored for people with diabetes. This mixture includes lavender, balsam fir needle, patchouli, palmarosa, geranium, and Roman chamomile essential oils.

Precautions: Never drink an essential oil. Some essential oils including thuja, wormwood, mugwort leaf, hyssop, tansy, and sage are poisonous, and can cause death. Do not apply undiluted essential oils to the skin, since most are so concentrated they can cause a skin rash or a burn. Tea tree oil and lavender are the only exceptions.

Do not get a massage with an essential oil after drinking, since this can cause hallucinations and nausea, Salter warns.

Pregnant women, people with allergies or chronic medical conditions such as high blood pressure, should consult a qualified practitioner for advice before using essential oils. Some essential oils such as spearmint, camphor, tea tree, and pepper can antidote homeopathic remedies and should therefore be avoided during homeopathic treatment.

Popular Essential Oils

Some essential oils that may be of interest are lavender, eucalyptus, frankincense, hyssop, geranium, cypress, ginger, marjoram, chamomile, rosemary, rosewood, thyme, and ylang ylang.

Lavender

Lavender is probably the most important essential oil used medicinally, and it is also the most versatile. Lavender is still used in Spanish folk medicine as an antidiabetic agent, and it is included in some Spanish over-the-counter herbal formulas for diabetes. Lavender's effects are said to be reviving, calming, soothing; to combat depression; and to help create emotional balance. Depression, tension, insomnia, high blood pressure, and stress are said to respond well to lavender.

In one study, when lavender was infused into rats with normal blood sugar, their blood sugars dropped. A small English study published in *The Lancet* found that lavender was about equal to hypnotic drugs in its ability to relieve insomnia, and provided more restful sleep for elderly patients. Used as an ingredient in massage oil, another study found that lavender penetrated the skin within five minutes, and was excreted within ninety minutes. Lavender is one of the few essential oils that may be directly applied to the skin, and it is sometimes used to treat burns and eczema. However, a few people with asthma or hay fever may be allergic to lavender. It should also be well-diluted if used simultaneously with homeopathic remedies.

Eucalyptus

Eucalyptus is one of the essential oils suggested for use by people with diabetes by aromatherapist Valerie Ann Worwood. As an adjunct treatment for diabetes, Worwood suggests two massages per week with eucalyptus oil in combination with other essential oils such as geranium, cypress, lavender, hyssop, or ginger, diluted in sweet almond oil. Made from the leaves and small branches of the eucalyptus tree, which is native to Australia, eucalyptus oil is quite pungent. It is versatile enough to cool the body in summer and warm it in winter. It repels insects.

Eucalyptus is anti-inflammatory, antiseptic, antibiotic, diuretic, analgesic, and deodorizing, and it also has an antiviral effect. It can help mitigate nerve pain. A massage with *Eucalyptus globulus* is said to relieve some of the pain of arthritis. In one experiment with rabbits with induced diabetes, blood sugars dropped when rabbits were exposed to the aroma of *Eucalyptus citriodora*. Do not use eucalyptus simultaneously with homeopathic remedies. It shouldn't be used more than a few days at a time. Don't use with babies or very young children.

Frankincense

Frankincense, or *olibanum*, is considered quite a spiritual oil, frequently used to perfume the air during meditation. It comes from the leaves of a tree found in North Africa. It measurably slows the rate of breathing, and calms the nerves and digestive system. Its aroma relieves anxiety and depression, and stimulates the immune system. Frankincense has wound-healing and antiseptic qualities but is safe enough to be used during pregnancy.

Hyssop

Hyssop was a revered cleansing herb in ancient Hebrew and Greek civilizations. It has stress- and anxiety-relieving qualities. Hyssop decreases fatigue while increasing alertness. Although it is something of a tonic to the circulatory system, note that hyssop can *increase* blood pressure. Do not use for more than a few days at a time or if you have epilepsy.

Geranium

Geranium balances the nervous system and helps to combat stress, apathy, anxiety, hyperactivity, and depression. Said to balance levels of hormones, geranium also acts as a tonic for the liver and kidneys. Although it is recommended for female problems such as premenstrual pain and tension, geranium should not be used during the first three months of pregnancy, or any time during pregnancy if a previous miscarriage has occurred.

Cypress

Cypress, distilled from the twigs and needles of the cypress tree, is a tonic for blood circulation. It can improve circulation, soothe cramps, and relieve the retention of fluids in the body.

Ginger

Ginger root is a common seasoning ingredient in Asian cooking, and it's been used medicinally by the Chinese for many years. Ginger essential oil, also made from the root of the plant, is a rubefacient that can help with the pain of rheumatism, muscle pain, or poor circulation. When inhaled, the aroma of ginger is said to ease mental confusion, to relieve fatigue, and to combat nerve-related exhaustion. When diluted, it's been used as a gargle for sore throat.

Sweet Marjoram

Sweet marjoram has a warm, somewhat spicy aroma. It is a vasodilator that may slightly lower high blood pressure while improving circulation. It is a tonic for the nerves, and a sedative that relieves nervous tension and can help induce restful sleep. It is also pain-relieving. Do not use during pregnancy.

Roman Chamomile

Roman chamomile essential oil is soothing and gentle. It can calm the nervous system and help induce sleep. It relieves pain, helps with digestion, and acts as a tonic for the liver. It is also said to be helpful with skin problems. However, chamomile causes skin rashes in some people. Don't get chamomile essential oil into the eyes. Don't use during the first three months of pregnancy.

Rosemary

Rosemary is said to be good for nervous exhaustion and an overstimulated brain. It reduces stress and infections. It's a stimulant of both the body and also of the mind, and an antiseptic that can be helpful in muscular problems, depression, fatigue, and diabetes, according to Worwood. In one experiment with animals, however, rosemary elevated blood sugar levels. The *Encyclopedia of Natural Remedies* recommends it be avoided by people with high blood pressure.

Rosewood

Rosewood comes from the rosewood tree of Brazil. Rosewood essential oil is said to be a tonic that is a mild painkiller, an antidepressant, and also an aphrodisiac. Rosewood is emotionally uplifting and is said to help balance the effects of stress on the nervous system.

Thyme

Thyme is believed to be one of the first plants to be used for health purposes, and it remains one of the most useful. Its fresh, outdoorsy scent is uplifting, and it can combat the blues, headaches, and the general effects of stress. An antiseptic, antibiotic, and disinfectant, thyme is said to be useful for infections, particularly those of the gastrointestinal tract and bladder. Thyme helps muscle and joint pain, stimulates the immune system, and improves circulation. Do not use thyme essential oil if you have high blood pressure, are pregnant, or taking homeopathic remedies.

Ylang Ylang

Ylang ylang is a sedative, an antidepressant, and something of a tonic for the nervous system. It can help reduce blood pressure and slow the heart rate during panic or rage. Said to be an aphrodisiac, ylang ylang is extracted from the fragrant flowers of a tropical tree that grows in countries such as Indonesia; fragrant ylang ylang flowers are traditionally spread across the nuptial bed after a wedding. In high concentrations, ylang ylang may cause nausea or headaches in some people, and also may irritate some people who are very sensitive.

Essential oils can rejuvenate and relax you, combating the ill effects of stress. Some oils may slightly lower blood sugar and blood pressure, or have a hormonal balancing effect. Aromatherapy can include a therapeutic massage by a professional aromatherapist, or self-treatment at home with aromas you like.

Part III

SPIRIT

"We are not human beings having a spiritual experience. We are spiritual beings having a human experience." —Pierre Teilhard de Chardin

SOME THERAPIES THAT MAY BE useful for people with diabetes have effects that cannot be fully explained. In this section, these are grouped together under the general heading of energy therapies.

Certain energy therapies may help some people manage symptoms of diabetes such as high blood sugar or high blood pressure. Used in tandem with good, conventional medical care, they work to strengthen the body or to heal in various ways. Some may relieve depression, provide emotional comfort, or help control symptoms such as neuropathic pain.

Many therapies included here have some connection to the subtle energies that are still being discovered in the universe. Subtle energies around us probably affect our health much more than we currently understand.

Energy therapies include acupuncture, homeopathy, Bach flower remedies, crystal therapy, light and color therapy, magnet therapy, therapeutic and healing touch, spiritual healing, and faith healing.

Chapter 18

Acupuncture

In China, the land of its inception, acupuncture is sometimes used as a primary treatment for diabetes. However, research in China shows that acupuncture is most effective when used as a complementary treatment along with diet, exercise, and medications.

Acupuncture as Therapy

Acupuncture was once used only as a pain treatment of last resort in the United States, but it is being utilized earlier now, with greater success. The World Health Organization recently added peripheral neuropathy to its list of diseases that respond well to acupuncture. Research in China shows that acupuncture treatment may lower blood sugar and blood pressure, perhaps by strengthening and rebalancing energy patterns in the body. It can be a useful treatment for anxiety or depression. Acupuncture beefs up the immune system and minimizes the chances for complications involving blood circulation. Acupuncture has also been effective as an aid in weight loss programs, if these are caused by food addictions.

Acupuncture is only one aspect of traditional Chinese medicine, but it is the part most frequently practiced in the West. Treatment involves fine needles gently pushed into one or several *acupoints* on the skin of

Moxibustion

Moxibustion is a traditional Chinese medical therapy involving the burning of mugwort over acupuncture points, which is believed to allow energy to enter the body. One small Chinese study suggests moxibustion could be a useful supplemental treatment for diabetes, according to Dr. Hui's review of diabetes treatment in the *Journal of Traditional Chinese Medicine* in 1995.

In a study of 13 people with diabetes conducted in the Fujian Province, nine of the subjects found moxibustion treatment improved the symptoms of diabetes. Blood sugar levels decreased and symptoms improved or disappeared with the use of moxibustion, according to this small study.

the body, ear, or hand. The 360 acupoints lie along 14 invisible energy pathways or circuits called *meridians*, about a dozen of which are believed to be tied into specific organs. These meridians are held to be channels for the ubiquitous life energy called *chi*, the invisible surging force of the universe believed to animate the body. In good health, according to Chinese theory, each person retains just the right amount of chi energy, balanced between its positive and negative forms, *yang* and *yin*. A shortage, excess, or imbalance of chi in parts of the body is said to result in diseases like diabetes.

Physicians in the West were initially quite skeptical about acupuncture, because acupoints and meridians do not correspond to any anatomical structure known in Western medicine. However, research has shown that acupoints have slightly different electrical and magnetic characteristics than the surrounding skin, and they contain high concentrations of nerves and blood vessels. Almost forty years ago a system of very fine ducts located where meridians are said to be was discovered by microscopic surgery. About two decades ago French researchers injected radioactive tracers into acupoints and discovered that they followed the path of the meridians channels almost exactly. When other points along the same meridian were stimulated, the flow of the tracer material also changed, indicating that the Chinese theory about changing the flow of chi was correct. A scientist in Russia also discovered that meridians conduct light, especially in the red and white spectral ranges.

Acupuncture should be administered by a licensed practitioner, or acupuncturist, many of whom are medical doctors. There are several ways to administer acupuncture, and some practitioners also use electrical devices to locate acupoints. Traditional acupuncturists use only needles, but others now use lasers, mild electricity, magnets, and even Vitamin B_{12} injections. Some practitioners heat the needles by burning mugwort or moxa on the handle of the needle before insertion. One group of practitioners uses corresponding points on the ear in a version called auricular acupuncture, or French acupuncture. Using acupoints on the hand is a Korean variation.

Some people respond better to one form of acupuncture than another. Treatment is usually described as uncomfortable or irritating rather than painful. Needles may remain in for twenty minutes or so.

It isn't a straight line from Western to Chinese medicine. For instance, high blood pressure is a very specific diagnosis in Western medicine, based on objectively measured blood pressure levels. In Chinese medicine, high blood pressure is usually called *liver heart fire*, and is not only treated differently, it's really a different diagnosis. Type 2 diabetes is also diagnosed in different ways by Chinese practitioners, depending on the type of energy imbalances sensed in the person through the taking of subtle pulses, examination of the tongue and other parts of the medical examination.

Research

In a 1988 study conducted at Royal Manchester Royal Infirmary at the University of Manchester, England, 46 patients with Type 2 diabetes who suffered chronic pain as a result of neuropathy were treated with acupuncture to determine its long-term effectiveness. Over ten weeks, patients received six courses of classical acupuncture, and 67 percent showed significant improvement. Followed up three to twelve months later, 67 percent said they were able to stop or significantly reduce their pain medication, and 77 percent noted significant improvement in their symptoms. Approximately 21 percent said their symptoms vanished completely. The authors concluded that acupuncture is a "safe and effective therapy for the long-term management of painful diabetic neuropathy."

An overview of the treatment of Xiao Ke (diabetes) by acupuncture was published in the *Journal of Traditional Chinese Medicine* in 1995. Professor Ho Hui of Bejing TCM University reviewed several Chinese studies of acupuncture treatments on people with diabetes. According to Dr. Hui, these studies show that blood sugar and insulin utilization is improved with acupuncture, allowing for a gradual reduction of medications. Generally, he said, people with Type 2 diabetes got better results from acupuncture than people with Type 1 diabetes. Approximately 25 treatments lasting about two to three months were usually required to produce results. Patients who had good dietary control and who utilized physical exercises, breathing exercises, or massage usually showed improved therapeutic effects.

In many of the Chinese studies examined by Dr. Hui, blood sugars were reduced an average of 50 percent or more. For instance, a 1980 study of people with diabetes, primarily people with Type 2, found that after acupuncture treatments, fasting blood sugars decreased almost 50 percent from an average of 308 mg./% to 160 mg./%. Postprandial blood sugars decreased 25 percent, falling from an average of 421 mg./% to 292 mg./%. In another small Chinese study of people with Type 2 diabetes, 76 percent of patients benefited from acupuncture. In this study, a greater percentage of patients benefited when acupuncture was combined with diabetes medications, although some improved when treated with acupuncture alone. Another study, of 246 people with diabetes treated by acupuncture, found the treatment markedly effective 62 percent of the time, effective 33 percent of the time, and ineffective about 4 percent of the time. In this study, average fasting blood sugar fell more than 50 percent after treatment, from an average fasting blood sugar of 383 mg./dl. to 117 mg./dl.

Acupuncture may also be helpful in the management of certain complications. According to Dr. Hui, one study in China showed acupuncture an effective treatment on diabetic urinary bladder lesions, with 90 percent effectiveness after three therapeutic courses involving a total of about 30 acupuncture treatments, versus no change in the placebo group. In another study of people with diabetic complications, including peripheral neuropathy, heart problems, and chronic diarrhea, a

---

Acupressure

Acupressure involves the use of the hands, fingers, and thumbs, which put pressure on acupuncture points. Acupressure may be administered by a trained acupressurist, but is also a form of treatment that may be self-administered or utilized at home.

Acupressure on appropriate points may help improve blood pressure and improve blood circulation. For instance, regularly pressing a acupoint called Spleen Six may help reduce blood pressure. The Spleen Six point is about four fingers up from the inner anklebone, near the edge of the shinbone. Practitioners would press this point with the thumb for about one minute, then switch legs. If you try this at home, you should feel a tingling sensation if you press the right spot. Books are available to provide guidance in finding appropriate points and in using acupressure at home.

Although acupressure is quite safe, pregnant women should avoid the abdominal area altogether and not use points such as Spleen Six and Large Intestine Four. As a matter of common sense, acupressure should never be applied to varicose veins, tumors, or wounded or infected areas, or areas where a bone may be broken.

---

marked improvement in clinical symptoms was observed after 15 treatments of acupuncture, with some beneficial effects observed on other complications such as cardiovascular lesions, hyperlipemia, and retinopathy.

While diagnoses in China varied between individuals and practitioners, Dr. Hui said about 80 percent of subjects with diabetes were diagnosed with a deficiency of chi and a deficiency of yang. The Bachshu, Front Mu, and limb points were the most frequently selected for treatment by practitioners. Some patients were treated using as many as 50 different acupoints. Treatments were given every day or two, for at least 21 treatments, and often more.

This blood sugar lowering effect also shows up in animal studies. At Hadassah University Hospital in Jerusalem, a study of rats that model insulin resistance and Type 2 diabetes in humans found that three elec-tropuncture treatments a week lowered blood sugar significantly when given for three weeks. Results were published in the European medical journal *Diabetologia* in the year 2000.

Some other forms of acupuncture have been effective. In Russia, research using microwave resonance therapy on acupuncture points on 195 people with diabetes concluded that acupuncture accelerated car-bohydrate metabolism compensation and improved blood circulation to peripheral areas, perhaps by lowering levels of stress hormones such as cortisol and adrenaline. A European study using laser acupuncture on people with diabetes with angiopathies of the lower extremities con-cluded that acupuncture reduced pain, increased blood circulation to peripheral areas, and raised skin temperatures.

Acupuncture may help people who are depressed. A Chinese study published in the *Journal of Traditional Chinese Medicine* in 1985 exam-ined people suffering a clinical or severe depression, treated either with acupuncture or with psychoactive medications. After five weeks of treatment, acupuncture was effective on 70 percent of patients, versus 65 percent cured or markedly improved on medications, according to Dr. Kenneth Pelletier. When the American Foundation of Medical Acu-puncture conducted a search of the world literature to determine the most successful applications of acupuncture, it concluded that acu-puncture benefits people with psychiatric problems such as depression or anxiety, as well as chronic pain and peripheral and central nervous system problems.

According to Time-Life's *Medical Advisor*, the use of a press nee-dle or a plastic device placed over special acupressure points on the ear can also help some people reduce cravings for food, when used as part of a program involving good diet and exercise. For this, consult an acupuncturist who is experienced in treating eating disorders.

Precautions: Acupuncture should be given by a licensed profes-sional. An estimated 2,000 or 3,000 of the more than 10,000 acupunc-turists in North America are also osteopaths or medical doctors. Sometimes, a mild depression, increased anxiety, or fatigue can follow treatment. Some people also may experience a slight rise in blood sug-ars when first treated with acupuncture, for as many as ten treatments, but this typically disappears after familiarity with the procedure. Risks of infection are minimal since practitioners now use disposable needles.

Acupuncture may help people with diabetes by strengthening the body, improving blood sugar fluctuations, and lowering blood pressure. Acupuncture may lift the spirits of people who are depressed and could be useful with certain types of eating disorders. Acupuncture can reduce the pain of diabetic neuropathy, and may be helpful with certain other complications. The next chapter examines another energy-based therapy, homeopathy, which works with a form of energy it calls the vital force.

Chapter 19

Homeopathy

Homeopathy, a gentle, energy-based medical treatment popular in the United States at the turn of the century, is regaining popularity. People as diverse as John D. Rockefeller, Henry James, and Mahatma Gandhi have been believers in homeopathic medicine. For several generations, Britain's royal family has been attended by homeopathic physicians. Approximately 3,000 health professionals practice homeopathy in the United States, including many who are medical doctors. At the moment, homeopathy is more frequently used in Europe and India than in this country. Homeopathy cannot cure diabetes, but it can greatly fortify the health of the person who has it. The greatest danger of homeopathic treatment, or any alternative therapy, is that it may delay the use of an effective conventional treatment. For this reason, people with diabetes are strongly advised to consult homeopathic practitioners who are also medical doctors or doctors of osteopathic medicine. These practitioners are most likely to understand the management of diabetes and to refer to other practitioners as necessary.

"You have to realize what Type 2 diabetes is," says Dr. Allen Neiswander, D.Ht., of Alhambra, California. "Exercise and diet are very important. You can use homeopathic remedies, and you can also use insulin and other medications." Dr. Neiswander, a distinguished medical doctor who was born into a family of homeopaths, has been practicing medicine and homeopathy for more than fifty years. "When you find your remedy, you can live much better with your diabetes. I can't promise any more than that," he says.

Homeopathy Defined

Homeopathy searches for *remedies*, plant or mineral substances that work against the physical, emotional, and psychological symptoms expressed by the patient, and stimulate healing by each person's life energy or "vital force." Remedies are made from very tiny amounts of particular substances, diluted many times in water, which are shaken vigorously between each dilution. Many doctors in the United States believe homeopathy is all placebo because they don't understand how such minute amounts of active ingredient can have an effect. However, homeopathy has a long tradition. Homeopathic preparations are pharmaceuticals and regulated by the FDA. Some companies that manufacture homeopathic remedies have been recently acquired by major pharmaceutical companies.

Homeopathic treatment is individualized according to the symptoms presented by the patient. Homeopathic doctors such as Dr. Neiswander believe the right remedy for a particular individual will hit the target every time and will not be antidoted by any form of diabetes medication.

"There are no incurable diseases, only incurable people," is a common saying in homeopathy. However, some homeopaths say there are people who do not respond to homeopathic medications. Dr. Neiswander says that understanding what remedy a patient actually needs is a fine, fine art that must be practiced for years to be accurately applied.

"Sometimes I can tell what remedy a person needs the minute they walk in the door, and other times I have to talk to them for three or four hours before I know—seeing them in the office, listening, talking on the telephone. Sometimes what the patient tells you isn't what's the problem at all," Dr. Neiswander observes. "It also takes some study on the part of the patient to know what they really want out of homeopathic treatment."

Sharon's Story

A woman we shall call Sharon was diagnosed with Type 2 diabetes at an unusually young age. Now the mother of two children, she believes that homeopathic treatment has helped her live with diabetes and other health problems for more than twenty years. As a matter of fact, Sharon was so impressed with the health benefits of homeopathy that she decided to become a homeopath herself.

"I think homeopathy has really made the difference in my not having all the problems and complications that most people with diabetes have," says Sharon, who is now 57, and approaching the age when her own father died from diabetes. "I feel like if I hadn't found homeopathy I'd be a basket case right now. I might not even still be alive."

Born in Kansas City, Missouri, Sharon was diagnosed with diabetes at the age of nineteen. Her blood sugars have fluctuated over the years, particularly in the first years after she was diagnosed, when she experienced several bouts of low blood sugar. A researcher from the Joslin Clinic told her a few years ago she might have a new type of diabetes they were identifying—a type with a strong hereditary component, somewhere between Type 1 and Type 2.

More than two decades ago Sharon was taking a sulfonylurea drug for diabetes when she also began to have problems with allergies. In addition, she experienced serious problems with blood sugar control when she became pregnant in 1972. Before she got pregnant, her blood sugars were higher than normal, but afterward, her blood sugars became very unstable, rising into the 300 mg./dl. range, and also falling so low she passed out several times from low blood sugar. Her medical doctor wanted to put her on insulin since diabetes pills cannot be taken during pregnancy, but Sharon refused to take insulin because her father hadn't done well on it. Instead, she did some medical research in a California medical library and put herself on the very low carbohydrate diet advocated by Dr. Richard Bernstein. This diet, she says, helped her normalize her blood sugars during pregnancy.

After her son was born, Sharon developed a yeast infection. Her medical doctor used cortisone to treat the allergies, but this made her diabetes worse. Medical treatment became a vicious circle, with each new medication aggravating a different medical problem. It got to the point where Sharon was allergic to all the medications that could help her, including antibiotic and antifungal drugs. She also suffered from allergies to pollens, chlorine, and certain perfumes. Finally, her doctors told her she'd just have to live with the yeast infection, since she was allergic to every medication they could use to treat it.

About this time, Sharon's old college roommate came to visit. A biochemist engaged in medical research at the University of Kansas, the old roommate opened her travel bag and gave Sharon a homeopathic remedy, *Sepia 6X*. After Sharon took it, the burning and itching from the yeast infection went away in twenty minutes. But the yeast infection returned a week later, after her roommate had gone home. The former roommate suggested to Sharon that she might consult a professional homeopath.

Sharon located a medical doctor who was also a homeopath in the town where she was then living. After filling out a written questionnaire, she answered some questions in a face-to-face interview in the doctor's office. She was given another remedy, *Sepia 10M*, which, she said, "worked in three seconds. I've always reacted. If it's the right remedy, I feel sort of woozy for a second or two."

Sharon was elated at the immediate relief. "Can you cure my diabetes, and my allergies, and treat my children, too?" she asked the homeopathic doctor.

"Well, diabetes isn't curable, so we'll have to be careful," he said. "We can stave off a lot of the problems, but as you get older, they'll come back. At some point, you will need more than homeopathy."

The homeopathic doctor did say that he could cure her allergies, but it would take a long time, probably two years. And he also said he could take care of her kids, if she'd assemble a small kit of homeopathic remedies she could work with at home, via telephone consultations.

Sharon continued on the Bernstein diet, and was treated with various homeopathic remedies. She saw her homeopath every month at first, then every three months. Within eight months, she says, her allergies were under control and her yeast infection had cleared up. Also, her diabetes had greatly improved. This showed up not only in home glucose testing, but in the results of the two glucose tolerance tests shown below. The first test was taken July 4, 1975, before Sharon began homeopathy. The second was taken June 20, 1979, six months after treatment by a homeopathic practitioner.

OGTT	Before Homeopathy	After Homeopathy
Fasting	89 mg./%	96 mg./%
Half hr	187	42
1 hour	205	140
2 hours	155	104
3 hours	101	92
4 hours	69	87
5 hours	80	98

For over twenty years now, Sharon has controlled Type 2 diabetes through attention to her diet and with homeopathy. All of her homeopaths have been medical doctors or doctors of osteopathy. She tested her blood sugars at home, several times a day, and apprised her physicians of her results. Her blood sugar levels were acceptable, enabling her to stay off diabetes medications and to continue with homeopathy. When her first homeopath retired, after training Sharon as a homeopath, she found another homeopath who was also a medical doctor to treat her. To take care of herself, Sharon has regularly seen eye doctors, and has her feet inspected on a regular basis by specialists.

"My ophthalmologist says that by looking at my eyes, he would never have guessed that I was diabetic, particularly for 37 years," Sharon says. "My podiatrist says the circulation in my feet is excellent. I attribute the lack of complications to homeopathy."

She adds, "Up until recently, other than the few times I was ill or had surgery, I've been able to keep my blood sugars normal with homeopathy for the last 22 years."

Her current homeopath, a medical doctor who was trained in the treatment of diabetes before he turned to homeopathy, suggested she see another medical doctor when her blood sugars began climbing about eight months before this interview.

Sharon's first HbA1c test was 7.6. She is currently on metformin, a diabetes medication, and working with her new diabetologist to stabilize her blood sugars, after which she plans to return to her homeopathic practitioner. At five foot two inches and 180 pounds, Sharon is admittedly overweight. She is unable to exercise because of back surgery she had as a young girl, which makes even a few minutes of walking painful. Still, she is controlling the symptoms of diabetes and her spirits are good. She now practices homeopathy at an integrated medicine clinic, supervised by a medical doctor, in a large city in the Midwest.

Homeopathic Remedies

Since the time of Samuel Hahnemann, the German physician who discovered homeopathy, homeopaths have conducted many "provings" of particular substances that document their effects. Symptoms recorded during provings are believed to be mirror images of the diseases the remedies are intended to cure. Homeopathic remedies may be diluted 10, 100, or 1,000 times, marked with a Roman numeral X, C, or M. After each dilution, remedies are given a vigorous shaking called a *descussion*. Remedies that are the most dilute are believed to be the most potent. Skeptics never get tired of pointing out that very dilute remedies that are the most potent probably do not contain one single molecule from the original formulation. But some homeopaths speculate that their remedies, which are in fact mostly water, may contain a powerful but subtle energy, or even a memory or an imprint of the original material, which makes them work.

Dana Ullman, a Berkeley, California, homeopathic practitioner who has written many books on homeopathy, notes that certain medications antidote homeopathic remedies. Some homeopathic remedies also antidote other remedies. A few homeopathic preparations are made from substances that are poisonous in large doses, such as arsenic or belladonna.

Classical Homeopathy

"Classical" homeopaths such as Dr. Neiswander prescribe only one remedy at a time. Before they prescribe, they question patients at length about their emotional state, taste preferences, aversions, climactic preferences, and location of their symptoms. The remedies they suggest, which are carefully matched with the symptoms of a particular person, are called *constitutional* remedies. As diagnostic aids, a few younger

Study Groups

One way to learn more about homeopathy is to join a homeopathic study group. Such informal study groups are part of a long tradition in homeopathic medicine, even among faculty members at homeopathic schools.

Some lay groups are similar to support groups, in that they allow patients who use homeopathy to discuss their thoughts and experiences about homeopathic treatment. Members share information with one another, and invite professional homeopaths in to discuss their treatment specialties. A few discussion and study groups are also conducted on the Internet.

The National Center for Homeopathy, listed in Appendix A, can provide a list of such groups upon request.

homeopaths also use kinesiology, or devices that measure electrical pressure at acupoints.

Each homeopathic remedy is given in a single dose or course of treatment, usually in the form of pills that dissolve under the tongue. With homeopathic remedies, once symptoms begin to go away, it's recommended that the medicine be stopped. Some liken this method to jump-starting a car. The same rule applies if a remedy is not working. It's recommended you stop taking the remedy, return to the practitioner for another evaluation, and then start another remedy, rather than increasing the dose of the remedy that isn't having an effect. After one remedy is tried, perhaps a month is given to clear the chemical out of the system before another is prescribed. Classical homeopathy is sometimes seen as similar to peeling an onion, in that the remedies can solve one problem only to unmask a deeper one, leading to a treatment process that sometimes takes months or years.

There are no over-the-counter homeopathic remedies for diabetes, as there are for colds and minor medical conditions.

Homeopathy may be helpful in managing the symptoms of diabetes such as high blood sugar, and other symptoms such as high blood pressure. However, Ullman notes, it's difficult to withdraw people with diabetes from their medications. People with diabetes should be carefully monitored, and medications such as insulin slowly reduced. Ideally, people with diabetes should be treated by a homeopath who is also a medical doctor.

Homeopathy can be tried as part of a weight reduction strategy. Over-the-counter mixtures such as *Argentum nitricum* are sometimes useful for intense sugar cravings. If you are attempting this type of treatment yourself, a professional homeopath should be consulted if you see no effect on your dieting in a month or two.

Research

Two studies in prestigious British medical journals have concluded that there is some scientific proof that homeopathy works. One study, a meta-analysis published in *The Lancet* in 1997, reviewed several dozen studies from around the world. The authors found patients treated homeopathically were 2.45 times more likely to receive positive therapeutic effects than patients receiving a placebo. A 1991 meta-analysis published in the *British Medical Journal* reviewed 107 studies, selected the 22 that were most rigorously conducted, and found that 15 of those contained evidence that homeopathy worked. The authors said the evidence they examined would "establish homeopathy as a regular treatment for certain indications."

There are few good research studies of homeopathy on people with diabetes. One of these is a double-blind, randomized, controlled study of the effects of *Arnica 5C* on diabetic retinitis, which was conducted in 1992. In this study, 47 percent of the patients who were given Arnica experienced measurable improvement in blood flow to the eye, while only 1 percent of the control group experienced improvement. In addition, 52 percent of patients given the *Arnica 5C* experienced improved blood flow to other parts of the body, while less than 2 percent of the control group showed similar improvements.

A 1992 study in Russia used a minimal homeopathic treatment on 68 patients with diabetes. Researchers found a statistically valid reduction in high blood sugar and glucosuria, allowing doctors to reduce the average dose of sugar reducing drugs.

Using Homeopathic Remedies

Here are a general few tips on using homeopathic medicines, which should be taken as directed by your homeopathic practitioner.

- Clean mouth of other flavors such as food, alcohol, coffee, or toothpaste twenty minutes before and after taking a homeopathic remedy.

- Before you take it, read the label. Make sure it is a homeopathic remedy, and also the one you wish to use at the proper potency.

- Nancy Bruning and Corey Weinstein, M.D., authors of *Healing Homeopathic Remedies*, advise the patient not to touch the pills— rather, tap each pill into the bottle cap or onto a clean piece of white paper, then take it. Throw away pills that are spilled.

- Pills should dissolve on the tongue or under it, unless chewable pills are prescribed.

- Avoid nasal sprays, liniments, camphorated medicines, and antiperspirants while taking homeopathic remedies, says Dr. A.C. Neiswander's *Homeopathic Guide for the Family*. Caffeine and nicotine can also interfere with the action of some remedies.

- Homeopathic remedies should be stored in a cool, dark, clean cupboard, out of reach of children. Remedies should be kept away from heat, light, and strong odors. Bottles should be kept closed when not in use.

A double-blind trial of adults and children who were anxious and had problems sleeping compared an over-the-counter French homeopathic preparation of plant extracts called Quietude with the well-known tranquilizer diazepam (Valium). Both preparations relieved sleeplessness and minor nervous tension 63 percent of the time. However, the homeopathic preparation produced no side effects, while some of subjects who took diazepam experienced daytime dizziness and drowsiness.

Homeopathy and Diabetes

Homeopathic remedies should be individualized, but Dr. Hahnemann stated that some forms of diabetes could be cured by *Argentum*, when symptoms called for it. Michael M. Bouko Levy, a French homeopath, wrote that diabetes cannot be cured by homeopathy but may be controlled and treated by remedies such as *Eugenia jambolana*, *Juglans regia*, *Iris versicolor*, *Natrum sulphuricum*, *Conium*, *Nux vomica*, *Sulfur*, and *Phosphorus*. Another well-known homeopath, George Vithoulkas, has written that homeopathy can benefit people with Type 2 diabetes if complications have not become serious. Homeopathy can sometimes make it possible to discontinue diabetes drugs, Vithoulkas wrote, allowing people to control it by diet and further treatment. Vithoulkas says that the administration of insulin does not interfere with the action of homeopathic remedies, although the amount needed may vary during treatment.

Writing in the *Journal of the British Homeopathic Association*, Janet Gray, a British homeopath, stated that constitutional homeopathic treatments can bolster the general health of a person with diabetes, steadying the secretion of insulin and blood sugar. While homeopathy is not suitable as a primary treatment for diabetes, depending on the person and their symptoms, Gray may suggest constitutional remedies such as *Syzgium*, *Uranium nitricum*, or *Phloridzin*.

As adjunct treatments, Gray suggests the complementary use of homeopathic remedies such as *Conium*, *Plumbum*, or a low potency *Calendula* lotion for symptoms of neuropathy. For retinopathy, homeopathy may complement conventional treatments such as laser therapy with remedies like *Lachesis* or *Mamamelis*. Homeopathic remedies such as *Apis mellifica*, *Natrum muriaticum*, *Lycopodium*, or *Sulfur* may help improve renal function in nephropathy, while maintaining good control of blood sugars will minimize the danger of kidney damage. For impotence, in addition to a constitutional remedy, *Coca*, Phosphoric acid, or *Moschu* might be tried with particular individuals, she suggests.

Steven L. Subotnick practices homeopathy in a managed care setting. A homeopath who was first trained as a podiatrist, Dr. Subotnick recommends appropriate vitamin and mineral supplements along with homeopathy. Many of his patients with diabetes are on several medications, and he works in tandem with their doctors. Writing in the *Journal of the American Institute of Homeopathy*, Dr. Subotnick stated he begins treating people with Type 2 diabetes using three to five drops of a combination "cocktail" containing *Psorinoheel, Lymphomyosot, Gallium*, and *Syzygesium* in a glass of water three times per day, sometimes adding *Secale, Coenzyme*, or *Ubichinon compositum* when indicated. Working with conventional physicians to monitor levels of medications and reduce them as necessary, he then proceeds to single remedies appropriate to each patient, at repetitively low doses.

Homeopathy can't cure diabetes, but it can be quite useful. Ideally, homeopathic practitioners should also be medical doctors. Classical homeopathy, which prescribes remedies tailored to the patient, is the best way to proceed. The next chapter examines the Bach flower remedies, developed by a homeopathic medical doctor, and other forms of subtle energy that could be useful in overcoming some of the strong emotions and upsets associated with diabetes.

Chapter 20

Bach Flower Remedies and Crystals

Bach flower essences and similar subtle energy products are said to relieve stress, rebalance the system, and help people deal with unpleasant emotions and emotional problems. Crystals and gems, two other New Age favorites, could be useful as an adjunct treatment, although there isn't much research that proves they work.

Bach Flower Remedies

English bacteriologist and homeopath Edward Bach, M.D., was a sensitive individual who spent much of his relatively short life searching for mild, nontoxic treatments for particular medical problems. Dr. Bach abandoned his medical practice in London and moved to the English countryside in 1930. His unusual discovery is said to have occurred as he was walking through the countryside early one morning. Overcome by intense emotions, Dr. Bach is said to have intuitively spread a bit of flower dew on his lips, which, amazingly, brought him back to a normal state of mind. Roaming the countryside over the next few years, through a process of trial and error, placing petals of particular flowers on his sensitive tongue, Dr. Bach eventually discovered 38 flowers of a "higher order." Now known as the Bach Flower Remedies, these are said to be useful in rebalancing emotional energy patterns and relieving certain types of mild emotional grief or pain.

Dr. Bach believed that emotions such as bitterness, lasting grief, terror, resentment, and doubt were precursors to illness. He theorized that these negative emotions were created when an individual's personality somehow became disconnected from its true spiritual purpose. He believed that his flower essences replaced or balanced negative emotions with more positive emotions such as love, wisdom, gentleness, courage, or joy. No reputable scientific studies of Bach's remedies have been completed, although one small and poorly designed trial done as part of a doctoral thesis in California did find a beneficial effect, according to the Bach Centre in Great Britain.

Bach's liquid tinctures are prepared by placing fresh flowers in bowls of spring water while dew remains on the flower petals, and then letting the flowers sit in sunlight for several hours. This process is believed to leave a shadow or "imprint" from the combination of flower, dew, and sunlight. After that, brandy is added to the water to create a mother tincture.

Flower essence practitioners can recommend particular remedies, or remedies may be self-selected. Dr. Bach meant his flower essences to be taken one at a time and targeted to particular problems. His *Rescue Remedy*, the only combination he devised, is a blend of clematis, cherry plum, papatiens, rock rose, and star-of-Bethlehem. Rescue Remedy is indicated for acute grief, anxiety, or panic attacks; shock or trauma of body or mind; or before or after stressful events such as a visit to the doctor or a stressful job interview. It is said to take effect within about twenty minutes.

Among the other Bach remedies, *white chestnut* is said to be good for obsessive thoughts, self-talk, or mental tapes occurring over and over, perhaps interrupting sleep, concentration, and peace of mind. *Wild rose* is intended for apathetic, pessimistic people or those suffering from a potentially terminal illness. *Walnut* is for people adapting to life transitions, such as marriage, divorce, menopause, or other stressful life changes. *Gentian, gorse,* and *sweet chestnut* are said to be useful in treating various levels of the blues, or depression. *Pine* is said to carry the vibration of forgiveness for people who are perfectionists and too critical of themselves. *Wild oat* purportedly carries a sense of purpose to people who feel dissatisfied with life. *Hornbeam* is for procrastinators who are weary and fatigued, carrying a vibration of internal vitality.

Other Flower Remedies

In addition to the original remedies devised by Dr. Bach, several competing flower essences are produced in different parts of the world. These include a few that are said to be helpful for people with diabetes.

Utilizing mostly native California and North American flowers, the Flower Essence Society produces *Apricot Flower Essence*, said to be useful for emotional ups and downs related to imbalances in blood sugar, particularly low blood sugar. Pegasus Products of Loveland, Colorado, sells a *Banana Flower Essence*, said to have a similar effect, as well as being helpful in weight-loss programs where the excess weight is produced by abnormal metabolism of sugar.

Other flower essences are the rare orchid essences developed by African Andreas Korte, and Australian Bush Flower Essences developed by Australian herbalist Ian White. These may be harder to find in the United States, but are available via mail order.

Crystals

Crystals and gemstones attempt to tap a different kind of energy found in stones.

Crystals are stones whose atoms are arranged in symmetrical patterns. Crystals of different colors, particularly those made of quartz, are believed to contain forms of subtle electromagnetic energy that may be useful in bolstering health. Amethyst, rose quartz, and herkimer quartz are piezoelectric stones that can store, receive, or emit electrical energy. Theoretically, thought is an electromagnetic activity.

There is not much research on crystals, but one doctor has found them useful during the treatment of depression. In the book *Miracles Can Happen*, neurologist C. Norman Shealy recounts an experiment using crystals as an adjunct therapy for people who were depressed. In

1988, at his Springfield, Missouri, pain clinic, half a group of 140 chronically depressed patients received either a clear quartz crystal, or a glass crystal that was a placebo. Patients were asked to "mentally program" the crystal using a short healing phrase or affirmation stating their health goal. After that, crystals were worn around the neck for two weeks. After two weeks Dr. Shealy found that 85 percent of both groups were improved. However, when they were followed up from three to six months later, 80 percent of the people who used the quartz crystals remained improved, while only 28 percent of those who used the glass crystals reported the same level of improvement. According to these results, Dr. Shealy states the probability is less than one chance in 1,000 that the quartz crystals didn't have a positive effect.

Since 1989, Dr. Shealy has recommended the use of crystals to reinforce results obtained from his program. He says that 85 percent of the people who finish the program when using a quartz crystal are improved. However, he admits that the way crystals work is certainly "beyond the known laws of science."

Crystals are said to hold positive and negative magnetic energy patterns. Practitioners recommend that they be cleansed of negative energy before being used. Cleaning may be accomplished by various methods— one is by placing the stone in water with a few drops of Pennyroyal flower essence for about fifteen minutes.

Although it might seem ridiculous, swallowing gemstone powders is a treatment for some disorders in Ayurvedic medicine. Gemstones are burned to the consistency of ash before being ingested. In the ancient Vedic texts, gemstones were said to have sprung from the demon, Vala, who ruled the universe until he was tricked and slain by demigods. According to this colorful legend, Vala's scattered body parts became precious gems with intrinsic potencies and talismanic powers.

In India, healers using gemstones often place various gemstones for twenty to forty-five minutes on the chakras of a client who is lying on his or her back. Gemstones of primary colors are used on particular chakras, in an effort to rebalance the body and to speed healing. For this, beginning from the lower chakra and working up, healers use red rubies or garnets for the first or lowest chakra, orange carnelian or orange jasper for the next, followed by amber, yellow citrine or yellow topaz, green emeralds or malachite, blue sapphires or lapis lazuli, vio-

Using Flower Essences

Flower essence practitioners are happy to make recommendations on particular essences. If you prefer to do it yourself, the literature may be studied for remedies that "sound right." For the Bach remedies, questionnaires allow self-testing for various life issues.

Dr. Bach himself made only one combination mixture, but he sometimes used several essences in treating other people. Today, experts recommend using a maximum of five to seven essences at a time. Once remedies are selected, brandy, apple cider vinegar, or vegetable glycerin should be added to the amber dropper bottle that holds the remedies; this helps curtail bacterial growth. After that, fill to the top with spring water and shake well.

Mixtures may be taken as drops under the tongue, or mixed with water or juice. Bottles should be kept away from excessive heat, cold, sunlight, and electrical appliances.

Most remedies should be taken a minimum of four times per day, for a minimum of six to eight weeks. Changes are usually gradual but may be seen in two weeks to a month, practitioners say.

let amethyst or violet fluorite, and rose quartz or magenta for the highest or crown chakra. More on the therapeutic use of color may be found in the next chapter on light therapy.

"Gem elixirs" are similar to flower essences. These are made from gemstones placed in water and left in direct sunlight, a process said to transfer an imprint of the gem's energy onto the water.

Tapping subtle energies from flowers and stones, flower essences and crystals may help you manage unpleasant emotions such as resentment, fear, and anger. There is very little scientific evidence in favor of these healing modalities so far, although one study did find quartz crystals useful as an adjunct treatment for depression.

The next chapter discusses a healing modality that enters the body through the eyes—light and color therapy.

Chapter 21

Light and Color Therapies

The full color spectrum of natural light, even in its invisible ultraviolet frequencies, may be beneficial to your overall health. Ultraviolet light helps lower blood pressure and has many other health benefits. Light therapies may relieve stress or help treat particular ailments such as depression. Using the vibrant visible color spectrum of light, color therapists also employ color to enhance healing.

Gods of the sun were probably the first worshiped by pagan man, an intuitive acknowledgment of sunlight's importance to life. Lights of various colors were used to treat illness by priests in ancient Egypt, and in ancient Rome. In the early 1900s, heliotherapy, the so-called "sun cure," a therapeutic exposure to sunlight, was often prescribed for diseases such as diabetes, tuberculosis, and gangrene. Research beginning in the 1930s used exposures to natural sunlight to lower blood pressure in people with high blood pressure. In some early experiments, just one treatment of sunlight measurably lowered blood pressure for up to six days.

Light and the Body

Natural light may be seen as a nutrient, an unacknowledged but important contributor to the smooth functioning of the body. Some doctors recommend daily exposure to the same natural, full-spectrum light that bathed our primitive ancestors for many hours a day. Jacob Liberman, O.D., Ph.D., author of *Light: Medicine of the Future*, recommends an hour a day of sunlight without glasses. Holistic physician Dr. C. Norman Shealy recommends, if possible, being outside in natural light without glasses for at least two hours a day for general health purposes, but avoiding the hours of peak intensity before and after noon.

Sunlight helps the body synthesize natural Vitamin D, which is different and probably better than the synthetic Vitamin D added to milk. In his book *Sunlight*, Dr. Zane Kime states that blood sugar, the rate of breathing, resting heart rate, and levels of lactic acid in the blood after exercise all *decrease* after a series of exposures to sunlight. Dr. Kime states that exposures to sunlight increase energy, strength, endurance, and stress tolerance, as well as the blood's ability to absorb and carry oxygen to the cells of the body.

Artificial light does not have the same beneficial effects as real sunlight, since it does not contain the entire spectrum of colors found in sunlight. Full-spectrum fluorescent lights sold for use at home, at school, or in the workplace are said to create a more pleasant and productive environment, which is beneficial to health.

The visible and invisible energy of light rockets through the sense organs of the eyes and directly up the nervous system to the hypothalamus of the brain, which Liberman calls the endocrine system's "master control center." This part of the brain helps regulate water balance, blood circulation, body temperature, and sugar and fat metabolism. The hypothalamus connects with the pineal gland and the pituitary gland, which help control the endocrine system. The hypothalamus balances body and mind as a nexus between the parasympathetic and sympathetic nervous systems, which switch on and off during stress and stress relief. The limbic system, which controls emotions, and the cerebral cortex are also impacted by the intake of light. Among their other benefits, emerging bright light therapies and full-spectrum light boxes may boost levels of serotonin, an important neurotransmitter. Low levels of serotonin are linked to many health problems, including depression and eating disorders.

John Ott, Sc.D., a leading light researcher, believes that a certain amount of light is necessary to support life. All the wavelengths found in sunlight, including the visible color spectrum and the invisible forms, such as X rays, microwaves, radio waves, and infrared and ultraviolet light, are beneficial in normal amounts. Dr. Ott believes that humans, like plants, utilize a type of photosynthesis. This involves solar energy cells on the skin and body, similar to the Langerhans cells in the pancreas, which help produce carbohydrates, proteins, and even DNA.

Earthly Rhythm

The rhythm of life on earth is the rhythm of light. Circadian rhythms are natural cycles or rhythms in living things, which are timed to the rotation of the earth and the passing of night and day. Circadian rhythms affect levels of hormones and almost a hundred body functions. The most obvious circadian rhythm is sleep, which we usually do in the absence of light.

Certain sleep disorders and certain forms of depression respond to light therapy. Light therapy boxes are devices that use light from 2,500 to 10,000 lux, which is about the strength of natural light around dawn or dusk. As a point of reference, 1 lux is the light of one candle. Bright light therapies sometimes work to treat forms of craving for carbohydrates, or *bulimia nervosa*, which strike some people during the winter months, when levels of light are low. Light therapies can be an effective first treatment for depression, with no side effects.

Light starvation is thought to intensify certain health problems such as depression, fatigue, difficulty concentrating, and the general effects of stress. In addition to seasonal factors, light starvation is believed to come from poor indoor lighting that does not contain the full spectrum of light.

Light is the treatment of choice for seasonal affective disorder, a form of depression that usually occurs during the winter months. Seasonal affective disorders affect from 1 to 5 percent of the populations of civilized countries, with incidence greater in the northern latitudes where there is less light during the winter. In Canada this disorder is so common that every university hospital has an SAD clinic, according to Dr. Raymond Lam of the University of British Columbia Faculty of Medicine in Vancouver. In research published in the year 2000 by Anna

Wirz-Justice, a professor of psychiatry at the University of Basel in Switzerland, 10,000 lux light boxes were used thirty minutes per day on people with seasonal affective disorder. "Light is as effective as antidepressant medications are, perhaps more so," she stated in the *Journal of the American Medical Association.*

Light could be an effective treatment for other forms of depression. Dr. Daniel Kripke, director of the Circadian Pacemaker Laboratory at the University of California at San Diego, looked at recent research on nonseasonal depression. He noted that bright light therapy produced reductions in mood symptoms of 12 to 35 percent, which is comparable with results with antidepressant medications.

Ultraviolet Light

The invisible ultraviolet light spectrum is important to good health and probably necessary in small doses. While overexposure is believed to increase the incidence of skin cancers, very small amounts of ultraviolet light may be used therapeutically to great effect. According to Dr. Liberman, studies have shown that ultraviolet light lowers blood pressure, reduces serum cholesterol, assists in weight loss, increases calcium absorption, increases levels of sex hormones, and increases heart efficiency. Solitrol, a hormone in the skin, produced by the action of ultraviolet light, influences circadian rhythms and the immune system. Scientists speculate that simple forms of communication between the cells in our body take place via the ultraviolet light cells emit in small quantities.

Research at the Tulane School of Medicine exposed 20 people to small amounts of ultraviolet light, and 18 of these averaged a 39 percent increase in the efficiency of their hearts, which could pump more blood. In another experiment, researchers in Russia used ultraviolet therapy on 169 patients with narrowed brain arteries, and found the circulation to their brains improved after treatment and at one year afterward.

Some experts also believe ultraviolet light stimulates the thyroid gland, causing an uptick in metabolism, which burns more calories. Farm animals fatten up faster when they are indoors, rather than when outdoors and exposed to light, Dr. Liberman says. Some studies have shown that animals lose weight when exposed to ultraviolet light. During the 1930s, the heyday of heliotherapy, doctors in Switzerland observed that their clients taking the sun cure had very little fat on their bodies, and well-developed muscles, even though they hadn't exercised in months. This is one reason to do some of your exercise outdoors, if you are trying to lose weight.

Contrary to conventional medical wisdom, Dr. Liberman says that wearing sunglasses that block ultraviolet rays, rather than being a good health behavior, actually may contribute to certain degenerative eye diseases such as macular degeneration, because ultraviolet light is necessary for the division of pigment epithelium cells in the eye. This is not widely accepted.

Precautions: Some ultraviolet wavelengths can be quite harmful. While a little natural sunlight is safe, any therapy involving ultraviolet light should only be performed under the supervision of a medical specialist specifically trained in UV therapy. Of course, never look directly into the sun.

Color Therapy

Most doctors agree that invisible forms of light such as X rays and microwaves have a role in maintaining human health. However, many remain skeptical about the effects of the visible light spectrum, which consists of all the colors we can see.

In the only form of visible light therapy that is accepted in conventional diabetes medical treatment, ophthamologists use green-argon lasers to treat diabetic retinopathy. In maternity wards, blue lights are also commonly used to rid premature babies of yellow jaundice. In an experiment at the San Diego State University School of Nursing, exposing the hands to blue light relieved some pain of rheumatoid arthritis. In another small study, a blinking red light relieved migraine headaches in 72 percent of patients.

In 1951 a Russian scientist found that the color red stimulates the sympathetic nervous system below the neck, and that the color blue stimulates the parasympathetic portion, which is mostly above the neck.

Dr. Liberman believes that colors may be medically coordinated with the chakras of yogic theory. The chakras, or energy centers, beginning near the sex organs and rising up through the body to the head,

Healing with Light

In the United States, the Society for Light Treatment and Biological Rhythms is setting standards for the use of light boxes and other devices, which may be used under a doctor's care.

One device, the Shealy Relaxmate, looks like a set of black plastic goggles. As you slip them on, you see a red adjustable flashing light pulsing in the slow, relaxing "alpha" range, or from 1 to 7.5 cycles per second. Dr. C. Norman Shealy, who developed the therapeutic goggles, says they operate on the principal of biological entrainment. Just as we automatically tap our feet in time to music, the brain responds to pulsing light, sound, or magnetic energy by gliding into sync with it. Using the goggles helps regulate beta endorphins and key hormones such as testosterone and estrogen, Dr. Shealy says. He claims that 90 percent of the people who use the Relaxmate feel deeply relaxed within ten minutes. People who are depressed and people with high blood pressure have measurably improved after using this device, according to research. Dr. Shealy recommends the goggles be used for fifteen minutes at a time, twice a day, plus an hour at night before retiring. Treatment may be combined with self-hypnosis audiotapes, he says, producing greater relaxation.

John Downing, O.D., Ph.D., has developed a color- and light-producing device said to improve symptoms of stress, hormonal imbalances, insomnia, depression, fatigue, fear, anxiety, and other disorders. The Lumatron Ocular Light Stimulator consists of a large light box mounted in front of a couch, at about eye level. During therapy, the patient looks into the lights flashing at frequencies corresponding to brain wave activity—red colors in the most rapid "beta" range, and violet colors pulsing in the much slower "theta" or "delta" ranges.

Precaution: People susceptible to epileptic seizures may have a seizure triggered by flashing lights, particularly at faster speeds, so Dr. Gerber advises that a neurologist should perform EEG brain wave testing with a flickering strobe light prior to the use of Downing's light box.

are roughly coordinated with the major glands of the endocrine system. Dr. Liberman matches red with the lower or first chakra, containing the genitals; orange with the second or spleen chakra; yellow with the third or solar plexus chakra, containing the pancreas; green with the fourth chakra, containing the heart and thymus; blue with the fifth chakra, containing the thyroid and parathyroid glands; indigo with the sixth chakra, containing the pituitary gland; and violet with the seventh or crown chakra, containing the pineal gland.

Dr. Liberman states that people are often unreceptive to particular colors, but that they coordinate almost 100 percent with the portions of their bodies that hold and develop disease. Under this theory, the color yellow would coordinate with diabetes.

In treating people with light, Dr. Liberman begins with exposures to colors some distance away on the color spectrum. Working for a few minutes at a time, he gradually brings people around to exposures of the color to which they are adverse. Sometimes, he writes, this triggers the release of old psychological trauma, which can be a breakthrough in the treatment of disease.

An older system of light therapy, developed by Dinshah Ghadiali in India, in 1920, held that yellow light strengthened the nerves and stimulated higher intellectual functioning. Yellow light was therefore considered a great restorer for people who were depleted by what we might term stress. The Dinshah Health Society in Malaga, New Jersey, has information on this form of light therapy.

Dr. Kate W. Baldwin, a surgeon, worked with Dinshah's color therapy system for several years at Woman's Hospital in Philadelphia. Dr. Baldwin was impressed by what color therapy could do. In an article in the *Atlantic Medical Journal*, April 1927, Dr. Baldwin said she could produce quicker and more accurate results using color for certain conditions than all other methods combined, with no side effects. Cardiac lesions, inflammatory conditions of the eyes, glaucoma, and cataracts all responded to color therapy, she wrote. Dr. Baldwin noted that each chemical element gives off a color wave: hydrogen emits red, oxygen emits blue, and so forth. This is useful in treatment. For example, Dr. Baldwin said, burns, caused by the red side of the color spectrum from hydrogen, could be treated with blue from oxygen—perhaps holding a

Healthy Colors

According to color therapists, particular colors are generally associated with health in the following manner:

Color	Alleged Health Benefit
Red	Stimulates nervous system, increases production of red blood cells
Orange	Stimulates vital energy, thyroid gland, and pulmonary regeneration
Yellow	Stimulates pancreatic and digestive function
Green	Stimulates mind/body balance, disinfects, helps liver or kidney toxicity, useful for cardiovascular
Blue	Calms the nervous system
Indigo	Eases pain, helps endocrine system
Violet	A spiritual color, calms nervous system

blue panel over the burn, 18 inches away for twenty minutes or so. Color treatment relieved nervous strain and made healing more rapid, she wrote.

At the moment, some acupuncturists are experimenting with a technique called *colorpuncture*, said to transfer light from acupoints to various organs. Some practitioners of reflexology use red LED light beams to stimulate reflex points on the feet, while a few use the entire mix of visible colors.

Color Reflexology

London reflexologist, color therapist, and author Pauline Wills, principal tutor of the Oracle School of Colour in London, believes that people are surrounded and interpenetrated by vibrational energies of color, which have an ability to accelerate healing. One of her tools, a light-emitting device called the "crystal torch," is designed to focus various colors onto reflex points on the feet. The color yellow is believed to particularly benefit the third or solar plexus chakra, probably the most important chakra to people with diabetes, since it is the location of the pancreas and digestive system. The solar plexus chakra is believed to supply pranic energy to the adrenal glands, which release stress hormones, as well as to the pancreas. If a particular chakra needs rebalancing—for instance, if the patient suffers from tension related to stress-induced high blood pressure—Wills's therapy might direct blue light, which is cooling and relaxing, onto the solar plexus chakra reflex points on the right and left feet.

In treating patients by color reflexology, Wills uses light that includes not only the selected therapeutic color but also its *opposite* on the color spectrum. Violet is a complementary color to yellow, for instance, which she says may be used on reflex points to help regulate blood sugar levels in patients with certain types of diabetes.

In general, color therapists believe that red light stimulates the nervous system and increases red blood cell production. Orange light is believed to stimulate the thyroid gland and regenerate lung tissue and vital energy. Green light is believed to be a mind/body balancer, a disinfectant, and useful for heart problems. With its complementary color, magenta, green is believed to be helpful in treating toxicity problems in the liver, kidneys, or colon. Blue is believed to have a calming influence on the nervous system, especially for someone who's overstimulated or afraid. Indigo, a combination of blue and violet, is believed helpful to the parathyroid or pituitary glands, and to help ease pain. Violet is believed to have a tranquilizing effect on the nervous system, and it is a color associated with spirituality.

Although it is a bit far-out, some color therapists even associate the colors of foods with how those foods might resonate in the chakras. Colors of foods in their natural state are said to be an expression of their light energy, which is very high in plants. Yellow foods, which would by this theory be beneficial to the third chakra, would include bananas, pineapples, yellow cheese, corn, lemons, grapefruit, honeydew melons, and egg yolks. As yet, no research has tested these ideas, which are called the "rainbow diet." Dr. Gabriel Cousens, author of *Spiritual Nutrition and the Rainbow Diet*, recommends a vegetarian diet composed of red, orange, and yellow foods in the morning; yellow, green, and blue foods at midday; and blue, indigo, violet, and golden foods in the evening. He says this diet matches the changing spectrum of natural light as it moves through the day.

Color Breathing

If you are visually oriented, a meditation technique called "color breathing" may be useful in relieving stress and achieving deep relaxation. Color breathing involves a visualization—breathing in particular colors through each chakra, from the bottom up, in successive order. Color therapist Wills, who is also a yoga instructor, teaches a simple color-breathing meditation believed to help "rebalance" the body. She suggests visualizing flowers or leaves of different colors to help the imagination focus on particular colors.

To begin color breathing, sit comfortably. Breathe in and out slowly, paying attention to your breathing. Relax. Imagine your stress melting away. Imagine a bright red leaf or vibrant red flower in your mind's eye. On the next inhalation, inhale and imagine yourself drawing up streams of red color from the earth, up through the soles of your feet and into your bottom or root chakra, which is between your legs, where the sex organs are located. When you exhale, imagine blowing or sending that red color energy out from the chakra into the entire area of the aura that surrounds your body. Inhale and exhale a vibrant shade of red three times. After red, do the same with orange, bright yellow, green, blue, indigo, and violet, working up the chakras from the bottom to the last chakra, located in the crown of the head. Wills suggests that imagery exercises be done focusing more on particular colors to deal with particular medical problems.

Color therapist Wills says objects such as your pajamas, nightgowns, sheets, and lamps may be illuminated with particular colors to help achieve a desired result. Even wearing clothes of a particular color can be of some health benefit. She says wearing blue clothes might help lower high blood pressure, for instance. In choosing clothing to wear, she recommends cotton or silk with natural dyes as the best choice, rather than synthetic fabrics.

Chapter 22

Magnets

Permanent magnets, another old therapy that has been rediscovered, may help relieve the pain of diabetic neuropathy. Pulsed electromagnetic fields are a more powerful emerging technology, probably more effective than permanent magnets, and may have benefits in wound and ulcer healing. Other electromagnetic devices may be helpful to relieve symptoms such as pain and depression.

Background

In ancient Egypt, Queen Cleopatra slept with a lodestone on her forehead to keep her young and beautiful. Magnets have gone in and out of fashion for years. They were all the rage in the United States until the 1920s, when lack of proof of their efficacy led to a reaction against them in the medical community and a banning of most magnetic healing devices. Their benefits are being rediscovered today.

In some sense, we are all electromagnetic beings. Electrical charges hold every atom in our bodies together. Thought is electromagnetic. We all have small flakes of a magnetic material called magnetite in the pineal gland near the center of our brains. European scientists have observed that dividing cells give off subtle electromagnetic signals.

Human DNA oscillates at between 52 and 78 gigahertz, which is about the same frequency as solar magnetic energy constantly sweeping over earth from the sun—the vibrating electromagnetic chord of life on our planet.

For years astronauts who left the earth's atmosphere suffered osteoporosis and other effects of "space sickness." Finally, scientists discovered that placing generators on spaceships to mimic the earth's slowly palpitating magnetic fields could keep astronauts healthy in space.

To live on earth, humans *need* the planet's constant weak magnetic pull, estimated at about one-half gauss, generated by the slow but constant rotation of earth's metal core. Certain areas of the earth experience what is called "geopathic stress," characterized by irregular or abnormal geomagnetic fields, which are linked to higher rates of cancer, arthritis, and other diseases. Other areas, like Lourdes, France, and Sedona, Arizona, have unused geomagnetic fields that may have healing effects. In 1976, Japanese research physician Kyoichi Nakagawa identified what he termed "magnetic field deficiency syndrome," a group of symptoms caused by a lack of exposure to natural magnetism of the earth, including stiff shoulders and neck, unexplained chest pains, weakness, insomnia, various forms of physical and mental fatigue, headaches, and habitual constipation. Dr. Nakagawa believes these symptoms are caused by our electronic culture, and the concrete and steel in our modern cities that cuts us off from earth's natural magnetic field. The Japanese treat these illnesses with magnetic sleeping pads, magnetic amulets, magnetic insoles, and many other permanent magnet-carrying devices. In the United States, several companies sell permanent magnets for use in sports medicine or as home remedies to relieve pain.

"Permanent magnets are of no value in the treatment of either Type 1 or Type 2 diabetes but may benefit diabetic neuropathy," says Dr. Paul Rosch, an expert on magnet technology and coauthor of the book *Magnet Therapy*. Dr. Rosch believes the future belongs to a more complex and mainstream technology—pulsed electromagnetic fields. Such fields will prove to be much more effective than permanent magnets in treating diabetic neuropathy, he predicts, with improvement noticeable in weeks rather than months. In the future, he added, pulsed electromag-

Magnetized Water

Water can be magnetized rather easily, and may have some health benefits. Magnetized water is used as a tonic in some Russian hospitals and in some countries, such as India. Some magnet therapists claim magnetic water can lower cholesterol levels and provide other health benefits.

For people with periodontal disease, brushing your teeth with magnetic water may reduce dental plaque, according to a study published in the *Journal of Clinical Periodontology* in 1993. When research subjects used a magnetic water treatment irrigator device on dental plaque and calculus, they experienced a 44 percent reduction in calculus volume compared to people who used the irrigator with regular water.

There are several methods of magnetizing water. Russians produce it by dripping water between both poles of a strong horseshoe magnet. Indians place a large, clean magnet in a jar full of water for 24 hours. Another method is to put a bottle of water on top of a large, flat magnet for at least 24 hours.

Some early experiments with magnets also found that plants germinated faster and grew bigger when they were watered with magnetized water.

netic fields may also prove to be effective in treating diabetic retinopathy and senile macular degeneration, areas where permanent magnets provide no benefit.

Research

In the United States, two studies show pain-relieving effects for people with diabetic neuropathy who wore magnetic insoles for several months.

A small study at Baylor University, in Houston, Texas, studied the effectiveness of magnetic insoles on people with diabetes who suffered painful diabetic neuropathy affecting their feet. Subjects wore magnetic insoles for four months, and several experienced a 75 percent reduction in chronic pain. However, this was a small study without a control group.

In a double-blind, placebo-controlled crossover study published in the *American Journal of Pain Management*, Dr. Michael Weintraub, a skeptical New York neurologist, tried magnetic foot insoles for four months on nineteen people with chronic foot pain caused by diabetes and other ailments. Subjects whose neuropathy resulted from diabetes achieved the greatest reduction in symptoms of burning, numbness, and tingling. Dr. Weintraub speculated that perhaps magnetic insoles were more effective in cases of severe nerve damage. A larger study is under way.

Of the five other double-blind, placebo-controlled studies conducted using permanent magnets for different types of pain, three found some benefit with magnets and two did not. Permanent magnets placed on the site of pain or on wounds that were healing had a healing, pain-relieving effect on people with postpolio syndrome and people recovering from liposuction surgery. Women with painful fibromyalgia improved after sleeping on magnetic mattress pads for four months.

Pulsating magnetic fields, used in a clinical setting, are stronger and work differently than permanent magnets. This technology has had an 80 percent success rate since the 1980s in healing previously unhealable bone fractures and it can also apparently speed healing of hard-to-heal diabetic ulcers.

A controlled, double-blind study of people with chronic diabetic ulcers treated with electrical nerve stimulation—80 hertz of alternating constant current for twenty minutes twice a day for three months—showed significant improvement and greater numbers of healed ulcers when compared to placebo, according to research published in 1992.

In his book, *Vibrational Medicine for the 21st Century*, Dr. Richard Gerber cites anecdotal evidence that patients who wear a strong neodymium magnet, with the south pole directly over their solar plexus chakra, can achieve better blood sugar control with reduced need for diabetes medications. However, no published studies demonstrate this.

CES for Depression

The cranial electric stimulator, or CES, a device developed by electrical engineer Saul Liss, may be helpful for depression. Although this small device is available over the counter in many countries, a doctor's prescription is necessary to purchase it in the United States.

The cranial stimulator uses only a thousandth of an amp of electric current, which can hardly be felt. CES leads to the normalization of endorphin and serotonin levels, according to Dr. C. Norman Shealy, who has been using the device since 1976. Dr. Shealy says CES is his "treatment of choice" for depression, and says it may also be used to treat insomnia and some forms of pain.

Magnets pop up here and there in other alternative therapies. Lodestone and magnetite gem elixirs are prepared from magnetic materials. Lodestone elixer is said to be useful in rebalancing the body, while proponents of magnetite claim it can enhance blood circulation through the endocrine system. After performing acupuncture, some acupuncturists tape magnets over acupuncture points as part of their treatment.

For several years, veterinarians have used magnetic devices to speed healing of broken legs of race and show horses. This is proof that magnets do have some effect, since animals experience no placebo effect.

How Magnets Work

Doctors interested in magnets speculate that placing a magnet on the skin may increase blood circulation by drawing blood to the area near a magnet. Theoretically, the increased blood flow brings more nutrients and carries away more waste products from the area. While the iron in hemoglobin found in red blood cells was previously not believed to be the type that would be attracted by a magnet, the deoxygenated hemoglobin molecule has recently been found to be magnetically sensitive, and might help red blood cells to respond to magnetic force. The presence of a magnet may also decrease the flow of calcium ions into the smooth muscle cells of the walls of blood vessels, causing them to relax and dilate, thereby bringing more blood to an area. Some researchers think that magnetic fields can affect the pH balance in body fluids. Other theories posit that magnets excite the nerves of the autonomic nervous system, or that they increase or decrease hormone production from the endocrine system.

Electromagnetic energy factors into health even down to the cellular level. The so-called "sodium-potassium pump," which pumps food into the cell and carries toxins out of the cell, is dependent on the movement of chemical ions, electrically charged molecules of sodium, potassium, calcium, and magnesium. This constant exchange of electrically charged minerals at the cellular level is the ebb and flow of life itself. Exposure to strong magnetic fields may slightly alter this flow and effect nerve cell function, including transmission of messages through the nervous system and the brain.

Magnets are presumed to be safe. Magnetic resonance imaging machines, or MRIs, subject people to powerful magnetic fields many times stronger than any magnet can produce. No ill effects have ever been reported from people who have undergone MRIs.

Precautions

Much remains unknown about the effects of permanent magnets, so prudence is advised. There are no standard recommendations as to what strength magnets should be used for what types of pain, what type of magnets to use, how and when magnets are applied, and so forth. Most experts advise against using strong magnets on the head, around cancer or infections, on the abdomen of pregnant women, on the chest region of people with pacemakers, or around the organs or glands for long periods on a daily basis. Some advise against sleeping on a magnetic bed or mattress pad for more than eight to ten hours at a time, although others dismiss that suggestion. If either pole of a magnet worsens the condition you are attempting to treat, stop using it. Always check with your doctor first, Dr. Gerber advises, especially in the case of recurrent pain.

Although we have more to learn about this form of treatment, permanent magnets may be helpful in relieving some types of pain. Magnetic insoles worn in the shoes may bring some relief to people with peripheral neuropathy. Electromagnetic energy, an emerging medical technology, speeds the healing of diabetic ulcers, and it may prove useful for other complications such as retinopathy. While magnets are presumed to be safe, common sense precautions are always in order.

Chapter 23

Therapeutic Touch

Therapeutic touch and the other therapies discussed in this chapter, which might be called "spiritual bodywork," could be seen as a modern-day extension of the "laying on of hands." They involve a transfer of vital energy from the hands of the therapist to the person receiving treatment, and they act by strengthening the body's natural energy. These therapies may be useful for pain and some other symptoms of diabetes; a few spectacular cures have been reported by users. Noncontact therapeutic touch, healing touch, chi gong, Reiki, and other energy therapies all must be given by expert practitioners.

Therapeutic Touch

Therapeutic touch is a medical variation of what was once, in biblical times, called the "laying on of hands." Simply being touched is therapeutic. Studies of premature babies, for instance, have found they are healthier when regularly touched by another person. Therapeutic touch is based on the idea that each person is surrounded by an energy field that is connected with the universal life energy. Practitioners center and steep themselves in that energy, then interact with the energy fields of patients. Practitioners are said to project a vital, healing energy into the patient's energy field, resulting in pain relief or healing.

Therapeutic touch was developed by Dolores Kreiger, Ph.D., a professor of nursing at New York University, and Dora Kunz, a healer. It is said to relieve stress, anxiety, and also to reduce pain, asthmatic breathing, and fever or inflammation. In its inception, it was often practiced in hospitals, although that is less true now. More than 30,000 people, many of them nurses, have been trained in the use of therapeutic touch.

An early experiment found that therapeutic touch raised blood hemoglobin levels, allowing the body to absorb more vital oxygen through the bloodstream. A study in 1990 found that skin wounds healed faster when therapeutic touch was utilized. A 1984 study found that patients in heart care units experienced less anxiety after experiencing therapeutic touch. In one study, the pain of tension headaches decreased 90 percent when therapeutic touch was employed.

Therapeutic touch begins when the therapist grounds himself or herself by meditation or prayer. Then, with intent and compassion, the therapist moves his hands along the patient's body from head to toe. The therapist is alert for imbalances or points of congestion, which are removed with gentle stroking or circular movements around the problem area.

There are anecdotal reports of patients with diabetes being helped by therapeutic touch. Rosa Mantonti, a certified diabetes educator and clinical nurse specialist at Presbyterian Health Care Services Hospital in Albuquerque, New Mexico, recalls visiting a homebound middle-age woman with diabetes who also suffered from neuropathy, renal problems, and gastropathy. Wheelchair bound, the woman was in constant pain. A nursing student at the time, Mantonti had studied therapeutic touch, and asked the woman if she wished to try it. The woman replied that she would try anything that might give her relief.

Mantonti first centered herself. She recalls that the lady was sitting up in her wheelchair, as she cautiously and carefully treated her with therapeutic touch. As she worked, the nurse noticed that the woman appeared to become very restful. She allowed Mantonti to do an entire treatment, which was surprising since the lady was quite sensitive to any stimulus and in nearly constant pain.

"Did that help?" Mantonti asked the woman afterward.

"Gosh, for that moment I just didn't feel any pain," the woman gratefully replied. "I just felt warm all over."

For the next several months, Mantonti utilized therapeutic touch on the same woman, whenever she saw her. The lady's blood sugars were very erratic, but leveled a bit. As long as Mantonti gave her therapeutic touch, it continued to help the woman deal with her chronic pain.

At Healing Sciences Research International, in Orinda, California, a small study of people with Type 1 diabetes combined therapeutic touch and prayer. Eleven of sixteen participants reduced their doses of insulin, although the reduction was not considered statistically significant.

Variations

Noncontact therapeutic touch, which is sometimes combined with therapeutic touch, is a form of spiritual healing that does not involve touching. The therapist sweeps his or her hands a few inches above the patient's body, from head to toe, looking for and attempting to dissipate perceived physical, mental, emotional, or even spiritual blockages. In examining eleven double-blind, randomized trials of noncontact therapeutic touch, the authors of a study published in *Annals of Internal Medicine* noted that seven of eleven trials showed a positive treatment effect on at least one outcome, three had no effect, and only one showed a negative outcome when results were compared to placebo.

Healing touch is a variation of therapeutic touch involving several additional energy modalities. As developed by Janet Mentgen, healing touch is a multilevel healing program that uses the hands to experience various layers of the natural energy field or aura, said to extend outward from the body in etheric, emotional, mental field, and spiritual field layers. A pendulum is used to locate chakras that are blocked; various techniques are employed to open the chakras and connections between them.

Specific Human Energy Nexus, or SHEN, is a healing touch type of therapy that is combined with polarity therapy. Used mostly for pain,

SHEN is said to release blocked energy currents caused by the repression of emotions in the body.

Reiki, which means "universal life energy" in Japanese, is another therapy involving the laying on of hands. Developed in the mid-19th century by Mikao Usui, a Japanese monk and educator, Reiki is said to transfer universal life energy from the body of the healer to the patient. Special Japanese symbols, drawn in the air by hand motions, are known and used only by the upper level or third degree Reiki practitioners. Believed to rebalance subtle energies within the body and mitigate stress. One study showed that Reiki raised hemoglobin levels. At its best, Reiki has a spiritual element for healer and patient. Unlike therapeutic touch, but like spiritual healing, Reiki is said to be effective at a distance, even when the healer and the patient are not proximate. At the University of Michigan, research is under way testing the effectiveness of Reiki in managing the pain of diabetic neuropathy.

Johrei, which means "spiritual purification" in Japanese, is another form of treatment using energy in the hands that has come west from Japan.

Chi gong, in its external form, practiced by a chi gong master, is an old, mystical healing method from China. Healers are said to gather and project chi energy from the hands of the healer to the patient, sometimes resulting in spectacular and miraculous healings.

Pranic healing, from the Philippines, also is said to direct healing energy through the hands and fingers, as well as the chakras. Pranic healing basically uses light "prana" energy visualized by healers and delivered through their hands to patients. Red prana, for instance, is believed to strengthen the body and aid healing and circulation. Orange prana is believed to expel toxins, cleaning and decongesting the body. Yellow prana is believed an aid to gluing together traumatized tissues and to help damaged cells repair themselves. Green prana breaks down and disinfects. Blue prana, which inhibits or contracts, is used to treat inflammations and pain and to reduce fevers. White prana is said to contain all the other colors.

Like Reiki, pranic healing is said to be effective on patients even when they are at a distance—when the healer is not present in the same physical place. According to Master Chao Kok Sui, a pranic healing and cleansing is useful on "donated" organs such as kidneys prior to transplant, which is said to decrease the incidence of rejection of the organ.

Therapeutic touch and several other therapies act by strengthening the body's natural energy field. They may be useful for pain and some other symptoms of diabetes. Non-contact therapeutic touch, healing touch, chi gong, Reiki and other energy therapies can relieve stress, assist in healing, and are said to sometimes miraculously improve health. The next chapter covers a form of therapy in which the transfer of energy is apparently all mental, spiritual healing or faith healing.

Chapter 24

Spiritual Healing

Spiritual healing or faith healing is rooted in the oldest mystical and religious traditions. People can sometimes improve their health due to the exercise of a healer's mental powers, the force of their spirit, their faith, their intuition, or through the transfer of some healing force. Real healers exist, and probably have connections to energies we don't yet understand, which are constantly washing through the universe. Although phony healers often make big promises, legitimate practitioners are relatively modest about what they can do, but sometimes achieve impressive results. This form of healing is gentle and without side effects, but it does involve a leap of faith, and a certain open-mindedness on the part of the person who seeks to be healed.

It is an expression of our humanity to believe in miracles. Myths, folk tales, and biblical legends contain stories of miraculous healings, people raised from the dead, and other symbolic conquests of human mortality. Every year, 5 million people or their loved ones go to Lourdes, France, in hope of being healed. Some people are healed. Of the 10,000-odd miracle cures that have been reported, more than 1,200 have been documented by a team of twenty skeptical doctors, including some who do not believe in God. In Great Britain, healers are licensed and eligible for payment from government health programs, if English patients request their services. Some hospitals in the United States and Canada are also becoming more open-minded in this regard.

Some research suggests that spiritual healing and various forms of prayer can make a difference in health outcomes, although improvements are sometimes modest. In this vast and relatively unexplored area, a great deal remains unknown.

Belief

A survey conducted in 1996 revealed that 82 percent of Americans believe in the power of prayer to heal. In a recent survey of users of alternative medicine, more than a third of respondents said they used prayer to address health-related problems, and 7 percent reported having tried some form of "spiritual healing."

An analysis of 23 randomized, double-blind clinical trials involving prayer, spiritual or mental healing, and other noncontact therapies was conducted at the University of Maryland School of Medicine in Baltimore. According to results published in the *Annals of Internal Medicine* in 2000, 57 percent of the trials showed a positive treatment effect on health. Two of five trials using prayer from distant locations showed a positive effect on patient health, while three had no effect. Of eleven studies utilizing noncontact therapeutic touch, seven showed a positive effect on at least one outcome, three showed no effect, and one showed a negative outcome. Of seven studies using some type of distant or paranormal healing, four produced positive treatment effects and three showed no significant effect. The authors concluded that spiritual healing merits further study.

The Research Council for Complementary Medicine in London conducted another study of healing as a complementary medical intervention, carefully examining fifty-nine randomized, double-blind clinical trials. Of twenty-two full trials studied, ten showed a "significant" effect on healing when compared with control. These included two large studies showing improvement in cardiac patients. However, several studies were poorly designed, and therefore of dubious value. Of fifteen pilot studies and dissertation abstracts examined in this study, eleven showed nonsignificant results.

The best-known study of the effects of prayer was conducted by cardiologist Randall Byrd at San Francisco General Hospital in San Francisco. This randomized, double-blind study assigned half a group of heart patients, without their knowledge, to be prayed for by a home prayer group given only their first names. A second group of heart patients was not prayed for. At the end of the ten-month study, heart patients who were prayed for had an easier time of it—they were less likely to need antibiotics, to develop a complication called pulmonary edema, or to require the emergency procedure known as intubation. The death rate of the group prayed for was slightly lower than the group that was not prayed for, although the difference was not statistically significant. Dr. Byrd's spectacular study is controversial in the medical world and raises many questions, but it does suggest that being praying for by others may have positive health consequences.

Healing

It's been known for years that people who participate in a religion have lower mortality rates and lower blood pressure than most. This may be because organized religion is a social undertaking, providing copious social support. But the concept of spirituality is larger and more nebulous than showing up for church or temple. Spirituality is intensely personal and includes various forms of prayer, meditation, and more.

Some religions strongly believe in the power of faith to heal. In addition to Christian Science and fundamentalist churches that sometimes make a tasteless show of faith healing, other denominations such as Methodists and many branches of Judaism are now organizing healing ministries to reclaim a religious tradition they say has been lost. A few churches hold prayer meetings for people with special problems such as overeating. Faith healing is different from spiritual healing in that it requires the healer and the person healed to share a common bond of faith. Sometimes faith healing works.

In a telephone survey of 500 adults who lived in Richmond, Virginia, 14 percent of respondents claimed they had been physically healed by some form of faith healing. While 12 percent said they were cured of colds or the flu, others claimed relief from conditions such as back problems, emotional distress, bone fractures, and even cancer due to prayer or divine intervention. People who conducted this survey made no attempt to corroborate these claims, but some may well have been true.

Some scientists speculate that healers are able to transfer energy in a way we don't understand, across normal boundaries of space and time. Kirlian photographs have documented the existence of what some healers call *auras*, or invisible energy fields that surround the physical body. At the University of California at Los Angeles, scientists used Kirlian photography to document decreases in the auras of healers after they have performed a healing, indicating a drain of electromagnetic energy. Distinguished medical research scientists such as Dr. Robert Becker, a pioneer of electromagnetic medicine, and Dr. Elmer Green, known for his work at the Menninger Clinic with biofeedback, have written of the great potential implicit in this type of healing, which is not far away from other strange but documented paranormal phenomena such as telepathy and extrasensory perception.

While it's true that average health outcomes have been improved in some research studies, most doctors believe that complete cures from chronic diseases are rare. Medical doctors call these mysterious and unexplainable healings "spontaneous remissions," and many have been recorded in the medical literature. The chance of having a complete spontaneous remission from a disease such as cancer by any nonconventional healing method including faith or spiritual healing has been estimated at between 80,000 and 100,000 to one. These are long odds, but they are greater than zero.

Spiritual Healing

Spiritual healing is more accepted in the British Isles than in the United States and Canada. There, more than 14,000 men and women are legally registered as healers and there are more practitioners of spiritual healing than practitioners of any other branch of alternative medicine. In England, spiritual healers are permitted to work on any patient who requests their services, and their work is reimbursed by Britain's national health insurance program.

The National Federation of Spiritual Healers, a British organization, defines spiritual healing as "the channeling of energies by the healer to reenergize the patient to deal with illness or injury." Spiritual healing may be done in person, or through *distant healing*— when the patient is not present. The federation's literature stresses that healing is a gentle healing modality, without side effects. The federation avoids promising any particular result or cure, but states: "It is not unusual for healing to be helpful in some way." They state that one healing treatment may help right away, but more may be necessary. The benefits of spiritual healing may appear at once, or emerge gradually. Benefits of spiritual healing may also be subtle, involving a simple change in attitude to life, or a feeling of greater stability and relaxation.

Florence Horn is a spiritual healer and teacher based in New York City, who also practices in England, Canada, and Israel. With a client who had diabetes, she says, she would tell them that a medical doctor must be seen for advice on medications, diet, and exercise.

"After we work, we never, never, under any circumstances say we've healed somebody. We never tell that person to go home and throw away their medication because they're healed," Horn says.

"We tell them after you go to the doctor you may be delighted with what you find out. But, do what your doctor tells you to do. You must be checked by a doctor, and not stop or reduce any medications until the doctor tells you it's all right."

Horn observes: "Sometimes people don't always *want* to be healed. If they don't, and you force the healing, you're going to cause more problems than you fix. The healing must be accepted by the client, and sometimes it does not 'take' immediately because the client is not ready to be healed."

Different states and different countries set various restrictions on healers, Horn observes. Customers can be called clients, but not patients, in the United States. On the other hand, English law allows them to be called patients. In most of the United States, it's against the law for healers to touch the body of the person being healed. Healers cannot legally diagnose illnesses, and they cannot mention a body part using the medical name.

Healers work in varied ways, says Horn, who is a member of several organizations for healers, including the Jewish Association of Spir-

Healing

Many healers believe that healing is an innate ability that all humans possess, and one that may be learned and practiced as part of a self-help technique. For people who wish to explore their healing capacity, Dr. Richard Gerber suggests the following exercise:

- Center the mind so it is free of anxiety and distraction, perhaps by progressive relaxation techniques or meditating.

- Listen to yourself breathe slowly. Ground yourself with an imaginary cord of gold or rainbow colors tied around your waist, the long end of the cord extending down your spine into the core of the earth. Imagine yourself protected by a sphere of bright white, blue, or gold light extending at least two feet above and below the body.

- Connect with a higher spiritual source, perhaps with a silent prayer that you might become a clear, pure channel of healing energy.

- Make a connection between yourself and the person you wish to assist to heal—stand behind them as they sit in a chair. Put your hands on their shoulders. Create an intimate connection between your hearts, visualized as a connecting beacon of golden white light. Imagine you are sending unconditional love, forgiveness, and complete acceptance of all aspects of the other person, whom you might see as a spirit locked into a body with some defects.

- Activate a channel of healing energy from a limitless source of energy such as the sun, Jesus Christ, Buddha, or any higher spiritual power. Bring this energy into your body through the head or up from the ground up to your heart, and send it through your hands to the other person.

- Imagine that the energy you are sending is correcting all the imbalances that influence the person's health problem. Allow it to flow for as long as you think appropriate, perhaps ten to thirty minutes.

Continued

- Afterward, physically and mentally disconnect yourself from the person by taking your hands away and telling yourself you are disconnected. Spend a few moments reenergizing yourself at this time.

itual Healers, an ecumenical group of more than a hundred spiritual healers in the United States Horn says a number of hospitals in the United States are expanding their menu of available treatments to include spiritual healing.

Healers

A wide variety of spiritual healing techniques exist in the world. This can be seen by examining the work of four well-known spiritual healers: Edgar Cayce, Carolyn Myss, Barbara Brennan, and Mietek Wirkus.

Edgar Cayce

The late Edgar Cayce, the so-called "Sleeping Prophet," was an American medical clairvoyant who astounded every medical doctor who observed him in the 1920s and 1930s. A humble man with an eighth-grade education, Cayce never accepted much money for utilizing what he saw as his gift from God. Going into a psychic trance, Cayce prescribed treatments and therapies that were sometimes sophisticated, sometimes quite simple, and occasionally unorthodox and bizarre. Cayce's remedies often worked when his instructions were followed exactly. Many distinguished medical doctors of the day were startled by his insights into the working of the human body when he was in a trance.

Cayce gave more than 9,000 documented medical "readings" that were transcribed word for word as he spoke them. He gave readings for individuals with almost every known disease, sometimes recommending unusual cures for people who had been pronounced "incurable" by medical specialists. Cayce often recommended holistic remedies such as a well-balanced diet, regular exercise, relaxation, and recreation. He warned against eating refined foods, and against eating when angry or upset. He clearly incorporated the role of attitudes and emotions into the process of healing, summarized in his statement: "Mind is the builder . . . the physical is the result."

Cayce's medical readings are cataloged and available to members of the Association for Research and Enlightenment, located in Virginia Beach, Virginia. A few hundred doctors in Phoenix, Arizona, and other locations continue to work with the Edgar Cayce therapies, with some using intuitive meditation as a diagnostic tool.

Carolyn Myss

Carolyn Myss, a medical intuitive, is the author of several books that examine the spiritual and emotional aspects of physical disease. A few years ago, in a study conducted by Dr. C. Norman Shealy, Myss achieved an astounding 93 percent success rate at diagnosing physical or psychological problems of patients she only heard about over the telephone. Myss lectures frequently about the spiritual aspects of healing, attempting to integrate Hindu, Christian, and Jewish mystical thought into a coherent metaphysical healing philosophy.

In her book *Why People Don't Heal and How They Can*, Myss links medical problems to particular chakras or energy centers in the body. She believes that each of the chakras corresponds to particular emotions, spiritual concepts, and states of mind that accompany disease.

According to Myss, diabetes is a problem of the third or solar plexus chakra, the physical location of the pancreas, liver, kidneys, spleen, and adrenal glands, as well as the stomach and intestines. From an emotional point of view, she writes, the third chakra relates most strongly to "the belief patterns we hold about ourselves," including our looks, intelligence, strength, and skills; in short, our self-esteem. Problems in changing personal behavior, and holding on to the change, are associated with the third chakra, Myss writes. For people with problems involving the third chakra, she says a commitment to yourself to go the distance can be considered the backbone of the healing challenge.

Mental and emotional issues associated with the third chakra include problems with trust, fear and intimidation, self-esteem, responsibility for making decisions, sensitivity to criticism, and personal honor. Myss says achieving spiritual qualities of honor, endurance, and personal integrity are particular challenges for people who have problems involving this chakra. What she calls the shadow side of the third chakra is shame, inadequacy, and self-conscious fear. Her writings stress the need to heal and respect yourself and your own life as an aspect of healing.

To evoke the power of the third chakra and give yourself strength, Myss suggests making promises to yourself and writing them down. She suggests making a written vow to yourself such as: "I promise to live and be in present time at all times. This means that I will put aside words and issues between me and my partner or me and my children. I will stop working myself too hard and make time for my exercise and new nutritional regimen. I will meditate twice a day and practice right speech and right action with myself and others." She suggests carrying this written pledge with you. She also suggests repeating the affirmation: "I am filled with the energy of endurance and honor. My thoughts and words carry the power of creation itself."

Building your personal self-esteem requires taking risks and building self-reliance, she says. As a ritual confirmation, she suggests writing your personal honor code in a journal and regarding it as a vow or a contract with yourself.

Barbara Brennan

Barbara Brennan is a former NASA physicist who became interested in healing in the 1970s. Her Barbara Brennan School of Healing in New York teaches a technique called *healing science*. It focuses on finding and healing areas of distortion in natural energy fields said to surround each person that can become repositories for childhood trauma and pain. In the healing process, she has said, facing the experience of early pain is often the most difficult part of a healing. Each person's energy field has at least seven levels that may be worked with during healing, she says. Brennan's healing technique is practiced with the patient lying down with shoes off. She teaches healers to begin at the feet, working their way up, charging and balancing energy fields. During healings, Brennan says she can see specific organs in the body, and describes her work as rebuilding lines of light, transforming energy from herself and her chakras through the hands of the healer to the body of the person healed.

Like most other healers, Brennan will not see a patient unless they are under the care of a medical specialist. She also recommends a healthy lifestyle, including eating a balanced, organic diet, exercising, and taking care of your personal needs.

Mietek Wirkus

Mietek Wirkus, another well-known healer, has performed many healings by focusing and directing the energy from his extraordinary hands. Born in Poland in 1939, Wirkus practiced under the auspices of the Polish state for many years, including at a school for deaf children where his healing efforts helped some of the children, including those born deaf, recover their hearing. Although his healing efforts drained energy from him at first, Wirkus reportedly learned to minimize this by using breathing techniques taught to him by a Tibetan monk. At one time, he was doing dozens of healings per day. After he came to the United States, he was studied by scientists at the Menninger Foundation in Topeka, Kansas. His hands were found to generate electrical surges of 80 volts and more during healings, something that astounded the doctors, since it was believed impossible for the human body to produce that much electricity.

Wirkus and his wife Margaret, who is also a healer, teach doctors and other practitioners the Wirkus bioenergy healing techniques at the nonprofit Wirkus Bioenergy Foundation in Bethesda, Maryland. Wirkus teaches that the body is surrounded by a silver energy field about three or four inches deep, about as far as the body's warmth can be felt, and other fields, including a third energy field called the astral or magnetic body. These various energy fields are the focus in Wirkus's style of healing, which is said to trigger self-healing mechanisms in the body.

Mietek and Margaret Wirkus told Canadian spiritual writer Tom Harpur: "What is of greatest importance is the healee's will to live. The bioenergy then supplies renewed energy for the body to heal itself. It's not a case of this type of healing helping some problems and not being appropriate for others. It stimulates the body's own mechanisms for healing itself—the immune system and other systems—and so it is a help in all fields and at all levels of the organism—mental, emotional, and physical. Once people get even one treatment, they say it's as if the clouds have moved away and their life feels as though it is taking on color again."

Final Thought

Spiritual healing has the enormous benefit of being harmless, gentle, and without side effects. Scientific studies suggest that various forms of prayer, faith healing, and spiritual healing can sometimes have an effect on health outcomes. Although the chance of a complete, instant cure of diabetes is remote, faith healers or spiritual healers may help you accept or work through certain aspects of the disease, or improve your physical or mental health in other ways. As a matter of common sense, beware of healers or other alternative practitioners who make big promises up front. Work with a reputable healer. Never abandon medical treatment for this, or any other, alternative form of healing.

Appendix A: Resources

A number of nonprofit and professional organizations exist to provide information on alternative therapies. On request, many professional organizations will direct you to a practitioner in your local area.

Acupuncture and Oriental Medicine

Acupuncture Foundation of Canada
2313 Lawrence Avenue East, Ste 204
Scarborough, Ontario, Canada M1R 5G4
afcinstitute.com/afc.html

American Association of Oriental Medicine
433 Front Street
Castasauqua, PA 18032
(888) 500-7999
aaom.org

National Certification Commission for Acupuncture
  and Oriental Medicine
11 Canal Center Plaza, Ste 300
Alexandria, VA 22314
(705) 548-9004
nccaom.org

Alternative Medicine

National Center for Complementary and Alternative Medicine
P.O. Box 8218
Silver Spring, MD 20907
(888) 644-6226
nccam.nih.gov

Aromatherapy

American Association for Holistic Aromatherapy
P.O. Box 17622
Boulder, CO 80308
(888) ASK NAHA
naha.org

International Federation of Aromatherapists
Stamford House
2-4 Chiswick High Road
London, W4 1TH United Kingdom
int-fed-aromatherapy.co.uk

Art Therapy

American Art Therapy Association
1202 Allanson Road
Mundelein, IL 60060
(888) 290-0878
arttherapy.org

Ayurvedic Medicine

Ayurvedic Institute
11311 Menaul NE, Ste A
Albuquerque, NM 87112
(505) 291-9698
ayurveda.com

Marahishi College of Vedic Medicine
2721 Arizona Street NE
Albuquerque, NM 87110
(888) 895-2614
mcumnm.org

Biofeedback

Association for Applied Psychophysiology and Biofeedback
10200 W. 44th Avenue, #304
Wheat Ridge, CO 80033-2840
(303) 422-8436
aaplo.org

Chelation Therapy

American College for Advancement in Medicine
23121 Verdugo Drive, #204
Laguna Hills, CA 92653
acam.org

Chiropractic

American Chiropractic Association
1701 Clarendon Boulevard
Arlington, VA 22209
(703) 276-8800
amerochiro.org

Diabetes

American Association of Diabetes Educators
Integrated Specialty Practice Group
100 W. Monroe
Chicago, IL 60603
(800) 338-3633; (312) 424-2426
aadenet.org

American Diabetes Association
1660 Duke Street
Alexandria, VA 22314
(800) 342-2383
diabetes.org

Canadian Diabetes Association
15 Toronto Street, Ste 800
Toronto, Ontario, Canada M5C 2E3
(800) BANTING
diabetes.ca

National Kidney and Urologic Diseases Information
Clearinghouse
3 Information Way
Bethesda, MD 20892-3580
(800) 891-5390
niddk.nih.gov/health/kidney/nkudic

Diet and Nutrition

American Dietetic Association
216 W. Jackson Boulevard, #800
Chicago, IL 60606
(800) 366-1655
eatright.org

Food and Nutrition Information Center
Agricultural Research Service, USDA
National Agricultural Library, Room 304
Beltsville, MD 20705-2351
(301) 504-5719
nal.usda.gov/fnic

National Institute of Nutrition
2565 Carling Avenue, #400
Ottawa, Ontario, Canada K1Z 8R1
nin.ca

Flower Essences

Flower Essence Pharmacy at Centergees
2007 NE 39th Avenue
Portland, OR 97212
(800) 343-8693
FlowerEssences.com

Nelson Bach USA, Ltd.
100 Research Drive
Wilmington, MA 01887
(978) 988-3833
bachcentre.com

Healing

Association for Research and Enlightenment
Edgar Cayce Foundation
215 67th Street
Virginia Beach, CA 23451
(800) 333-4499; (757) 428-3588
are-cayce.com

The Barbara Brennan School of Healing
P.O. Box 2005
East Hampton, NY 11937
(800) 432-5377
barbarabrennan.com

The Biofield Research Institute
20 YFH Gate Six Road
Sausalito, CA 94965
(415) 332-2593

Jewish Association of Spiritual Healers (nondenominational)
106 Cabrini Boulevard
New York, NY 10033
(212) 928-4275

National Federation of Spiritual Healers
Old Manor Farm Studio, Church Stress, Sunbury-on-Thames
Middlesex, United Kingdom, TW16 6RG
U.K. Telephone: 01932 783164; International: +44 1932 783164
nfsh.org.uk

Wirkus Bioenergy Foundation
9007 Fleming Avenue
Bethesda, MD 20814
(301) 652-3480
mietekwirkus.com

Herbal Medicine

American Herbalists Guild
P.O. Box 70
Roosevelt, UT 84066
(435) 722-8434
healthy.net/herbalists

Canadian Natural Health Association
439 Wellington Street
Toronto, Ontario, Canada M5V 2H7
(416) 977-2642

Herb Research Foundation
1007 Pearl Street, #200
Boulder, CO 80302
(800) 748-2617
herbs.org

Homeopathy

British Homeopathic Association
27A Devonshire Street
London, WC1N 1RJ United Kingdom

British Institute of Homeopathy
Hahneman Center for Heilkunst
14445 St. Joseph Blvd.
Ottawa, Ontario KIC 7K9
(613) 830-2556
homeopathy.com

National Center for Homeopathy
801 N. Fairfax Street, #306
Alexandria, VA 22314
Telephone (703) 548-7790; fax (703) 548-7792
healthy.net/nch/index.html

Humor Therapy

The American Association for Therapeutic Humor
222 S. Meramec, #303
St. Louis, MO 63105
(314) 863-6232
aath.org

The Humor Project
480 Broadway
Saratoga Springs, NY 12866
(518) 587-8770
humorproject.com

Hypnosis

American Society of Clinical Hypnosis
33 W. Grand, #402
Chicago, IL 60610
(312) 645-9810
asch.net

Light Therapy

College of Syntonic Optometry
1200 Robeson Street
Fall River, MA 02720-5508
(508) 673-1251
syntonicphototherapy.com

Dinshah Health Society
100 Dinshah Drive
Malaga, NJ 08328
(609) 692-4686
members.aol.com/mystuff66/page1.htm

The Oracle School of Colour
9 Wyndale Avenue
Kinsbury, London, England NW9 9PT
lighttrust.co.uk/the_trustees

Society for Light Treatment and Biological Rhythms
P.O. Box 591687, 174 Cook Street
San Francisco, CA 94159-1687
(415) 751-2758
sltbr.org

Magnet Therapy

Bioelectromagnetics Institute (sells an information packet on
    magnetic products)
2490 W. Moana Lane
Reno, NV 89509
(702) 827-9099

The North American Academy of Magnetic Therapy
28240 West Agoura, #202
Agoura, CA 91301
(800) 457-1853

Massage

American Massage Therapy Association
820 David Street, Suite 100
Evanston, IL 60201
(847) 864-0123
amtamassage.org

American Reflexology Certification Board
P.O. Box 740875
Arvada, CO 80006-0879
(303) 933-6921
arcb.net/index.htm

International Council of Reflexologists
P.O. Box 30513
Richmond Hill, Ontario, Canada L4C OC7
(905) 770-2464
icr.reflexology.org

Rosen Institute
825 Bancroft Avenue #A
Berkeley, CA 94710
(510) 845-6606
rosenmethod.org

Meditation

Maharishi International University
Fairfield, Iowa 52557
(888) 532-7686
tm.org

Mind/Body Medical Institute
New England Deaconess Hospital
110 Francis Street
Boston, MA 02215
(617) 632-9530
mindbody.harvard.edu

Stress Reduction Clinic (mindfulness meditation)
University of Massachusetts Medical Center
Worcester, MA 01655
(508) 856-1616
umassmed.edu/behavmed/clinical.cfm

Mental Health

American Association for Marriage and Family Therapy
1100 17th Street NW, 10th Floor
Washington, DC 20036
(800) 374-2638

American Association of Sex Educators, Counselors, and
   Therapists
P.O. Box 238
Mount Vernon, IA 52314-0238
aasect.org

American Psychiatric Association
1400 K Street NW
Washington, DC 20005
(202) 682-6000

American Psychological Association
750 First Street NE
Washington, DC 20002-4242
(202) 336-5700
apa.org

National Institute of Mental Health
Information, Resources and Inquiries
5600 Fishers Lane, Room 7C-02
Rockville, MD 20857
nimh.hih.gov

Music Therapy

American Music Therapy Association
8455 Colesville Road, #1000
Silver Spring, MD 20910
musictherapy.org

Canadian Music Therapy Association
Wilfrid Laurier University
Waterloo, Ontario, Canada N2L 3C5
(800) 996-CAMT
musictherapy.ca

Naturopathy

American Association of Naturopathic Physicians
2366 Eastlake Avenue East, #322
Seattle, WA 98012
(206) 323-7610
naturopath.org

Canadian College of Naturopathic Medicine
60 Berl Avenue
Etobicoke, Ontario, Canada M8Y 3CZ
ccnm.edu

Nurses

American Holistic Nurses Association
P.O. Box 2130
2133 E. Lakin Drive, #2
Flagstaff, AZ 86003-2130
(800) 278-2462
ahna.org

Osteopathic Manipulation

The American Academy of Osteopathy
3500 DePauw Boulevard, #1080
Indianapolis, IN 46268-1136
(317) 879-1811
academyofosteopathy.org

Pranic Healing

American Institute of Asian Studies
Attn: Mr. Stephen Co, Certified Pranic Healing Instrctor
P.O. Box 1605
Chino, CA 91708-1605
(909) 465-0967
pranichealing.com

Reiki

Reiki Outreach International
P.O. Box 609
Fair Oaks, CA 95628
(916) 863-1500
annieo.com/reikioutreach

Support Groups

American Diabetes Association
(800) 342-2383

Friends Health Connection
P.O. Box 114
New Brunswick, NJ 18903
(800) 48-FRIEND

National Self-Help Clearinghouse
33 W. 42nd Street
New York, NY 10036
(212) 642-2944

Stress

The American Institute of Stress
124 Park Avenue
Yonkers, NY 10703
(914) 963-1200
stress.org

Therapeutic Touch

Healing Touch International
12477 W. Cedar Drive, #202
Lakewood, CO 80228
(303) 989-7982
healingtouch.net

Nurse Healers Professional Associates
1211 Locust Street
Philadelphia, PA 19107
(215) 545-8079
theraputic-touch.org

The Therapeutic Touch Network (Ontario)
P.O. Box 85551
875 Eglinton Avenue West
Toronto, Ontario, Canada M6C 4A8
(416) 65-TOUCH
therapeutictouchnetwk.com

Yoga

International Association of Yoga Therapists
P.O. Box 2418
Sebastopol, CA 95413
(707) 928-9898
iayt.org

Appendix B: Internet and World Wide Web

In addition to the web sites listed previously, here are several others of possible interest.

acupuncture.com
Listings of practitioners of acupuncture by state.

healthfinder.gov
U.S. Dept. of Health and Human Services maintains this gateway site.

graylab.ac.uk/omd
On-line medical dictionary with in excess of 65,000 definitions.

cdc.gov
United States Centers for Disease Control and Prevention.

ama-assn.org/aps/amahg.htm
The American Medical Association Physician selector.

fda.gov
Food and Drug Administration site includes information on prescription drugs, food safety, dietary supplements, and medical devices.

http://altmedicine.com
News and opinion about some aspects of alternative medicine.

acupuncture.org.uk
Information on acupuncture from the British Acupuncture Council.

shealyhealthnet.com
Dr. C. Norman Shealy website.

randomhouse.com/chopra
Dr. Deepak Chopra website.

drweil.com
Dr. Andrew Weil website.

http://chili.rt66.com/hrbmoore/HOMEPAGE/HomePage.html
Herbalist Michael Moore website.

herbalgram.org
American Botanical Council, Herb Research Council, and *HerbalGram* magazine site contains information on medicinal herbs, herbalism, Commission E Monographs, and available books on many related topics.

ars-grin.gov/duke
The USDA's Agricultural Research Service phytochemical and ethnobotanical databases containing information on medicinal plants.

www.imagerynet.com
Imagery and visualization website run by Dr. Dennis Gersten as an educational effort.

pitt.edu/~cbw/altm.html
University of Pittsburgh's site for links to sources of information on alternative medicine.

http://odp.od.nih.gov/ods/databases/ibids.html
The International Bibliogaphic Information on Dietary Supplements
(IBIDS) Database is produced by the National Institutes of Health and
contains more than 380,000 scientific citations and abstracts on dietary
supplements, vitamins, minerals, and botanicals, plus a journal list of
more than 1,500 publications with links to their websites where full
journal articles may be ordered.

Bibliography

Abbot, N. C., "Healing as a therapy for human disease: a systematic review," *Journal of Alternative and Complementary Medicine*, April 2000.

Achterberg, Jeanne. *Imagery in Healing: Shamanism and Modern Medicine*. Boston: New Science Library, 1985.

Adler, J. H., et al., "The diabetic response of weanling sand rats (Psammomys obese) with diets containing different concentrations of salt bush (Atriplex halimus)," *Diabetes Research and Clinical Practice*, March 1986.

Agrawal, P., et al., "Randomized placebo-controlled, single blind trial of holy basil leaves in patients with non-insulin-dependent diabetes mellitus," *International Journal of Clinical Pharmacology and Theraputics*, September 1996.

Aikens, J. W., "Thermal biofeedback for claudication in diabetes: a literature review and case study," *Alternative Medicine Review*, April 1999.

Ajabnoor, M. A., "Effect of aloes on blood glucose levels in normal and alloxan diabetic mice," *Journal of Ethnopharmacology*, February 1990.

Alexander, C. N., "Transcendental meditation, mindfulness, and longevity: an experimental study with the elderly," *Journal of Personality and Social Psychology*, 1989.

Alghadyan, A. A., "Retinal vein occlusion in Saudi Arabia: possible role of dehydration," *Annals of Opthamology*, October 1993.

Al-Hadar, M. B., et al., "Hyperglycemic and insulin release inhibitory effects of Rosmarinus officinalis," *Journal of Ethnopharmacology*, 1994.

American Diabetes Association, "Clinical Practice Recommendations 1998," *Diabetes Care*, January 1998.

Anderson, James, M.D. *Live Longer Better: Dr. Anderson's Antioxidant, Anti-aging Program*. New York: Carroll & Graf, 1996.

Anderson, Richard A., et al., "Cinnamon extracts boost insulin sensitivity," *Agricultural Research*, July 2000.

Anderson, Richard A., et al., "Elevated intakes of supplemental chromium improve glucose and insulin variables in individuals with type 2 diabetes," *Diabetes*, November 1997.

Astin, J. A., et al., "The efficacy of 'distant healing': a systematic review of randomized trials," *Annals of Internal Medicine*, June 6, 2000.

Atkins, Robert, C., M.D. *Dr. Atkins New Diet Revolution*. New York: M. Evans, 1999.

Atkins, T. W., et al., "The treatment of poorly controlled non-insulin dependent diabetes subjects with granulated guar gum," *Diabetes Research and Clinical Practice*, May-June 1987.

Aro, A., et al., "Improved diabetic control and hypocholesterolaemic effect induced by long-term dietary supplementation with guar gum in type 2 (insulin-independent) diabetes," *Diabetologia*, July 1981.

Baily, C. J., and C. Day, "Traditional plant medicines as treatments for diabetes," *Diabetes Care*, September 1989.

Baldwin, K. W., M.D., "Therapeutic value of light and color," *Atlantic Medical Journal*, April 1927.

Baskaran, K., et al., "Antidiabetic effect of a leaf extract from Gymnema sylvestre in insulin-dependent diabetes mellitus patients," *Journal of Ethnopharmacology*, October 1990.

Batmanghelidj, F., M.D. *Your Body's Many Cries for Water: You Are Not Sick, You Are Thirsty*. Falls Church, Virginia: Global Health Solutions, 1997.

Becker, Robert, M.D., and Gary Selden. *The Body Electric: Electromagnetism and the Foundation of Life*. New York: William Morrow, 1985.

Ben, G., et al., "Effects of chronic alcohol intake on carbohydrate and lipid metabolism in subjects with type II (non-insulin-dependent) diabetes," *The American Journal of Medicine*, January 1991.

Benson, Herbert, M.D., with Marg Stark. *Timeless Healing: The Power and Biology of Belief*. New York: Scribners, 1996.

Bernstein, Richard K., M.D. *Dr. Bernstein's Diabetes Solution: The Complete Guide to Achieving Normal Blood Sugars*. Boston: Little, Brown & Company, 1997.

Berrio, L. F., et al., "Insulin activity stimulatory effects of cinnamon and brewer's yeast as influenced by albumin," *Hormone Research*, 1992.

Bloomfield, Harold H., M.D. *Healing Anxiety Naturally*. New York: Harper Perennial, 1998.

Blumenthal, Mark, editor. *The Complete German Commission E Monographs: Therapeutic Guide to Herbal Medicines, Integrative Medicine Communications*. American Botanical Council, 1998.

Boden, G., et al., "Effects of ethanol on carbohydrate metabolism in the elderly," *Diabetes*, January 1993.

Boden, G., et al., "Effects of vanadyl fulfate on carbohydrate and lipid metabolism with non-insulin-dependent diabetes mellitus," *Metabolism*, September 1996.

Boehm, S., et al., "Predictors of adherence to nutrition recommendations in people with non-insulin dependent diabetes mellitus," *Diabetes Educator*, March-April 1997.

Bonanome, A., et al., "Carbohydrate and lipid metabolism in patients with non-insulin-dependent diabetes mellitus: effects of a low-fat, high-carbohydrate diet vs. a diet high in monounsaturated fatty acids," *The American Journal of Clinical Nutrition*, 1991.

Bonnefont-Rousselot D., et al., "Consequences of the diabetic status on the oxidant/antioxidant balance," *Diabetes and Metabolism*, June 2000.

Borcea, V., et al., "Alpha-Lipoic acid decreases oxidative stress even in diabetic patients with poor glycemic control and albuminuria," *Free Radical Biology and Medicine*, June 1999.

Bordia, A., et al., "Effect of ginger (Zingiber officinale Rosc.) and fenugreek (Trigonella foenumgraecum L.) on blood lipids, blood sugar and platelet aggregation in patients with coronary artery disease," *Prostaglandins, Leukotrienes, and Essential Fatty Acids*, May 1997.

Bradley, E., "Spiritualcise mind-body exercise program," *Diabetes Educator*, March-April 1996.

Brala, P. M., and R. L. Hagen, "Effects of sweetness perception and caloric value of a preload on short term intake," *Physiology and Behavior*, January 1983.

Brent, L., and D. Weaver, "The physiological and behavioral effects of radio music on singly housed baboons," *Journal of Medical Primatology*, October 1996.

Broadhurst, C. L., et al., "Insulin-like biological activity of culinary and medicinal plant aqueous extracts in vitro," *Journal of Agriculture and Food Chemistry*, March 2000.

Broady, Tom, "Vitamin tests," *The Gale Encyclopedia of Medicine*. Farmington Hills, Michigan: Gale Research, 1999.

Bruning, Nancy, and Corey Weinstein. *Healing Homeopathic Remedies*. New York: Dell, 1996.

Bursell, S. E., "High-dose vitamin e supplementation normalizes retinal blood flow and creatinine clearance in patients with type 1 diabetes," *Diabetes Care*, August 1999.

Byers, J. F., and K. A. Smyth, "Effect of a music intervention on noise annoyance, heart rate, and blood pressure in cardiac surgery patients," *American Journal of Critical Care*, May 1997.

Capaldo, B., et al., "Carnitine improves peripheral glucose disposal in non-insulin-dependent diabetic patients," *Diabetes Research and Clinical Practice*, December 1991.

"Carnitine deficiency," editorial, *The Lancet*, March 17, 1990.

Cefalu, W. T., et al., "Effect of chromium picolinate on insulin sensitivity in vivo," *The Journal of Trace Elements in Experimental Medicine*, 1999.

Chakravarthy, B. K., et al., "Functional beta cell regeneration in rats by epicatechin," *The Lancet*, 1981.

Chattopadhyay, R. R., "A comparative evaluation of some blood sugar lowering agents," *Journal of Ethnopharmacology*, November 1999.

Choate, Clinton J., L.Ac., "Diabetes mellitus from conventional scientific and TCM perspectives," Chinese Medicine website healingpeople.com

Christensen, Alice. *The American Yoga Association Wellness Book*. New York: Kensington Publishing, 1995.

Collinge, William. *The American Holistic Health Association Complete Guide to Alternative Medicine*. New York. Warner Books, 1996.

"Compliance with physical activity recommendations by walking for exercise—Michigan, 1996 and 1998," *Morbidity and Mortality Weekly Report*, June 30, 2000.

Cooke, B., and E. Ernst, "Aromatherapy: a systematic review," *British Journal of General Practice*, June 2000.

Cooper, M. G., and N. N. Aygen, "Effect of transcendental meditation on serum cholesterol and blood pressure," *Harefuah, the Journal of the Israel Medical Association*, 1978.

Cousins, Norman. *Anatomy of an Illness as Perceived by the Patient: Reflections on Healing and Regeneration*. New York: W. W. Norton & Co., 1979.

Cox, R. H., et al, "Pain reduction and relaxation with brain wave syncronization (photo stimulation)," *The Journal of Neurological and Orthopaedic Medicine and Surgery*, 1996.

Critchfield, T., and A. Burris, "Chromium supplements: what's the story," *Diabetes Forecast*, April 1996.

Cummings, Stephen, M.D., and Dana, Ullman, MPH. *Everybody's Guide to Homeopathic Medicine*. Los Angeles: Jeremy Tarcher, 1991.

Das, U. N., "Essential fatty acids in health and disease," *The Journal of the Association of Physicians of India*, September 1999.

Deng, X. J., and Y. P. Xie, "Preliminary study on the treatment of diabetic retinopathy utilizing with nourishing yin, tonifying kidney and blood-activating herbs," *Chung Kuo Chung His I Chieh Ho Tsa Chih*, 1992.

De Palo, E., et al., "Plasma and urine free L-carnitine in human diabetes mellitus," *Acta diabetologia Lat*, 1981.

Dillon, R. S., "Improved serum insulin profiles in diabetic individuals who massaged their insulin injection sites," *Diabetes Care*, July-August 1983.

Dossey, Larry, M.D. *Healing Words: The Power of Prayer and the Practice of Medicine*. New York: HarperCollins, 1993.

Drum, David, and Terry Zierenberg, R.N., CDE. *The Type 2 Diabetes Sourcebook* (2nd edition). Los Angeles: Lowell House, 2000.

Edelstein, J., and M. W. Linn, "The influence of the family on control of diabetes," *Social Science & Medicine*, 1985.

"Effect of treatment with capsaicin on daily activities of patients with painful diabetic neuropathy." Capsaicin Study Group, *Diabetes Care*, February 1992.

Efimov, A. S., et al., "The effect of microwave resonance therapy on the clinical and metabolic indices of diabetic patients," *Ter Arkh*, 1991.

Elam, M., et al., "Effect of niacin on lipid and lipoprotein levels and glycemic control in patients with diabetes and peripheral arterial disease," *Journal of the American Medical Association*, September 13, 2000.

Elson, D. F., and M. Meredith, "Therapy for type 2 diabetes mellitus," *WMJ:Official Publication of the State Medical Society of Wisconsin*, March 1998.

Eriksson, B. S., and U. Rosenqvist, "Social support and glycemic control in non-insulin dependent diabetes mellitus patients: gender differences," *Women's Health Issues*, 1993.

Ernst, E., "Chelation therapy for coronary heart disease: An overview of all clinical investigations," *American Heart Journal*, July 2000.

Ernst, E., and M.H. Pittler, "Yohimbine for erectile dysfunction: a systematic review and meta-analysis of randomized clinical trials," *Journal of Urology*, February 1998.

Evans, M. B., "Emotional stress and diabetic control: a postulated model for the effect of emotional distress upon intermediary metabolism in the diabetic," *Biofeedback Self-Regulation*, September 1985.

Ewins, D. L., et al., "Alternative medicine: potential dangers for the diabetic foot," *Diabetic Medicine: a Journal of the British Diabetes Association*, 1993.

Ezrin, Calvin, M. S., and Robert E. Kowalski. *The Type II Diabetes Diet Book*. Los Angeles: Lowell House, 1995.

Fahim, M. A., et al., "Water deprivation reveals early neuromyopathy in diabetic mice," *Endocrine Research*, February 2000.

Filina, A. A., and N. A. Sporova, "Effect of lipoic acid on tyrosine metabolism in patients with open-angle glaucoma," *Vestn Oftalmol*, May-June 1991.

Filina, A. A., et al., "Lipoic acid as a means of metabolic therapy of open-angle glaucoma," *Vestn Oftalmol*, October-December 1995.

Fox, K. R., "The influence of physical activity on mental well-being," *Public Health Nutrition*, September 1999.

Frati-Munari, A. C., et al, "Effect of a dehydrated extract of nopal (Optunia ficus indica Mill.) on blood glucose," *Archivos de Investigacion Medica (Mex)*, 1989.

Frati-Munari, A. C., et al., "Hypoglycemic action of different doses of nopal (Opuntia streptacantha Lemaire) in patients with type II diabetes mellitus," *Archivos de Investigacion Medica (Mex)*, April-June 1989.

Frati-Munari, A. C., et al., "Influence of nopal intake upon fasting glycemia in type II diabetics and healthy subjects," *Archivos de Investigacion Medica (Mex)*, 1991.

Fuessl, H. S., et al., "Guar sprinkled on food: effect on glycaemic control, plasma lipis and gut hormones in non-insulin dependent diabetic patients," *Diabetic Medicine: a Journal of the British Diabetes Association*, September-October 1987.

Fukunishi, I., et al., "Perception and utilization of social support in diabetic control," *Diabetes Research and Clinical Practice*, September 1998.

Furnham, A., and R. Hayward, "A study and meta-analysis of lay attributions of cures for overcoming specific psychological problems," *The Journal of Genetic Psychology*, September 1997.

Garay-Sevilla, M. E., et al., "Adherence to treatment and social support in patients with non-insulin dependent diabetes mellitus," *Journal of Diabetes Complications*, April-June 1995.

Garg, A., et al., "Comparisons of effects of high and low carbohydrate diets on lipoproteins and insulin sensitivity in patients with mild NIDDM," *Diabetes*, October 1992.

Garg, A., "High-monusaturated-fat diets for patients with diabetes mellitus: a meta-analysis," *The American Journal of Clinical Nutrition*, 1998.

Gerber, Richard, M.D. *Vibrational Medicine for the 21st Century: The Complete Guide to Energy Healing and Spiritual Transformation.* New York: Eagle Brook/HarperCollins, 2000.

Ghannam, N., et al., "The antidiabetic activity of aloes: preliminary clinical and experimental observations," *Hormone Research*, 1986.

Ghen, Mitchell J., "Treating diabetes mellitus," *American Journal of Natural Medicine*, October 31, 1998.

Giancaterini, A., et al., "Acetyl-L-carnitine infusion increases glucose disposal in type 2 diabetic patients," *Metabolism*, June 2000.

Gilden, S. P., et al., "Diabetes support groups improve health care of older diabetic patients," *Journal of the American Geriatric Society*, 1992.

Gill, G. V., et al., "Diabetes and alternative medicine: a cause for concern," *Diabetic Medicine: a Journal of the British Diabetes Association*, March 1994.

Goldfine, A., "Vanadium," Joslin Diabetes Center website www.joslin. harvard.edu/research

Goleman, Daniel, Ph.D., and Joel Gurin, editors. *Mind Body Medicine: How to Use Your Mind for Better Health*. Yonkers, New York: Consumer Reports Books, 1993.

Gorie, M., and R. K. Campbell, "Natural products and diabetes treatment," *Diabetes Educator*, March-April 1998.

Gray, A. M., and P. R. Flatt, "Insulin-releasing and insulin-like activity of the traditional anti-diabetic plant Coriandrum sativum (coriander)," *British Journal of Nutrition*, March 1999.

Gray, A. M., and P. R. Flatt, "Pancreatic and extra-pancreatic effects of the traditional anti-diabetic plant, Medicago sativa (lucerne)," *British Journal of Nutrition*, August 1997.

Gray, J., "Homeopathy in the Management of Diabetes Mellitus," *The Journal of the British Homeopathic Association*, April 30, 1997.

Griffith, L. S., et al., "Life stress and social support in diabetes: association with glycemic control," *International Journal of Psychiatry in Medicine*, 1990.

Gumeniuk, V. A., et al., "Systems analysis of colour music corrective effect," *Vestn Ross Adak Med Nauk*, 1998.

Guthrie, Diana W., Ph.D., CDE, with Richard Guthrie, M.D. *Alternative and Complementary Diabetes Care: How to Combine Natural and Traditional Methods*. New York: John Wiley & Sons, 2000.

Hamilton, Kirk, "Diabetes mellitus, alpha lipoic acid, vitamin C and vitamin E," *Health Counselor*, July 31, 1997.

Hanser, S. B., and L. W. Thompson, "Effects of a music therapy strategy on depressed older adults," *Journal of Gerontology*, November 1994.

Hardy, M., et al., "Replacement of drug treatment for insomnia by ambient odour," *The Lancet*, September 9, 1995.

Harpur, Tom. *The Uncommon Touch: An Investigation of Spiritual and Energy Field Healing*. Toronto, Canada: McClelland & Stewart, 1995.

Harvery, Claire, and Amanda Cochrane. *The Encyclopedia of Flower Remedies*. Great Britain: Thorsons/HarperCollins, 1995.

Helmrich, S. P., et al., "Physical activity and reduced occurrence of non-insulin-dependent diabetes mellitus," *New England Journal of Medicine*," July 18, 1991.

"Herbal medicines: where is the evidence?" editorial, *British Medical Journal*, August 12, 2000.

Herpetz, S., et al., "Patients with diabetes mellitus: psychosocial stress and use of psychosocial support: a multicenter study," *Medizinische Klinik*, July 2000.

Hilz, M. F., et al., "Diabetic somatic polyneuropathy. Pathogenesis, clinical manifestations and therapeutic concepts," *Fortschr Neurol Psychiatr*, June 2000.

Hoffer, Abram, M.D., and Morton Walker, DPM. *Smart Nutrients: A Guide to Nutrients That Can Prevent and Reverse Senility*. Garden City, New York: Avery Publishing Group, 1994.

Holman, R. R., et al., "No glycemic benefit from guar administration in NIDDM," *Diabetes Care*, January-February 1987.

Hong, C. Z., et al., "Magnetic necklace: its therapeutic effectiveness on neck and shoulder pain," *Archives of Physical Medicine and Rehabilitation*, October 1982.

Horrobin, D. F., "Essential fatty acids and the complications of diabetes mellitus," *Wien Klin Wopchenschu*, April 14, 1989.

Horrobin, D. F., "The use of gamma-linolenic acid in diabetic neuropathy," *Agents Actions Supplement*, 1992.

"How Does Catalyst Altered Water Work?" The Official Willard Water Website www.dr-willardswater.com

Huebner, Peter, "Research on Diabetes," Medical Resonance Therapy website www.medicalresonancetherapymusic.com

Hui, Hu, "A Review of Treatment of Diabetes by Acupuncture During the Past Forty Years," *Journal of Traditional Chinese Medicine*, 1995.

Ikemoto, S., et al., "High-fat diet-induced hyperglycemia and obesity in mice: differential effects of dietary oils," *Metabolism*, December 1996.

"Illness and Injuries Associated with the Use of Selected Dietary Supplements," U.S. Food and Drug Administration Center for Food Safety and Applied Nutrition, 1993. No author listed.

Inouye, M., et al., "Levels of lipid peroxidation product and glycated hemoglobin in the erythrocytes of diabetic patients," *Clin Chim Acta*, August 1998.

Jain, S. C., et al., "A study of response pattern of non-insulin dependent diabetics and yoga therapy," *Diabetes Research and Clinical Practice*, January 1993.

Jamal, G. A., "The use of gamma linolenic acid in the prevention and treatment of diabetic neuropathy," *Diabetic Medicine: a Journal of the British Diabetes Association*, March 1994.

Jamal, G. A., and H. Carmichael, "The effect of gamma-linolenic acid on human diabetic peripheral neuropathy: a double-blind placebo-controlled trial," *Diabetic Medicine: a Journal of the British Diabetes Association*, May 1990.

Janssen, G. W. H. M., "The Maharishi Ayur-Veda treatment of ten chronic diseases—a pilot study," *Nederlands Tijdschrift voor Integrale Geneeskunde*, 1989.

Jenkins, D. J., et al., "Dietary fibres, fibre analogues, and glucose tolerance: importance of viscosity," *British Medical Journal*, May 27, 1978.

Jialal, I., and S. Devaraj, "High intake of Vitamin E can help reduce heart disease and stroke risk in Type II diabetics," *Circulation*, July 11 2000.

Johnson, K. E., et al., "The effectiveness of a magnetized water oral irrigator (Dyrdr Floss®) on plaque, calculus and gingival health," *Journal of Clinical Periodontology*, May 1993.

Jones, D. B., "Low-dose guar improves diabetic control," *Journal of the Royal Society of Medicine*, July 1985.

Kahn, A., et al., "Insulin potentiating factor and chromium content of selected foods and spices," *Biological Trace Element Research*, March 1990.

Kant, Ashima K., "Consumption of energy-dense, nutrient-poor foods by adult Americans: nutrition and health implications. The Third National Health and Nutrition Examination Survey, 1988–1994," *The American Journal of Clinical Nutrition*, October 2000.

Kaptchuk, Ted. *The Web That Has No Weaver: Understanding Chinese Medicine*. New York: Congdon and Weed, 1992.

Karlstrom, B., et al., "Effects of leguminous seeds in a mixed diet in non-insulin-dependent diabetic patients," *Diabetes Research*, 1987.

Keen, R. W., et al., "Indian herbal remedies for diabetes as a cause of lead poisoning," *Postgraduate Medical Journal*, 1994.

Keen, H., et al., "Treatment of diabetic neuropathy with gamma-linolenic acid. The Gamma-Linolenic Acid Multicenter Trial Group," *Diabetes Care*, January 1993.

Kelleher, D. J., "Do self-help groups help?" *International Disability Studies*, 1990.

Kelly, Gregory, N. D., "Insulin resistance: lifestyle and nutritional interventions," *Alternative Medicine Review: a Journal of Clinical Therapeutic*, April 2000.

Khamaisi, M., et al., "Lipoic acid acutely induces hypoglycemia in fasting nondiabetic and diabetic rats," *Metabolism*, April 1999.

Khanna, P., et al., "Hypoglycemic activity of polypeptide-p from a plant source," *Journal of Natural Products*, November-December 1981.

Kingery, W. S., "A critical review of controlled clinical trials for peripheral neuropathic pain and complex regional pain syndromes," *Pain*, November 1997.

Kleinjnen, J., et al., "Clinical trials of homeopathy," *British Medical Journal*, February 9, 1991.

Kleinjnen, J., et al., "Garlic, onions and cardiovascular risk factors. A review of the evidence from human experiments with emphasis on commercial available preparations," *British Journal of Clinical Pharmacology*, November 1989.

Koutsikos, D., et al., "Oral glucose tolerance test after high-dose i.v. biotin administration in normoglucemic hemodialysis patients," *Renal Failure*, January 1996.

Krause, R., et al., "Ultraviolet B and blood pressure," *The Lancet*, August 29, 1998.

Kreiger, Dolores, Ph.D., R.N. *The Therapeutic Touch: How to Use Your Hands to Help or to Heal.* New York: Prentice Hall, 1986.

Kubo, K., et al., "Anti-diabetic activity present in the fruit body of Grifola frondosa (Maitake)," *Biological & Pharmaceutical Bulletin*, 1994.

Kurtzweil, P., "An FDA guide to dietary supplements," *FDA Consumer*, September-October 1998.

Lamberg, L., "Dawn's early light to twilight's last gleaming," *Journal of the American Medical Association*, November 11, 1998.

Lamparski, D. M., and R. R. Wing, "Blood glucose discrimination training in patients with type II diabetes," *Biofeedback Self-Regulation*, 1989.

Landis, B. J., "Uncertainty, spiritual well-being, and psychosocial adjustment in chronic illness," *Issues in Mental Health Nursing*, May-June 1996.

Landon, K., et al., "Guar gum improves insulin sensitivity, blood lipids, blood pressure, and fibrinolysis in healthy men," *American Journal of Clinical Nutrition*, January 2001.

Lanthony, P., and J. P. Cosson, "The course of color vision in early diabetic retinopathy treated with Ginkgo biloba extract. A preliminary double-blind versus placebo study," *J Fr Opthalmol*, 1988.

Lark, Susan, M.D. *The Chemistry of Success: Six Secrets of Peak Performance*. San Francisco: Bay Books, 2000.

The Lawrence Review of Natural Products, Facts and Comparisons, St. Louis, Missouri. Ongoing.

Lawrence, Ron, M.D., Ph.D.; Paul Rosch, M.D., FACP; and Judith Plowden. *Magnet Therapy: The Pain Cure Alternative*. Rocklin, California: Prima Publishing, 1998.

Leatherdale, B. A., et al., "Improvement in glucose tolerance due to Momordica charantia (karela)," *British Medical Journal*, June 6, 1981.

Liberman, Jacob, O. D., Ph.D. *Light: Medicine of the Future*. Santa Fe: Bear & Company, 1991.

Liljeberg, H., and I. Bjorck, "Bioavailability of starch in bread products. Postprandial glucose and insulin responses in healthy subjects and in vitro resistant starch content," *European Journal of Clinical Nutrition*, March 1994.

Liljeberg, H., and I. Bjorck, "Delayed gastric emptying rate may explain improved glycaemia in healthy subjects to a starchy meal with added vinegar," *European Journal of Clinical Nutrition*, May 1998.

Lima, M de S., et al., "The effect of magnesium supplementation in increasing doses and control of type 2 diabetes," *Diabetes Care*, May 1998.

Linde, K., et al., "Are the clinical effects of homeopathy placebo effects? a meta-analysis of controlled trials," *The Lancet*, September 20, 1997.

Lininger, Skye, D.C., editor. *The Natural Pharmacy*. Rocklin, California: Prima Publishing, 1998.

Luks, Allen, with Peggy Payne. *The Healing Power of Doing Good: The Health and Spiritual Benefits of Helping Others*. New York: Fawcett Columbine, 1992.

Lundeberg, T. C., et al., "Electrical nerve stimulation improves healing of diabetic ulcers," *Annals of Plastic Surgery*, 1992.

Luthe, Wolfgang. *Introduction to the Methods of Autogenic Therapy*, training manual, 1977.

Lynch, J., et al., "Moderately intense physical activities and high levels of cardiorespiratory fitness reduce the risk of non-insulin-dependent diabetes mellitus in middle-aged men," *Archives of Internal Medicine*, June 24, 1996.

Madar, Z., et al., "Glucose-lowering effect of fenugreek in non-insulin dependent diabetes," *European Journal of Clinical Nutrition*, January 1988.

Mahdi, G. S., and J. D. Naismith, "Role of chromium in barley in modulating the symptoms of diabetes," *Annals of Nutrition and Metabolism*, 1991.

Malter, R., "Trace mineral analysis and psychoneuroimmunology," *Townsend Letter for Doctors and Patients*, April 30, 1996.

Mamchenko G. F., and G. P. Kolesova, "The use of homeopathy in treating diabetics," *Lik sprava*, November-December 1992.

Manisha, Chandalia, M.D., et al., "Beneficial effects of high dietary fiber intake in patients with type 2 diabetes mellitus," *New England Journal of Medicine*, May 11, 2000.

Matsumoto, J., "Vanadate, molybdate and tungstate for orthomolecular medicine," *Medical Hypotheses*, 1994.

Maxwell, A. E., et al., "Effects of a social support group, as an adjunct to diabetes training, on metabolic control and psychosocial outcomes," *Diabetes Educator*, 1992.

McCarty, M. F., "High-dose biotin, an inducer of glucokinase expression, may synergize with chromium picolinate to enable a definite nutritional therapy for type II diabetes," *Medical Hypothesis*, May 1999.

McCarty, M. F., "High-dose pyridoxine as an 'anti-stress' strategy," *Medical Hypotheses*, May 2000.

McCarty, M. F., "Toward a wholly nutritional therapy for type 2 diabetes," *Medical Hypotheses*, March 2000.

McCarty, M. F., "Toward practical prevention of type 2 diabetes," *Medical Hypotheses*, May 2000.

McGrady, A., "Effects of group relaxation training and thermal biofeedback on blood pressure and related physiological and psychological variables in essential hypertension," *Biofeedback Self Regulation*, March 1994.

McInnis, K. J., "Exercise and obesity," *Coronary Artery Disease*, March 2000.

The Medical Advisor: The Complete Guide to Alternative and Conventional Treatments. Alexandria, Virginia: Time-Life Books, 1997.

Miller, M., and R. Rahe, "Life changes scaling for the 1990s," *Journal of Psychosomatic Research*, September 1997.

Mingrone, G., et al., "L-carnitine improves glucose disposal in type 2 diabetic patients," *Journal of the American College of Nutrition*, February 1999.

Mohan, I. K., and U. N. Das, "Effect of L-arginine-nitric oxide system on the metabolism of essential fatty acids in chemical-induced diabetes mellitus," *Prostaglandins Leukotrines, and Essential Fatty Acids*, January 2000.

Mooradian, A., et al., "Selected vitamins and minerals in diabetes," *Diabetes Care*, May 1994.

Murphy, D. R., "Diagnosis and manipulative treatment in diabetic polyneuropathy and its relation to intertarsal joint dysfunction," *Journal of Manipulative and Physiological Theraputics*, 1994.

Murray, Michael, N. D., and Joseph Pizzorno, N.D., *The Encyclopedia of Natural Medicine* (2nd edition). Rocklin, California: Prima Publishing, 1998.

Murray, Michael, N. D. *Diabetes and Hypoglycemia*. Rocklin, California: Prima Publishing, 1994.

Murray, Michael, N. D., "Vitamin C in diabetes mellitus: abstracts and commentary," *The American Journal of Natural Medicine*, May 1996.

Myss, Caroline, Ph.D. *Why People Don't Heal and How They Can*. New York: Harmony Books, 1997.

Naismith, D. J., et al., "Therapeutic value of barley in the management of diabetes," *Annals of Nutrition and Metabolism*, 1991.

Nakaya, Y., et al., "Taurine improves insulin sensitivity in the Otsuka Long-Evens Tokushima Fatty rat, a model of spontaneous type 2 diabetes," *American Journal of Clinical Nutrition*, January 2000.

Naylor, G. J., et al., "A double-blind placebo controlled trial of ascorbic acid in obesity," *Nutritional Health*, 1985.

Neil, H. A., et al., "Garlic powder in the treatment of moderate hyperlipidaemia: a controlled trial and meta-analysis," *Journal of the Royal College of Physicians of London*, July-August 1996.

Neiswander, A. C., M.D. *Homeopathic Guide for the Family*. St. Louis, Missouri: American Foundation for Homeopathy, 1986.

Nelson, W. A., "Diabetes mellitus: two case reports," *Chiropractic Technique*, May 31, 1989.

Nesse, Randolph M., M.D., and George C. Williams, Ph.D. *Why We Get Sick: The New Science of Darwinian Medicine*. New York: Random House, 1994.

Nicholson, A., "Toward improved management of NIDDM: a randomized, controlled, pilot intervention using a lowfat, vegetarian diet," *Preventive Medicine*, 1999.

Norbiato, G., et al., "Effects of potassium supplementation on insulin binding and insulin action in human obesity: protein-modified fast and refeeding," *European Journal of Clinical Investigation*, December 1984.

Nothwehr, F., and T. Stump, "Health-promoting behaviors among adults with type 2 diabetes: findings from the Health and Retirement Study," *Preventive Medicine*, May 2000.

"Nutrition and diabetes resource list for consumers," Food and Nutrition Information Center, Agricultural Research Service, USDA, Beltsville, Maryland.

Nuttall, F. Q., "Dietary fiber in the management of diabetes," *Diabetes*, April 1993.

Oettle, G. F., et al., "Glucose and insulin responses to manufactured and whole-food snacks," *American Journal of Clinical Nutrition*, 1986.

Olszewer, E., and J.P. Carter, "EDTA chelation therapy in chronic degenerative disease," *Medical Hypotheses*, September 1988.

Olszewer, E., et al., "A pilot double-blind study of sodium-magnesium EDTA in peripheral vascular disease," *Journal of the National Medical Association*, March 1990.

Ornish, Dean, M.D. *Dr. Dean Ornish's Program for Reversing Heart Disease*. New York: Ballantine Books, 1990.

Paolisso, G. et al., "Daily vitamin E supplements improve metabolic control but not insulin secretion in elderly type II diabetic patients," *Diabetes Care*, November 1993.

Parillo, M., et al., "A high-monusaturated-fat/low-carbohydrate diet improves peripheral insulin sensitivity in non-insulin-dependent diabetic patients," *Metabolism*, December 1992.

Pauling, Linus. *How to Live Longer and Feel Better.* New York: Avon, 1986.

Peeke, Pamela, M.D., MPH. *Fight Fat After Forty: The Revolutionary Three-Pronged Approach That Will Break Your Stress-Fat Cycle and Make You Healthy, Fit, and Trim for Life.* New York: Viking Press, 2000.

Pelletier, Kenneth R., Ph.D. *The Best Alternative Medicine: What Works? What Does Not?* New York: Simon & Schuster, 2000.

Pelletier, Kenneth R., Ph.D. *Holistic Medicine: From Stress to Optimum Health.* New York: Dell Publishing, 1979.

Perschel, W. T., et al., "Susceptibility to infections in diabetes—effects on metabolism," *Immun Infekt*, December 1995.

Peshko, A. A., "Laser puncture in the treatment of diabetic angiopathies of the lower extremeties," *Vrach delo*, 1992.

Plantel, K., and K. Srinivasan, "Effect of dietary intake of freeze dried bitter gourd (Momordic charantia) in streptozotocin induced diabetic rats," *Nahrung*, 1995.

Plantel, K., et al., "Influence of bitter gourd (Momordica chrantia) on growth and blood constituents in albino rats," *Nahrung*, 1993.

Plantel, K., and K. Srinivasan, "Plant foods in the management of diabetes mellitus: vegetables as potential hypoglycaemic agents," *Nahrung*, April 1997.

Poirier, P., et al., "Impact of time interval from the last meal on glucose response to exercise in subjects with type 2 diabetes," *The Journal of Clinical Endocrinology and Metabolism*, August 2000.

Ratner, H., et al., "A hypnotherapeutic approach to the improvement of compliance in adolescent diabetics," *American Journal of Clinical Hypnosis*, January 1990.

Rice, B. I., and J.V. Schindler, "Effect of thermal biofeedback-assisted relaxation training on blood circulation in the lower extremities of a population with diabetes," *Diabetes Care*, July 1992.

Rider, M. S., et al., "The effect of music, therapy, and relaxation on adrenal corticosteroids and the reentrainment of circadian rhythms," *Journal of Music Therapy*, Spring 1985.

Rosch, Paul, M.D., "Stress and the diabetes epidemic," *Health and Stress*, the newsletter of the American Institute of Stress, October 2000.

Ryan, A. S., "Insulin resistance with aging: effects of diet and exercise," *Sports Medicine*, November 2000.

Ryan, M., et al., "Diabetes and the Mediterranean diet: a beneficial effect of oleic acid on insulin sensitivity, adipocyte glucose transport and endothelium-dependent vasoreactivity," *Monthly Journal of the Association of Physicians*, February 2000.

Ruhnau, K. J., et al., "Effects of 3-week oral treatment with the antioxidant thioctic acid (alpha-lipoic acid) in symptomatic diabetic polyneuropathy," *Diabetic Medicine: a Monthly Journal of the British Diabetes Association*, December 1999.

Sabo, Carolyn E., Ed.D., R.N.; Susan Rush Michael, DNSc., R.N., CDE; and Lori L. Temple, Ph.D., "The use of alternative therapies by diabetes educators," *The Diabetes Educator*, November/December 1999.

Sadhukhan, B., et al., "Clinical evaluation of a herbal antidiabetic product," *Journal of the Indian Medical Association*, 1994.

Salmeron, J., et al., "Dietary fiber, glycemic load, and risk of NIDDM in men," *Diabetes Care*, April 1997.

Sanchez de Medina, F., et al., "Hypoglycemic activity of juniper berries," *Planta Medica*, June 1994.

Sargent, L. A., et al., "Vitamin C and hyperglycemia in the European Prospective Investigation into Cancer—Norfolk (EPIC-Norfolk) study: a population-based study," *Diabetes Care*, June 2000.

Sauvaire, Y., et al., "4-Hydroxyisoleucine: a novel amino acid potentiator of insulin secretion," *Diabetes*, February 1998.

Schimizu, H., et al., "Long-term effect of eicosapentaenoic acid ethyl (EPA-E) on albuminuria of non-insulin dependent diabetic patients," *Diabetes Research and Clinical Practice*, April 1995.

Schlitz, M., and W. Braud, "Distant intentionality and healing: assessing the evidence," *Alternative Therapies in Health and Medicine*, November 1997.

Schmidt, Lois E., and K. E. Yarasheski, "Magnesium and diabetes: a call for concern," *Practical Diabetology*, March 1995.

Schmidt, Lois E., R.D., MPH, CDE, "Practical mineral recommendations: translation to clinical practice," *The Diabetes Educator*, January/February 1995.

Sears, Barry, Ph.D. *The Zone: A Dietary Road Map*. New York: Regan-Books, 1995.

Seiler, G., and V. Seiler, "The effects of transcendental meditation on periodontal tissue," *Journal of the American Society of Psychosomatic Dentistry and Medicine*, 1979.

Selye, Hans, M.D. *The Stress of Life*. New York: McGraw-Hill, 1976.

Seneff, John A. *Numb Toes and Aching Soles: Coping with Peripheral Neuropathy*. San Antonio, Texas: MedPress, 1999.

Shani, J., et al., "Insulin-potentiating effect of salt bush (Atriplex halimus) ashes," *Israeli Journal of Medical Sciences*, June 1972.

Shanmugasundaram, E. R., et al., "Possible regeneration of the islets of Langerhans in streptozotocin-diabetic rats given Gymnema sylvestre leaf extracts," *Journal of Ethnopharmacology*, 1990.

Shanmugasundaram, E. R., et al., "Use of Gymnema sylvestre leaf extract in the control of blood glucose in insulin-dependent diabetes mellitus," *Journal of Ethnopharmacology*, October 1990.

Sharma, R. D., et al., "Effect of fenugreek seeds on blood glucose and serum lipids in diabetes," *European Journal of Clinical Nutrition*, April 1990.

Shaw, S., "Guided imagery and diabetes—is wellness all in your mind?" *Diabetes Interview*, September 1997.

Shigeta, Y., et al., "Effect of Coenzyme Q7 treatment on blood sugar and ketone bodies of diabetics," Journal of Vitaminolgy, 1966.

Shoji, M., et al., "Pharmacological effects of Gosha-jinki-gan-ryo extract: effects on experimental diabetes," *Nippon Yakurigaku Zasshi*, 1992.

Shealy, C. Norman, M.D., Ph.D. *Miracles Do Happen: A Physician's Experience with Alternative Medicine*. Rockport, Massachusetts: Element Books, 1995.

Shealy, C. Norman, M.D., Ph.D., editor. *The Illustrated Encyclopedia of Natural Remedies*. Rockport, Massachusetts: Element Books, 1998.

Silagy, C., and A. Neil, "Garlic as a lipid lowering agent—a meta-analysis," *Journal of the Royal College of Physicians of London*, January-February 1994.

Silagy, C. A., and H. A. Neil, "A meta-analysis of the effect of garlic on blood pressure," *Journal of Hypertension*, April 1994.

Simopoulos, Artemis P., "Essential fatty acids in health and chronic disease," *American Journal of Clinical Nutrition*, September 1999.

Simpson, I., et al., "A high carbohydrate leguminous fiber diet improves all aspects of diabetic control," *The Lancet*, 1981.

Singh, R. B., et al., "Effect of hydrosoluble coenzyme Q10 on blood pressures and insulin resistance in hypertensive patients with coronary artery disease," *Journal of Human Hypertension*, March 1999.

Skrha J., et al., "Insulin Action and fibrinolysis influenced by vitamin E in obese subjects with Type 2 diabetes mellitus," *Diabetes Research and Clinical Practice*, April 1999.

Snowden, D. A., and R. L. Phillips, "Does a vegetarian diet reduce the occurrence of diabetes?" *American Journal of Public Health*, May 1985.

Sorensen, L., and K. E. Ibsen, "Purulent myofascititis in a patient with diabetes treated with a vacuum boot by a zone therapist," *Ugeskr Laeger*, 1993.

Spiegel, D., "Imagery and hypnosis in the treatment of cancer patients," *Oncology*, August 1997.

Sreedevi, Chaturvedi A., "Effect of vegetable fibre on post prandial glycemia," *Plant Foods for Human Nutrition*, July 1993.

Storlien, L. H., et al., "Skeletal muscle membrane lipids and insulin resistance," *Lipids*, March 1996.

Stoudenmire, J., "A comparison of muscle relaxation training and music in the reduction of state and trait anxiety," *Journal of Clinical Psychology*, July 1975.

Strokov, I. A., "The efficacy of the intravenous administration of the trometamol salt of thioctic (alpha-lipoic) acid in diabetic neuropathy," *Zh Nevrol Psikhiatr Im SS Korsakova*, 1999.

Subotnick, Steven L., "Diabetes mellitus: an integrated homeopathic approach," *Journal of the American Institute of Homeopathy*, March 31, 1997.

Sullivan, Karin Horgan, "Herb dos and don'ts," *Natural Health*, February 2000.

Surwit, R. S., and M. N. Feinglos, "The effects of relaxations on glucose tolerance in non-insulin dependent diabetes," *Diabetes Care*, 1983.

Surwit, R. S., and M. S. Schneider, "Role of stress in the etiology and treatment of diabetes mellitus," *Psychosomatic Medicine*, July-August 1993.

Suzuki, Y., et al., "Effects of gosha-jinki-gan, a kampo medicine, on peripheral tissue blood flow in streptozotocin-induced diabetic rats," *Methods and Findings in Experimental and Clinical Pharmacology*, May 1998.

Swanson-Flatt, S. D., et al., "Glycaemic effects of traditional European plant treatments for diabetes. Studies in normal and streptozotocin diabetic mice," *Diabetes Research*, February 1989.

Tagliaferro, V., et al., "Moderate guar-gum addition to usual diet improves peripheral sensitivity to insulin and lipaemic profile in NIDDM," *Diabetes and Metabolism*, December 1985.

Tattersall, R. B., et al., "Group therapy in the treatment of diabetes," *Diabetes Care*, 1985.

Tawata, M., et al., "The effects of goshajinkigan, a herbal medicine, on subjective symptoms and vibratory threshold in patients with diabetic neuropathy," *Diabetes Research and Clinical Practice*, 1994.

"Things that push your blood sugar level up or down," *Mayo Clinic Health Letter*, February 1998.

Thorne, M. D., et al., "Factors affecting starch digestibility and the glycemic response with special reference to legumes," *American Journal of Clinical Nutrition*, 1983.

Tjokroprawiro, A., et al., "Metabolic effects of onion and green beans on diabetic patients," *The Tohoku Journal of Experimental Medicine*, December 1983.

Torjesen, P. A., et al., "Lifestyle changes may reverse development of the insulin resistance syndrome. The Oslo Diet and Exercise Study: a randomized trial," *Diabetes Care*, January 1997.

Tosiello, L., "Hypomagnesia and diabetes mellitus: a review of clinical implications," *Archives of Internal Medicine*, June 10, 1996.

Trachtman, H., et al., "Taurine ameliorates chronic streptozocin-induced diabetic nephropathy in rats," *American Journal of Physiology*, September 1995.

Trejo-Gonzales A., et al., "A purified extract from prickly pear cactus (Optunia fuliginosa) controls experimentally induced diabetes in rats," *Journal of Ethnopharmacology*, December 1996.

Tremble, J. M., and D. Donaldson, "Is continued weight gain inevitable in type 2 diabetes mellitus?" *Journal of the Royal Society of Health*, December 1999.

Ulene, Art, M.D. *Nutribase Nutrition Facts Desk Reference*. Garden City, New York: Avery Publishing Group, 1995.

Ullman, Dana, MPH. *The Consumer's Guide to Homeopathy*. New York: Tarcher/Putnam, 1996.

Urban, J., et al., "Folk healing causing severe diabetic coma," *Cas Lek Cesk*, 1992.

Usuki, Y., et al., "Successful treatment of a senile diabetic woman with cataract with goshajinkigan," *American Journal of Chinese Medicine*, 1991.

Uusitupa, M., et al., "Long-term effects of guar gum on metabolic control, serum cholesterol and blood pressure levels in type 2 (non-insulin dependent) diabetic patients with high blood pressure," *Annals of Clinical Research*, 1984.

Van Loon, Luc J. C., et al., "Plasma insulin responses after ingestion of different amino acid or protein mixtures with carbohydrate," *American Journal of Clinical Nutrition*, July 2000.

Vegitarian Diets Position of ADA, *Journal of the American Dietetic Association*, 1997.

Velussi, M., et al., "Long-term (12 months) treatment with an antioxidant drug (silymarin) is effective on hyperinsulinemia, exogenous insulin need and malondialdehyde levels in cirrhotic diabetic patients," *Journal of Hepatology*, April 1997.

Vessby, B., "Dietary fat and insulin action in humans," *British Journal of Nutrition*, March 2000.

Vogler, B. K., and E. Ernst, "Aloe vera: a systematic review of its clinical effectiveness," *British Journal of General Practice*, October 1999.

Vuksan, V., et al., "American Ginseng (panax quinquefolius L) Reduces Postprandial Glycemia in Nondiabetic Subjects and Subjects with

Type 2 Diabetes Mellitus," *Archives of Internal Medicine*, April 10, 2000.

Vuksan, V., et al., "Konjac-mannan (glucomannan) improves glycemia and other associated risk factors for coronary heart disease in type 2 diabetes. A randomized controlled metabolic trial," *Diabetes Care*, June 1999.

Walker, Morton, DPM. *The Chelation Answer: How to Prevent Hardening of the Arteries and Rejuvenate Your Cardiovascular System.* Atlanta: Second Opinion, 1994.

Walker, Morton, DPM. *DMSO: Nature's Healer.* Garden City, New York: Avery Books, 1993.

Wallace, R. K., et al., "Decreased blood pressure in hypertensive subjects who practiced meditation," *Circulation/Supplement II*, 1972.

Wallace, R. K., et al., "Systolic blood pressure and long-term practice of the Transcendental Meditation and TM-Sidhi program: Effects of TM on systolic blood pressure," *Psychosomatic Medicine*, 1983.

Wang, C. Y., and M.M. Fenski, "Self-care of adults with non-insulin dependent diabetes mellitus: influence of family and friends," *Diabetes Educator*, September-October 1996.

Wang, X. M., "Treating type II diabetes mellitus with foot reflexotherapy," *Chung Juo Chung His I Chieh Ho Tsa Chih*, 1993.

Wang, Z., and Z. Yin, "Effect of ke-tang-Ling administration on the function of pancreatic islets cells in non-insulin-dependent diabetes mellitus," *Chung Juo Chung His I Chieh Ho Tsa Chih*, 1990.

Wascher, T. C., et al., "Effects of low-dose L-arginine on insulin-mediated vasodilation and insulin sensitivity," *European Journal of Clinical Investigation*, August 1997.

"Water/Hydration . . . Water Works," American Dietetic Association website, www.eatright.org

Watkins, G. R., "Music therapy: proposed physiological mechanisms and clinical implications," *Clinical Nurse Specialist CNS*, March 1997.

Webb, D., "Traditional Chinese Herbal Medicines in Taiwan Adulterated with Synthetic Conventional Drugs," *HerbalGram*, 1998.

Weintraub, M., "Magnetic bio-stimulation in painful diabetic peripheral neuropathy: a novel intervention—a randomized, double-blind placebo crossover study," *American Journal of Pain Management*, 1999.

Welihinda, J., et al., "Effect of Momordica charantia on the glucose tolerance in maturity onset diabetes," *Journal of Ethnopharmacology*, September 1986.

Wenneberg, S. R., et al., "The effect of transcendental meditation on ambulatory blood pressure and cardiovascular reactivity," presented at the 52nd Annual Meeting of the American Psychosomatic Society, Boston, April 1994.

White, J. M., "Effects of relaxing music on cardiac autonomic balance and anxiety after acute myocardial infarction," *American Journal of Critical Care*, July 1999.

Wichowski, H. C., and S. M. Kubsch, "Increasing diabetic self-care through guided imagery," *Complementary Therapies in Nursing and Midwidery*, December 1999.

Will, J.C., et al., "Serum vitamin C concentrations and diabetes: findings from the Third National Health and Nutrition Examination Survey, 1988-1994," *American Journal of Clinical Nutrition*, July 1999.

Wilson, W., and C. Pratt, "The impact of diabetes education and peer support upon weight and glycemic control of elderly persons with noninsulin dependent diabetes mellitus (NIDDM)," *American Journal of Public Health*, May 1987.

Windsor, R., "Healing with the human energy field to harmonize the body, mind and spirit: An interview with Barbara Brennan," *Spectrum Magazine*, as reprinted at www.barbarabrennan.com.

Winter, M. F., et al., "Music reduces stress and anxiety of patients in the surgical holding area," *Journal of Post Anesthesia Nursing*, December 1994.

Wirz-Justice, A., and P. Graw, "Phototherapy," *Ther Umsch*, February 2000.

Wolever, T.M., "Dietary carbohydrates and insulin action in humans," *British Journal of Nutrition*, March 1983.

Wolever, T. M., et al., "Effect of canning on the blood glucose response to beans in patients with type 2 diabetes," *Human Nutrition, Clinical Nutrition*, 1987.

Wolever, T. M., et al., "Effect of method of administration of psyllium on glycemic response and carbohydrate digestibility," *Journal of the American College of Nutrition*, 1991.

Wolf, S. and J. G. Bruhn. The Power of Clan: The Influence of Human Relationships on Heart Disease. New Brunswick, NJ: Transaction Publishers, 1998.

Worwood, Valeria Anne. *The Fragrant Pharmacy*. New York: Bantam Books, 1995.

Wright, D. W., et al., "Sucrose-induced insulin resistance in the rat: modulation by exercise and diet," *The American Journal of Clinical Nutrition*, 1983.

Yaniv, Z., et al., "Plants used for the treatment of diabetes in Israel," *Journal of Ethnopharmacology*, March-April 1987.

Yarnell, E., "Strengthening the Link Between Zinc Deficiency and Diabetes Mellitus," *Quarterly Review of Natural Medicine*, December 1997.

Yee, A. C, and A.S. Dissanayake, "Glucose tolerance and the Transcendental Meditation program (a pilot study)," paper presented at International Congress on Research on Higher States of Consciousness at the Faculty of Science, Mahidol University, Bangkok, Thailand, December 1980.

Yongchaiyudha, S., et al., "Antidiabetic activity of Aloe vera L. Juice. II. Clinical trial in diabetes mellitus patients in combination with slibenclamide," *Phytomedicine*, 1996.

Zettler, A., et al., "Coping with fear of long-term complications in diabetes mellitus: A model clinical program," *Psychotherapy and Psychosomatics*, 1995.

Ziegler, D., and F. A. Gries, "Aplha-lipoic acid in the treatment of diabetic peripheral and cardiac autonomic neuropathy," *Diabetes*, September 1997.

Index